# JESUS AND THE CONSTRAINTS OF HISTORY

# Jesus and the Constraints of History

*The Bampton Lectures, 1980*

A. E. HARVEY

Duckworth

First published 1982 by
Gerald Duckworth & Co. Ltd.
The Old Piano Factory,
43 Gloucester Crescent, London NW1.

© 1982 by A. E. Harvey

ISBN 0-7156-1597-1 (Cased)

British Library Cataloguing in Publication Data

Harvey, A. E.
    Jesus and the constraints of history. – (The
    Bampton lectures; 1980)
    1. Jesus Christ
    I. Title    II. Series
    232.9'08        BT303.2

    ISBN 0-7156-1597-1

Photoset by
The Allen Lithographic Co. Ltd.
Kirkcaldy
and printed by
Redwood Burn Limited
Trowbridge

# Contents

Preface      vii

List of Abbreviations      viii

1. Introduction: Jesus and Historical Constraint      1

2. Political Constraints: The Crucifixion      11

3. The Constraint of Law      36

4. Jesus and Time: the Constraint of an Ending      66

5. The Intelligibility of Miracle      98

6. Jesus the Christ: the Options in a Name      120

     *Note: A pre-Christian interpretation of Isaiah 61*      152

7. Son of God: the Constraint of Monotheism      154

*Appendix I: The Interpretation of Acts 13:27-8*      174
     *II: Alleged Messianic Pretenders*      175
     *III: The Divinity of Jesus in the New Testament*      176

*Index: Primary Sources*      179
     *Modern Authors*      181
     *Subjects*      183

# Preface

Each of the eight Bampton Lectures which I had the privilege of giving in the University Church, Oxford, in 1980 was constrained by the Sunday morning worship of that church to be delivered in the space of little more than half an hour. In my first lecture I used this limitation as a trivial example of the constraints to which all human communication is in fact subject, a notion which I have found helpful when seeking to understand that master communicator, Jesus of Nazareth. This limitation of time has had a further consequence: the Lectures are required to be published, but in the form in which they were delivered they would barely have been sufficient to provide the substance of a book. Moreover, the argument is of a kind that, to carry conviction when studied at leisure, and to sustain the scrutiny of those expert in the subject, it must necessarily be presented in considerable detail. Indeed, to do it justice I should have had to devote many more years to its investigation and many more pages to its discussion. But the result would have then had little relationship to the original Lectures. In the event I have sought a compromise. I have included what seemed necessary by way of scholarly support and elaboration; but I have preserved so far as possible the arrangement and style of the argument as I first presented it. In any case, in a field where virtually every statement needs to be qualified in the light of the incessant research of countless others, it would have been pretentious to offer more than tentative conclusions. I shall be content if, on the strength of a few examples, I have succeeded in encouraging those who still, despite the apparently destructive effect of much recent New Testament scholarship, feel respect for the basic historical reliability of the gospels.

I have received invaluable help from colleagues and friends who faithfully attended the Lectures and generously shared their comments with me. I am also particularly indebted to Professors J. Duncan, M. Derrett and Maurice Wiles, and to Dr. Geza Vermes, who each read a chapter in draft and made the kind of observations which, had I been able to digest them more throroughly, would have saved me from still more errors of judgment. Finally, I must record my gratitude to the SPCK for permission to reproduce in my Introduction certain paragraphs from one of my contributions to *God Incarnate, Story and Belief* (1981). The same argument was appropriate in each case, and I have to confess that I lacked both the time and the fertility of mind to find more than one way of expressing it.

Wolfson College, Oxford, 1981                                         A.E.H.

# Abbreviations

| | |
|---|---|
| b | Babylonian Talmud |
| BC | F. Foakes Jackson and K. Lake, *The Beginnings of Christianity* (1920–33) |
| Bl.-D. | Blass–Debrunner, *A Greek Grammar of the New Testament and other Early Christian Literature,* ed. R. Funk (1961) |
| BZ | *Biblische Zeitschrift* |
| BZNW | *Beiheft zur Zeitschrift für die Neutestamentliche Wissenschaft* |
| CIJ | *Corpus Inscriptionum Judaicarum* |
| CPJ | *Corpus Papyrorum Judaicarum* |
| CR | *Classical Review* |
| DSSE | *The Dead Sea Scrolls in English*² (1975), translated by Geza Vermes |
| Enc. Jud. | *Encyclopaedia Judaica* |
| Eph ThLouv | *Ephemerides Theologicae Lovanienses* |
| E.tr. | English translation |
| HST | R. Bultmann, *History of the Synoptic Tradition* (E.tr. 1968) |
| HThR | *Harvard Theological Review* |
| IEJ | *Israel Exploration Journal* |
| IG | *Inscriptiones Graecae* |
| JBL | *Journal of Biblical Literature* |
| JE | *Jewish Encyclopaedia* |
| JHS | *Journal of Hellenic Studies* |
| JJS | *Journal of Jewish Studies* |
| JRS | *Journal of Roman Studies* |
| JSNT | *Journal for the Study of the New Testament* |
| JTS | *Journal of Theological Studies* |
| LXX | Septuagint |
| M. | Mishnah |
| MM | J. Moulton and G. Milligan, *Vocabulary of the Greek Testament* (1930) |
| NTS | *New Testament Studies* |
| Nov. T. | *Novum Testamentum* |
| PBSR | *Papers of the British School at Rome* |
| PGM | *Papyri Graecae Magicae* |
| RAC | *Reallexikon für Antike und Christentum* |
| RB | *Revue Biblique* |
| Rev. de Qum. | *Revue de Qumran* |
| RHR | *Revue de l'Histoire des Religions* |
| RHPhR | *Revue d'Histoire et de Philosophie Religieuses* |
| RTh Louv | *Revue Théologique de Louvain* |
| Str.-B. | H. L. Strack und P. Billerbeck, *Kommentar zum N.T. aus Talmud und Midrasch* (1926–8) |
| Supp. Nov.T. | *Supplement to Novum Testamentum* |
| T. | Tosefta |
| Tg | Targum |
| T.R. | *Textus Receptus* |
| TWNT | *Theologisches Wörterbuch zum Neuen Testament* (1933–73) (the references are to the German edition; the page numbers in the English Translation (1964–76) are virtually identical) |
| v.l. | varia lectio |
| y | Jerusalem Talmud |
| ZNW | *Zeitschrift für die Neutestamentliche Wissenschaft* |
| ZThK | *Zeitschrift für Theologie und Kirche* |
| ZRGG | *Zeitschrift für Religions- und Geistesgeschichte* |

# 1

# Introduction: Jesus and Historical Constraint

One fundamental discovery governs the thought of all who are engaged in serious and critical study of the New Testament, and is becoming increasingly widely known and understood among thinking Christian people. The gospels, it is now recognised, can no longer be regarded simply as records (differing from each other only to the extent that different witnesses to the same facts will always give slightly divergent testimony) of what in fact took place. They are rather the product of the situation in which the first, or even the second or third, generation of Christians found themselves, a situation which not only determined what they chose to preserve out of their traditions and memories about Jesus, but also influenced their manner of recording them, forcing them to tell the stories in such a way that their own problems and questions should be met and answered by them, and even to introduce material which they doubtless believed to be authentic but which was in reality the product of their own pious reflection upon the remembered origins of their faith. I referred to this as 'a discovery'. But New Testament scholars must beware of their own rhetoric. Nothing new has been discovered. The evidence is exactly the same as it always was – the bare text of the gospels which is preserved in any pocket edition of the Bible just as faithfully (subject to minor variations in text and translation) as in the critical edition on my desk. There is no discovery, only a hypothesis – a way of explaining why the four gospels manifest those peculiarities in their relationships with each other which any attentive reader can discern for himself. But this is a hypothesis which has been singularly successful, so much so that it is now taken for granted in virtually every scholarly commentary and indeed in most of the more popular books about the New Testament. It also carries with it a disconcerting consequence. If the reports about Jesus in the gospels are the creation of the church, rather than the testimony of eye-witnesses to the original events, then it follows that it is no longer possible to regard any New Testament statement about Jesus as historically reliable. In almost every instance it has become debatable whether a given word or action goes back to Jesus or is the creation of the early church. In other words, the more successful the hypothesis in explaining why the written gospels are as they are, the more it seems to take away from us the possibility of ever knowing anything for certain about Jesus. No wonder the progress of modern biblical studies seems to many people today to be, not only negative, but threatening.

What to lay Christians seems a threat, to theologians should be a challenge. And in fact theologians have reacted to the progress of New Testament study – or rather, as I would prefer to say, to the success of its most popular working hypothesis – by a notable shift of the ground of their arguments. Until recently it was taken for granted that theological statements about the nature and status of Christ would be ultimately based on certain passages in the New Testament – and mainly, for Christological purposes, in the Fourth Gospel.[1] But not only can the modern critical approach to the New Testament show that this gospel is the least reliable of the four from the point of view of history; but biblical scholars have now placed question marks over the historical value of almost every verse of all the gospels. Theologians have therefore naturally come to assume that the New Testament is no longer the place from which Christian theology must begin. As Professor Maurice Wiles has written: 'It is essential that the doctrinal theologian recognises . . . that the kind of information about Jesus that theology has so often looked to New Testament scholars to provide is not available.'[2] In brief, the assumption is gaining ground, both among theologians and among Christian people at large, that it is no longer possible to say anything for certain about the historical figure of Jesus. If this is so, it would follow that the ultimate basis of our faith must be looked for elsewhere: in the impact which he made on his followers, or the movement which resulted from his death and resurrection, or even (and this seems fashionable today) the lasting value of his story regarded as a myth – one of those myths which lives on because of its timeless and universal significance, but which does not require, for this purpose, to be firmly rooted in history.

Stated thus crudely, this scepticism appears to be a somewhat extreme reaction to the exaggeratedly reverent attitude of the past; and indeed it would be fair to say that New Testament scholars themselves (largely, it seems, unnoticed by systematic theologians) have retreated some way from the radical scepticism which followed the first impact of form-criticism. As a symptom of this, one may take the question of the very existence of the person who is the centre of all the gospel narratives, Jesus of Nazareth. For a time it seemed possible seriously to advance the suggestion that this person never existed at all, but that a new religion which swept the eastern half of the

[1] Cf. E. Schillebeeckx, *Jesus* (E.tr. 1979) 570 on the implications of this for the subsequent development of Christology.

[2] *The Remaking of Christian Doctrine* (1975) 48.

Roman Empire in the first century A.D. took as its symbolic founder a divinity named after the Joshua-saviour-figure of the Old Testament, and then wove such legends around him that an actual biography of a first-century Galilean began to emerge.[3] Such a development would not be without analogy, either in the history of world religions, or in the ancient history of mediterranean civilisation.[4] But in the case of Jesus it runs against such formidable objections that the theory has had little success even among the bitterest critics of Christianity. The case of Nazareth, however, was somewhat different. The place-name occurs nowhere in ancient literature before the New Testament; there was no evidence, literary or archaeological, that there was any settlement on the modern site of Nazareth before the fourth century A.D.; and no inscription had ever been found bearing the village's name. Now even in the New Testament there are signs that the designation 'of Nazareth' was seen to have more than topographical significance. Was not Jesus in some sense a 'Nazirite', one of those Old Testament shaman-figures of whom Samson is the best-known representative? Was he not also a branch (Hebrew *netser*) from the root of Jesse, as Isaiah (11.1) had long ago described the coming Messiah? In which case, what more natural than that in due course these cult-titles should be transformed into a fictitious place of origin, which was then actually located on the map of Palestine? But then, in 1955, excavations under the Church of the Annunciation in the modern town of Nazareth revealed that the place was in fact occupied well before the Christian era.[5] And in 1961 an inscription was discovered in Caesarea, dating from the early Roman period, in which the name Nazareth is there for all to read.[6]

This little episode by no means stands alone. It is symptomatic of the way in which archaeology has tended in recent years to enhance the credibility of the gospel narratives. A conspicuous instance of this, though it is still not widely known, is a discovery that was made some ten years ago by Israeli archaeologists in a burial ground just outside Jerusalem.[7] It was the custom of the Jews, some years after the burial of a corpse in a tomb of rock, to gather the bones of the deceased and preserve them in small stone boxes called ossuaries. One of these ossuaries, dating from the first century A.D., was found in a cemetery on the Mount of Olives, and contained the bones of a man named Jehohanan who had died in his mid-twenties and who had apparently been crucified. The nail which had been driven through his anklebones to secure him to the cross had evidently proved impossible to remove and was still in place, with fragments of wood adhering to it. The bones of the lower part of the legs had been broken by a transverse blow.

[3] E.g. Archibald Robertson, *Jesus: Myth or History?* (1946).
[4] Cf. A. Deissmann in *Mysterium Christi* (ed. A. Deissmann and G. Bell, 1930) 4-5.
[5] C. Kopp, *The Holy Places of the Gospels* (E.tr. 1963) 60-1.
[6] *IEJ* 12 (1962) 137-9.
[7] For the original report, see *IEJ* 20 (1970) 38-59. For subsequent discussion and bibliography, see H.-W. Kuhn in *Theologia Crucis - Signum Crucis* (Dinkler Festschrift, 1979) 303-34.

Here, then, is totally independent evidence for the crucifixion of a contemporary of Jesus. In a number of significant details – the nail, the breaking of the legs – it agrees precisely with the account given in the gospels. That is to say: it is no longer possible (if it ever was) to regard the gospel narratives as pious legend or irresponsible fabrication. The gruesome episode of the crucifixion is recorded without either rhetorical exaggeration or fanciful elaboration. Henceforth the gospels must be taken seriously as historical documents purporting to record events as they would in fact have happened in that place and at that moment in history.[8] But of course, impressive though such confirmation is, it does not take us very far. It can prove that in certain respects the gospel accounts are plausible; but it can make no contribution to the question whether they are true. That is to say: many of the details of their narrative may turn out to be historically correct; but this does not of itself help us to decide whether the authors were deliberately composing a fictitious story that would sound convincing to their readers, or whether they were recording what they believed to have actually happened. Archaeological discovery may force us to treat the gospels as serious historical evidence; but it cannot tell us whether that evidence is to be trusted.

If, however, the effect of these discoveries is to force us to take the gospels seriously as historical witnesses, then there is one important consequence of this which does bear upon our question. For some years now it has been realised that radical scepticism about the historical value of the information contained in the gospels rests upon a logical fallacy. It may be true that, in the light of modern critical study, there is virtually no single report of any of the words and deeds of Jesus of which we can be certain, and there is indeed quite a large number of them which are likely to be either fictitious or fashioned by the tradition into something very different from the original. But it does not follow from this that we can know nothing for certain about Jesus. Your estimate of a respected friend or teacher will normally be based on a large number of pieces of information about him, all (or virtually all) of which seem to add up to the kind of personality and achievement which is worthy of respect. Of course it may happen that one of these stories about him turns out to have no basis in fact, and that another has grown considerably in the telling; and you may have to admit that, at least in theory, the same could be true of any of the others. But if so, you will not immediately abandon all possibility of reliable information about this person and transfer your respect elsewhere. What impresses you is the fact that there is so much information which all points in the same direction and allows you to infer a character of consistency and integrity. The mere possibility that any particular source of information may

[8] The striking agreement between the ossuary remains and the gospel narrative may of course be partly due to chance: it is unlikely that crucifixion was always carried out in exactly the same way. Cf. M. Hengel, *Crucifixion* (E.tr. 1977) 24–5.

turn out to be unreliable would certainly not lead you to think that you could no longer make any reasonable judgment about him at all. And so it is in modern New Testament study. Attention has moved away from establishing the truth or falsity of any particular report about Jesus,[9] and is now directed more towards the impression made by the narrative as a whole. Writers who string together stories which are devised purely to give credit to the hero will succeed only in presenting a one-sided description of his character, lacking in any real depth or originality; others who are content to collect any anecdotes regardless of historical plausibility will fail to portray a character of any consistency. Neither fault can be laid to the charge of the evangelists. The Jesus who emerges from their accounts has both originality and consistency – some of the apocryphal gospels, which present by comparison a cardboard figure, offer an instructive contrast. Unless these authors were the most consummate and imaginative artists, able to create a striking and consistent character out of scanty and unreliable sources, we have every reason to think that, in broad outline (whatever may be the case with some of the details), the Jesus whom they portray is the Jesus who actually existed. To this extent, no New Testament scholar today would be prepared to say that we can know nothing for certain about Jesus.

But now a word must be said about this notion of certainty. For the greater part of the history of Christianity the statements of fact contained in the Bible seemed to enjoy a quite exceptional degree of certainty, in that their truth was guaranteed by the divine inspiration of scripture. This doctrine of the literal inerrancy of the Bible is no longer so widely held; but the recollection of the splendid assurance it provided has subtly influenced the judgment of many theologians. It is agreed that the information contained in scripture should be subjected to investigation with all the tools and methods of historical study. It is then found that, though it often comes surprisingly well out of the process, it is seldom possible to say more at the end of the day than that, as a piece of historical reporting, it is probably true. An alarming degree of relativity seems now to attach even to statements of historical fact which are at the very heart of our religion. But such uncertainty need be a cause for dismay only when it is contrasted with the supernaturally guaranteed certainty which seemed to be offered on an earlier understanding of the authority of scripture. The appropriate comparison today is not with statements which may be believed true on divine authority, but with other historical statements made on the basis of comparable evidence. What we have to ask is not whether a given statement is true with a kind of supernatural certainty but whether the fact which it reports may be regarded as at least as well established as any other fact which comes down to us from antiquity. On this test we shall find that the evidence for at least the main facts of the life and

---

[9] Cf. N. Dahl, *The Crucified Messiah* (1974) 67: 'Whether the historicity of individual words or episodes remains uncertain is consequently of lesser importance.'

death of Jesus is as abundant, circumstantial and consistent as is the case with any other figure of ancient history.

There are of course many points of detail in the gospels which are by no means reliably established as historical facts. The witnesses may be isolated and biassed, the evidence may be in conflict with other evidence, and the report itself may have an inherent improbability. But there are also certain facts about Jesus which, by any normal criterion of historical evidence, it would be altogether unreasonable to doubt. Such facts are that Jesus was known in both Galilee and Jerusalem; that he was a teacher; that he carried out cures of various illnesses, particularly demon-possession, and that these were widely regarded as miraculous; that he was involved in controversy with fellow-Jews over questions of the Law of Moses; and that he was crucified in the governorship of Pontius Pilate. These facts are attested by at least as much reliable evidence as are countless others which we take for granted as historical facts known to us from the ancient world. Now it may of course be said that statements of such a general kind about Jesus are too colourless and imprecise to be of much interst to us. And indeed it is certainly the case that theologians, when seeking to define the nature and significance of the incarnation, have looked to the gospels, not for the bare bones of Jesus' biography, but for information about such subtle and intimate matters as his so-called messianic consciousness, his moral perfection or his relationship with his heavenly father. On all these questions the evidence of the gospels is both insufficient and controversial.[10] They are questions to which we can never know the certainly correct answer. For this reason it may easily be felt that the New Testament offers no firm foundation for the beliefs which a Christian must necessarily hold about the unique nature and status of Jesus Christ. The words I quoted of Professor Wiles were carefully chosen: '. . . *the kind* of information about Jesus that theology has looked to New Testament scholars to provide is not available.'[11] Nothing I have said so far materially affects this judgement. It can still be argued that we can have no reliable historical knowledge about Jesus with regard to anything that really matters.

It is at this point that I believe it is possible to give a new turn to the argument by introducing the notion of historical constraints.[12] No individual, if he wishes to influence others, is totally free to choose his own style of action and persuasion: he is subject to constraints imposed by the culture in which he finds himself. If communication is to take place, there must be constraints which are recognised by both the speaker and his listeners, the artist and his public, the leader and his followers. Utterances that are interminable or spasmodic; artistic works or performances without recognisable

[10]The point is fairly made by D. E. Nineham, *The Myth of God Incarnate* (ed. J. Hick, 1977) 188.

[11]Cf. id. ib., 49: 'Our knowledge about him *in himself* is at every point tentative and uncertain.'

[12]My use of the term is arbitrary and non-technical. I am indebted for the idea to J. Bowker, *The Sense of God* (1973), esp. 60-1, 87-9, where however the notion is explored systematically with the help of recent information-theory.

form; leadership which appears random or impractical – all these fail to communicate because they do not work within the constraints imposed by the rhythm of human activity and the conventions of culture and civilisation. Indeed it is only by taking account of such constraints that any of these activities can be fully understood. Now Jesus was, at the very least, a speaker, an artist, a leader. It is evident that he succeeded in communicating with his hearers, his followers, and indeed his enemies. To do so, he had to speak a language they could understand, perform actions they would find intel- ligible, and conduct his life and undergo his death in a manner of which they could make some sense. This is not to say, of course, that he must have been totally subject to these constraints. Like any truly creative person, he could doubtless bend them to his purpose. But had he not worked from within them, he would have seemed a mere freak, a person too unrelated to the normal rhythm of society to have anything meaningful to say.

It is possible to claim, I believe, that for the study of these constraints modern research has made available a wealth of detail which was simply not known, or whose significance was not apparent, to previous generations of scholars. Archaeological discovery, the substantial body of new Jewish literature contained in the Dead Sea Scrolls, and the application of modern critical methods to post-biblical Jewish writings in Greek and other languages, have greatly increased our knowledge of the environment in which Jesus lived, and enable us to bring a new precision to the study of the constraints to which he was exposed. In the light of this, we shall find that those bare biographical statements, which are established with a high degree of historical certainty but which seem at first to convey little information that is of interest to the theologian, take on considerable significance. The state- ment, for example, that Jesus was a teacher, when set in the context of the constraints which bore upon any teacher of his time and culture and of the relatively small number of options which was open to anyone who wished to give a new lead in religious understanding while remaining intelligible to the majority of his hearers – such a statement is capable of yielding a surprising amount of information about the kind of person Jesus must have been and the kind of achievement at which he aimed; and this information is of great relevance to the ultimate question of Christology: who and what was Jesus?

Much of the material which is discussed in the following chapters consists of evidence which is drawn from sources outside the New Testament and which helps us to give definition to the historical constraints within which Jesus must have lived, worked and died. These constraints, in turn, allow us to establish the options which were open to a person such as we believe Jesus to have been, and give objective content to those general statements about him which we regard as historically established. In this way we can begin to build up a profile of Jesus which is independent of Christian sources and which offers some kind of test by which the reliability of these sources can be checked. But let me admit at once that it would be quite unrealistic to suggest that this method allows us to work independently of the New Testament evidence. At every point it will be necessary to check our results against the data provided by the Christian tradition and indeed to supplement them by drawing on episodes and sayings which are preserved only in the gospels. I have already remarked that New Testament scholars themselves (who tend to be the severest critics of their own methods) no longer regard all information offered by the gospels as in principle untrustworthy. For some time now they have been experimenting with criteria which would enable us to distinguish systematically between material that is likely to have derived from Jesus and that which may have originated in the early church. Not all these criteria have stood up to rigorous criticism, but there are two in particular which have won general assent, and which I shall make use of in what follows. One I have already mentioned: this is the sheer consistency and originality of the broad outlines of the portrait of Jesus as they emerge from the entire gospel tradition.[13] Material which has this recurring and characteristic quality (for example, the mixed – and to many of his contemporaries shocking – company kept by Jesus, his unprecedented attitude towards children *as* children, the importance he attached to the sharing of a meal, both for promoting the solidarity of his followers and for conveying religious truth) can be confidently regarded as having considerable historical reliability. The other is that known to scholars as the criterion of 'dissimilarity', which may be crudely decribed as the principle that 'odd is true'. If we come across something in the gospels which appears strikingly original and for which there is no known parallel or precedent in the ancient world; and if we can see no possible reason for anyone to have invented such a thing and foisted it upon the story of Jesus; then it seems reasonable to assume that we have at least an echo of something which happened in historical fact. Its very oddity is an argument for its truth. The criterion needs to be used with caution,[14] since it is always vulnerable to the acquisition of new knowledge: what was once thought to be unparalleled and unprecedented may be shown by new discoveries to have been well established in the culture. Moreover, the criterion must never be used in isolation. It would be impossible to build up a credible portrait of Jesus entirely out of material selected because of its peculiarity: no one has or could ever have a character composed entirely of idiosyncrasies. The method can be used only to supplement those more normal characteristics for which we have reliable evidence. But there are elements of the gospel tradition (such as the episode of Jesus' mounted entry

[13] A variant on this is the so-called 'principle of multiple attestation'. When a saying or episode is attested by a number of apparently independent testimonies (particularly if these occur in different contexts, or, best of all, are noted *en passant* for no apparent purpose), it has a strong claim to authenticity.

[14] For a just evaluation of the limitations of this criterion, cf. R. S. Barbour, *Traditio-Historical Criticism of the Gospels* (1972) 5-20.

into Jerusalem) which, as we shall see, are inexplicable unless they derive from authentic reminiscence, and which provide us with invaluable clues to the specific options which were actually chosen by Jesus amid the constraints to which he was subjected.

The following chapters represent a preliminary attempt to study some of the constraints which bore upon the activity of Jesus, and to define them with such precision as has been made possible by recent research. Within those constraints, only a certain number of options, a relatively small range of styles of action, was open to Jesus, and by making use of the criteria I have mentioned it is possible to use the evidence of the gospels to make a well-founded judgment on the question of which of these options was actually adopted by him. In this way I believe that we can turn those apparently dry and general facts which are certainly known about Jesus (such as that he was a teacher, a healer, a controversial figure) into material of great interest, not only to theologians, but to every Christian. Let me conclude this introduction with a preliminary example of the way I conceive these constraints to have operated.

We have, in the writings of St. Luke, a remarkable thumbnail sketch of Jesus. In Acts 10.37f. Peter is made to describe him as one who 'went about doing good and healing all those who were in the power of the devil'. The second clause – the statement that Jesus performed exorcisms – is one of those pieces of information about him which we may regard as historically well established, and which will be considered in more detail later on. But what about the first? That Jesus 'went about doing good' is a phrase which does not usually catch our attention: we probably interpret it, almost unconsciously, in terms of whatever particular goodness we have ourselves discerned in the person of Jesus. But the Greek word for 'doing good', *euergetōn*, permits us no such liberty. Among the Jews its normal meaning was that of giving alms to the poor;[15] among the Gentiles, it meant 'conferring benefits', and was mainly used as a term of flattery to describe the activities of a ruler who liked to be known as a benefactor, *euergetēs*, towards his people.[16] Neither of these senses is appropriate to Jesus; and when Luke used the word here, there is only one remaining connotation he can have had in mind. The word crops up in a philosophical cliché, variously attributed to Pythagoras and Aristotle, to the effect that 'doing good' is something that men have in common with God;[17] that is to say, the word was a way of describing a person whose

---

[15] Cf. Str. -B. 4.563f. εὖ ποιεῖν occurs only once in LXX, and with this meaning (Prov. 3.27); cf. Hebr. 13.16, where εὐποιία has the same connotation.

[16] Cf. A. D. Nock in S. E. Johnson (ed.) *The Joy of Study* (1951) 135 = *Essays* 2.725: 'a regular term in civic decrees . . . it could describe continued helpfulness as well as sudden aid in an emergency.'

[17] Aelian *Var. Hist.* 12.59: Πυθαγόρας ἔλεγε δυὸ ταῦτα ἐκ τῶν θεῶν τοῖς ἀνθρώποις δεδόσθαι κάλλιστα, τό τε ἀληθεύειν καὶ τὸ εὐεργετεῖν. Wiener Gnomologikon: Ἀριστοτέλης ἐρωτηθεὶς ὑπό τινος τί ἄνθρωπος ἴσον ἔχει θεῷ εἶπε τὸ εὐεργετεῖν. Cf. Philo *Spec. leg.* 4.73; Edict of Germanicus (A.D. 19) in

activity showed him to have a particularly close relationship with the divine. Luke in fact drives the point home when, immediately after the sentence I have quoted, he adds the words, 'because God was with him'. We glimpse here – though it is only a glimpse – the historical constraints under which Jesus lived and worked. Not many styles of action were available to him which would have been regarded as expressive of what I shall call his divine agency (his unique relationship with his heavenly father). The passionate and exclusive monotheism of the Jewish people excluded any style of action which might have suggested that he claimed to be divine; and only a small number of options would have been open to him which would express an exceptional degree of authorisation by God, and which would have led people to acknowledge that 'God was with him'. Luke's readers will have known instinctively what these constraints and options were. For us, it demands accurate historical enquiry. But it is an enquiry for which, I believe, the materials are now available, and which will enable us to understand better what it might mean to claim that 'God was with' a person of history in such a unique and decisive way that he could be regarded as an actual agent of the divine, and become thereby an object, not only of our endless and fascinated study, but of our love and worship.

---

A. Hunt and C. Edgar, *Select Papyri* (1956) 2.76, no. 211, ll.35–6, quoted by Nock, op. cit. 132=724; cf. also H. Bolkestein, *Wohltätigkeit und Armenpflege im Urchristlichen Altertum* (1939) 434 and P. van den Horst, *The Sentences of Pseudo-Phocylides* (1978) 129–30 for discussions of the difference between Jewish and Hellenistic attitudes to 'well-doing'. The proverb is regularly applied to almsgiving in Jewish literature; cf. Ep. Diogn. 10.6; Philo, loc. cit.

# 2
# Political Constraints: The Crucifixion

*He was crucified under Pontius Pilate.* It would be no exaggeration to say that this event is better attested, and supported by a more impressive array of evidence, than any other event of comparable importance of which we have knowledge from the ancient world. Not only is it described in considerable detail in all four canonical gospels, and referred to on countless occasions in the other New Testament writings; it is also explicitly mentioned by Tacitus,[1] and its historicity is assured by the unusual circumstance that it occurs in the ancient creeds of the church. These creeds represented the faith of Christians under persecution. It was a faith for which they were prepared to die. All the other clauses in these creeds contain propositions of a religious character. That God is creator of heaven and earth, that Jesus was born of a virgin, that there is such a thing as the forgiveness of sins and life everlasting are articles of faith. No evidence could ever be produced by historical research to prove them either true or false. By contrast, that Jesus was crucified under Pontius Pilate is a statement of historical fact. As such, it is exposed, like any other historical statement, to the possibility of contradiction in the light of further evidence. Had there been the smallest chance of this taking place, Christians who were living little more than a century after the event would hardly have incorporated it in their profession of faith. The slightest suspicion, then or subsequently, that Jesus had *not* been crucified would have robbed their religion of any credibility. Had this danger existed, they would surely have omitted such a vulnerable clause. But in fact they knew it to be established beyond any reasonable doubt. And so, alongside the tremendous theological assertions contained in the rest of the creed, they boldly recited a fact of history which they knew that no one could possibly deny: *crucifixus est sub Pontio Pilato.*

Here then is at least one piece of information about Jesus which we may regard as historically certain. Expressed as a theological doctrine, it is something of immense significance: that the Messiah, the Son of God, met

[1] *Ann.* 15.44.

his death in this way presented the supreme challenge to the religious under-standing of Paul, as it has to countless Christian thinkers ever since. But from the point of view of a historical reconstruction of the life of Jesus it seems at first sight to be less promising. It is one of those bare statements of bio-graphical information which looks too colourless and summary to take us much further. But this is to reckon without those historical constraints to which I referred in the Introduction. Our knowledge of the times in which Jesus lived and died does not allow us to imagine that anyone might be crucified in any manner on any pretext. On the contrary, those who inflicted the penalty acted within the constraints imposed by the rule of law and the pressure of political circumstances. From the bare fact that Jesus was crucified we can infer some significant information about the circumstances which led up to his death; and this in turn will have a bearing on the kind of person Jesus must have been if he met his death in this way. We must look at the crucifixion, not as an isolated event, but as one conditioned by the constraints under which it took place.

I have already mentioned the Mount of Olives ossuary, which confirms several of the physical circumstances of crucifixion which are described in the gospels, and suggests that Jesus was crucified according to a standard procedure. There are also numerous references by classical authors to the horror and cruelty of this form of execution.[2] But the significant evidence, from our point of view, bears upon the nature of the offence for which this punishment was imposed. The first question to which we require an answer is, By whom would it have been carried out? Although there is evidence for a Jewish tyrant having ordered mass crucifixions some two centuries before,[3] we can say with absolute confidence that at the time with which we are concerned this form of execution in a Roman province could have been carried out only by the Roman officials, and only on the orders of the Roman governor.[4] *Sub Pontio Pilato* is therefore true, not only as a means of dating the event,[5] but as an indication of the authority under which it took place. It follows that the offence for which it was imposed must have been one of which the Roman administration took cognisance. Our evidence from pagan sources leaves us in no doubt about the nature of such offences.[6] Apart from its infliction upon slaves and hardened criminals, crucifixion was reserved for the punishment of rebels against the Roman state. It was a deliberately public form of execution. The victim was impaled outside the city near a public highway, so that his punishment should have the maximum deterrent effect.[7]

[2] Cf. M. Hengel, *Crucifixion* (E.tr. 1977) passim.
[3] Alexander Jannaeus, Jos. *B.J.* 1.97, often thought to be referred to in 4QpNah 1.6-7; cf. G. Vermes, *DSSE* 65.
[4] H.-R. Weber, *The Cross* (E.tr. 1979) 9 and numerous other writers.
[5] Its function in the Creeds; cf. J. N. D. Kelly, *Early Christian Creeds*[3] (1972) 150.
[6] M. Hengel, op. cit. 33ff.
[7] *Digest* 48.19.28.15; cf. M. Hengel, op. cit. 50.

Josephus records a large number of such crucifixions outside Jerusalem under the Roman Procurators, and always for the same reason: rebellion against the Roman authority.[8] There can be no reasonable doubt that Jesus met a death which was reserved for those whom the Roman governor regarded as a threat to the peace and security of the state.

This conclusion is of course strikingly confirmed by the evidence of the gospels. We have been taking as our starting point a fact which may be regarded as historically certain quite independently of the testimony of the New Testament, and our purpose is to see how far these basic facts will take us. We must allow ourselves at most a sideways glance at the gospel evidence, since its authors necessarily stand under the suspicion of having a dogmatic Christian bias in their presentation. But the piece of evidence which interests us at this point is extraordinarily unlikely to be the product of any such bias. All the four gospels record that a notice was affixed to the cross of Jesus on which was written, in three languages, the charge on which he had been convicted. The textbooks maintain, with astonishing unanimity, that this practice of writing the charge over the crucified victim's cross was well-established in the Roman Empire. In which case it could perhaps be said that the gospel writers eagerly provided such a notice in the case of Jesus in order to give their story the greatest possible verisimilitude. Looked at more closely, the available evidence appears to establish nothing of the sort.[9] Criminals, before their execution, were sometimes forced to display in public a notice showing why they were to be put to death.[10] But we know of no other instance of such a notice actually being fixed to the cross.[11] The first historians of Jesus' death can therefore have been under no compulsion to invent one. On the other hand, the exact manner of crucifixion certainly varied according to circumstances, and there is nothing in the least improbable in their account of the so-called *titulus*. What is unlikely is that they should have invented the wording. All four accounts contain the phrase, King of the Jews.[12] It was precisely the suggestion that Jesus represented some kind of political threat to the Roman authorities that Christians of the early centuries had most strenuously to deny. It is hard to believe that they would have fabricated a piece of evidence which could so easily be turned against them.[13] The only plausible explanation for its appearance in their

[8] *B.J.* 2, 75, 241, 253.

[9] Cf. H.-W. Kuhn, *ZThK* 72 (1975) 5 n.13. Noted also by E. Haenchen, *Interpretation* 24 (1970) 218.

[10] Dio Cass. 54.3.7; Suet *Cal.* 32 (2); *Dom.* 10 (1).

[11] The notice in Hesychius s.v. σανίς (τίθεται δὲ καὶ ἐπὶ τοῦ [σταύρου]) may derive from the gospels.

[12] That pretensions to kingship were held by Jewish rebels is shown by Jos. *Ant.* 17.285; *B.J.* 2.444. E. Haenchen (art. cit. 218), who denies that the charge 'King of the Jews' is historically plausible, appears to overlook these parallels.

[13] Though some scholars have not found it so. Cf. Bultmann, *HST* 307; E. Haenchen, loc. cit., 'the claim of the early Christian community'. For a well-documented argument in favour of authenticity, cf. M. Hengel, *Nachfolge und Charisma* (1968) 42ff; *Son of God* (E.tr. 1976) 61 n.113.

accounts is that it was actually seen by a large number of people and could not be omitted. In which case it offers welcome confirmation of the conclusion we have reached by another route: that Jesus was convicted and executed on a charge of sedition against the Roman authority.

This conclusion, reached (as we have seen) by a strong chain of historical inference from the well-established fact of the crucifixion, confronts us with our first major difficulty. Jesus was crucified as an actual or potential enemy of the Roman authority. But if we now turn to the gospels, there is virtually nothing which gives any colour to such a charge. Indeed we can go further. The portrait of Jesus, as it is presented to us not only in the gospels but throughout the New Testament, is utterly irreconcilable with this explanation of his death. Moreover, had Jesus in fact been executed as a rebel, he would undoubtedly have had followers and sympathisers who would have applauded him. The first century A.D. had already seen, and would soon see again, a great number of Jewish freedom-fighters (as we would now call them) who met their end in this way. Had Jesus been one of them, he would have fallen into place beside many others, and there would surely be some echo in the records of the admiration felt for his fortitude and determination right up to the end.[14] But not merely is there barely a hint that Jesus left any such reputation;[14a] the movement which grew up after his death and in his name was far removed from the ideology of anyone who would have been involved in violent resistance against the Roman regime.

This stark opposition between the evidence derived, on the one hand, from our simple historical reconstruction, and on the other from the Christian tradition, forces us to make a choice between clearly defined alternatives. One possible explanation is that the gospels are utterly tendentious from beginning to end. Jesus was in fact a rebel, a freedom-fighter, an insurgent, and the gospels represent an elaborate attempt by the early church to cover up all traces of such activity, and to portray Jesus as a harmless religious teacher who was convicted through the malign intrigues of his fellow Jews. This explanation is by no means to be dismissed as implausible. It has had some distinguished advocates,[15] and in fact it is very difficult to prove wrong. And this for good reason. It starts from the assumption that the gospels present a fictitious account of the events leading up to Jesus' death, and are therefore worthless as evidence for those events. It cannot therefore be shown wrong by appeal to any detail in that evidence – and there is no other evidence which we can appeal to. Everything hangs upon the opinion which we hold of the only evidence we possess. Now documents which are deliberately composed to cover up the truth have a tendency to give themselves away. In

[14] As there is for John the Baptist, Jos. *Ant.* 18.116.
[14a] The only hints of a recollection of Jesus as a martyr for the Jewish cause are in Heb. 12.2; 1 Tim 6.13.
[15] Especially S. G. F. Brandon, *Jesus and the Zealots* (1967).

the first place, they are liable to preserve, as it were by accident, tell-tale traces of what really happened; and in the second place their own version of the events is likely to reveal flaws and inconsistencies which ultimately undermine their credibility. Those who hold this view point triumphantly to the fact that one of Jesus' followers was called 'the Zealot' (a name subsequently associated with violent guerilla activity against the Romans); that Jesus was involved in a discussion of the propriety of paying tax to Caesar; that he made an open attack on the temple institutions; and that (according to Luke) his followers had two swords at the time of his arrest in Gethsemane. Here are the tell-tale pointers to Jesus' true intentions, carelessly left lying in the narrative by the evangelists. As for the general plausibility of their accounts, particularly with regard to the trial of Jesus, these critics again and again find details which they describe as 'improbable', 'preposterous' or 'absurd'.[16]

As I have said, we cannot prove this explanation wrong. On the other hand, we can still ask whether this opinion of the gospel evidence is the most appropriate one. With regard to the alleged traces of violent activity, we may observe that the meaning of Simon's added name 'Zelotes' is by no means certain; that it is difficult to rewrite the episode of the discussion of Roman taxation in such a way as to incriminate Jesus; that the so-called cleansing of the temple appears to have been aimed at the abuse of Jewish institutions, not at the Roman authority; and that the two swords in Gethsemane hardly amount to evidence for violent intentions. As for the general estimate of the reliability of the gospel accounts, it is of course true (as we shall see) that the trial narratives in particular offer considerable difficulties to the historian; but words like 'preposterous' and 'absurd' are not those which have normally occurred to the readers of these stories, whether or not these readers were sympathetic to Christianity. On the contrary, for all the difficulties they contain, the gospels have commended themselves again and again as serious records of what actually happened, just as the narrative of the crucifixion has now been proved by archaeological finds to be, in certain respects at least, a piece of plausible historical reporting.

We are therefore asked to make a decision, not between one interpretation of the gospel evidence and another, but between accepting or rejecting that evidence in its entirety. To anyone who is prepared to reject it as entirely tendentious, there is nothing more to say. We cannot prove him wrong – though we are entitled to press him hard on the consequential question of how the Christian religion could have flourished as it has if it were really based on such fraudulent documents. But if we make our decision in favour of the general reliability of the Christian tradition, we have to look for some other explanation of the apparent contradiction between the activity and

---

[16] These words occur frequently in Brandon. Cf. also H. Cohn, *The Trial and Death of Jesus* (1972) 189 ('. . . ridiculous').

character of Jesus as preserved by that tradition and the nature of the charge on which he was sentenced to death. We have to ask in effect how a person such as we believe Jesus to have been could have met his end as an alleged rebel against the Roman occupying power.

In theory, it could have been an accident. Jesus could be one of those innocent victims who are picked up (as we say) by police action at a time when peace-keeping has become difficult and the forces of law and order are over-stretched, and then arbitrarily put to death. History, not least in our own time, has many examples of such brutal police methods. The explanation is perfectly plausible. But a moment's reflection shows that it will not fit this particular case. Had Jesus been the victim of sheer misgovernment by a hated alien administration, his fellow-countrymen woud have lost no time in exploiting the fact. His legend would have been that of any national hero who had been unjustly condemned to death. But of this there is not a hint in our sources. Moreover, once again, its consequence was not a national movement devoted to mourning and avenging an innocent victim's death but the totally different ideology of the Christian church.

In any case, everything that we know of the administration of justice in the Roman provinces points in a different direction. The governor could put a subject to death only after trial.[17] It follows therefore, from the statement that Jesus was crucified – a form of execution which, as we have seen, could have been imposed only by the authority of the governor – that he also stood trial before Pontius Pilate. We have already established the charge on which he must have been arraigned: that of sedition. The normal procedure would have been for this charge to have been brought against him by his fellow-countrymen.[18] Pilate must have accepted this charge as well-founded and ordered Jesus' execution. It was, that is to say, a miscarriage of justice. And to the question why Pilate should have given a false judgment in this case, the only possible answer is that which is offered by the gospels. His verdict was influenced by pressure from Jesus' Jewish accusers.

This conclusion is not absolutely secure. We cannot be certain that Pilate followed the proper procedure in this case. In the course of a rhetorical attack on Pilate's character, Philo of Alexandria (who is a contemporary witness) accuses him of frequent executions carried out without trial.[19] Indeed the Jews, according to Philo, threatened to send an account of these irregularities to the Emperor Tiberius – which is itself a precious piece of evidence confirming that the governor would have been acting illegally if he had sentenced a subject without first placing him on trial. It is therefore possible that Pilate acted in this summary and illegal manner in the case of Jesus, and

---

[17] Fourth edict of Augustus, V. Ehrenburg and A. Jones, *Documents* (1955) no. 311; cf. A. N. Sherwin-White, *Roman Society and Roman Law in the New Testament* (1963) 17-18.
[18] *Delatores:* Pliny *Ep.*10. 97.1. Cf. Sherwin-White, loc. cit.
[19] *Leg. ad G.* 302 τοὺς ἀκρίτους καὶ ἐπαλλήλους φόνους.

sent him straight to the cross without a hearing. Possible, but surely improbable. Such an action would undoubtedly have evoked some word of criticism in our sources. It is true that the tendency of the Christian accounts of Jesus' end is to place the responsibility for it firmly upon the Jews and so far as possible to exonerate the Romans. But had Pilate dealt with Jesus so summarily that there was no opportunity for the Jews even to make an accusation against him, we would surely hear at least a murmur in Christian sources of criticism of such high-handed illegality. But of this, once again, there is not so much as a hint. We may take it as established that Jesus was executed only after due trial.

We still have to ask, of course, whether, if Jesus was in fact plainly innocent, it is plausible that any Roman governor would have yielded to popular pressure to the extent of convicting him. It is true that Pilate's conduct of the trial involved some irregularities by the book,[20] and that its issue does no credit to the record of justice administered in the Roman provinces. On the other hand, we have no reason to suppose that Pilate was a model governor. If we compare him with Cicero, such conduct may seem unacceptable; if we compare him with Verres, a single venal judgment in a capital case involving an unknown provincial troublemaker would hardly amount to a serious delict. Moreover his province was notoriously difficult to govern; and we have plenty of instances in our own time of occupied countries where both the police and the judiciary are frequently accused, and perhaps occasionally with good reason, of perverting the course of justice. In short, the only alternative to regarding the gospel narrative as a complete fabrication is to accept, in broad outline, the solution which it offers to the paradox from which we started – the paradox that the Jesus who was certainly executed on a charge of sedition was a person who could not possibly have been guilty of such an offence.

The solution offered is that in this case the judge was so influenced by the Jewish prosecution that he convicted the prisoner even though the evidence against him was insufficient to prove his guilt. We can test the plausibility of this solution by turning the question round and asking, suppose that this is in fact what happened, what kind of account of it would we be likely to find in our Christian sources? We must assume, to start with, that those who first reported the trial had no means of knowing what had actually passed in Pilate's court. Proceedings are not likely to have been held in public,[21] and the suggestion that one of the judges was Joseph of Arimathea, who could subsequently have related the trial to his Christian friends, is a last resort to save the reputation of the gospels as eye witness accounts. All that is likely to have been known is that Jesus had been tried before Pilate; that the charge on which he was convicted was publicly displayed on the cross and involved a

[20] Exploited by H. Cohn, op. cit. 142ff.
[21] Cohn, op. cit. 146.

claim to be in some sense King of the Jews; that this charge was brought by Jewish accusers; and that Jesus, though certainly innocent of any such political offence, was convicted, doubtless owing to the pressure exerted by influential Jews in the courtroom. To these basic inferences we may add two further recollections. There was from early times a strong tradition that Jesus, like the victim in Isaiah 53, opened not his mouth before his accusers, but was like a sheep that before the shearers is dumb. If so, then it could be assumed that he had said nothing in self-defence before Pilate. The other recollection concerned Barabbas. The question whether Pilate would have had the right to grant amnesty to a prisoner held on a serious charge is still debated by historians.[22] But no decisive reason has been found to rule it out of court. The evangelists or their sources may well have known that, in releasing Barabbas, the governor showed himself to have been amenable to popular demand. If so, it would have seemed that much less improbable that he might at the same time have been so influenced by popular clamour that he sentenced an innocent man to death.[23] This would have provided further colour, as it still does, to the account of events according to which Pilate's judgment was influenced by pressure exerted upon him by the Jewish leaders.

Apart from such anecdotal additions as Pilate's wife's dream, or the involvement of Herod Antipas, the entire trial narrative in all the gospels is accounted for by this reconstruction. John's gospel, for understandable reasons of its own, uses the scene to define the nature of Jesus' kingship – an issue raised by the charge – and offers a mise-en-scène which makes possible a private dialogue between Pilate and the prisoner. But apart from this, every detail without remainder is accounted for by the supposition that the one circumstance of which the evangelists had certain knowledge in the trial before Pilate was that Jesus' conviction was the result of intervention by the Jews. And since this, as we have seen, represents also the only plausible explanation available to us of the fact that Jesus was convicted on the charge of sedition, it must be accepted as historically established. In which case we are furnished with one further historical inference of far-reaching importance: Jesus must have been a person who, by his words or actions, attracted a high degree of animosity, fear or jealousy on the part of his fellow Jews, so much so that they were prepared to secure his condemnation in a pagan court.

If we now go on to ask in more detail what chain of events could have led to such a strange dénouement, the answer which seems at first sight to be suggested by the gospel accounts, and which is offered by the great majority of commentators, is simple and cogent: the Roman trial was preceded by a trial in a Jewish court, at which Jesus was found guilty on a capital charge. But

[22] J. Blinzler, *The Trial of Jesus* (E.tr. 1959) 205-8, 218-21 argues for its historicity; P. Winter, *On the Trial of Jesus*[2] (1974) 131-4 replies that it is 'nothing but a figment of the imagination'. It is arguable that the reading Ἰησοῦν Βαραββᾶν at Matthew 27.16 guarantees at least the existence of the man; cf. F. Bovon, *Les derniers jours de Jésus* (1974) 67.

[23] The possible influence of *vox populi* on a trial is discussed by F. Bovon, op. cit. 68-9.

since the Sanhedrin at this period did not have the power to carry out the death penalty (a piece of information happily preserved for us in John's gospel) it was necessary for the Jews to bring their prisoner before the Roman court and secure his conviction there if the desired execution were to take place. According to this reconstruction, therefore, there must have been a case against Jesus such that he could be formally accused before a Jewish court on a capital charge; and since the relatively small number of offences which carried the death penalty under Jewish law is known to us,[24] it should not be too difficult to establish, by a process of elimination, the charge which was laid against Jesus. If we can do this, we shall have a further highly significant piece of evidence about Jesus, obtained independently of the gospel narrative, and providing us with a criterion by which we may sift the reports of his teaching and activity. We shall be able, in effect, to interrogate our sources and ask how far they allow us to answer the question, what must Jesus have said or done such that he was in due course arraigned on such a charge?[25]

Unfortunately the matter is a great deal more complicated than this simple summary suggests; moreover, as we shall see, this explanation does not even do justice to the evidence of the New Testament itself. In the first place, it places very great strain on a piece of information which is itself of doubtful historical reliability and which in any case is not reported in order to answer the question in which we are primarily interested. According to John's gospel the Jews, in answer to Pilate's challenge to take Jesus and judge him according to their own law, reply that it is illegal for them to put anyone to death (18.31). The evangelist comments that it was this that enabled Jesus' prophecy to be fulfilled, the prophecy that he would die by being 'lifted up', that is, by being crucified. He does not say that this was the practical hinge of the story, without which the whole train of events would have been incomprehensible; indeed, it stands in contradiction to a number of occasions earlier in the gospel on which the Jews in fact (whether legally or illegally) attempted to carry out a sentence of death on Jesus, but were prevented from doing so by various impediments.[26] From the point of view of the dramatic structure of the gospel, the protestation of their legal impotence by the Jews is simply the last of a series of providential obstacles (such as that Jesus was not to be found, or that his hour was not yet come) which prevented Jesus from meeting his death by stoning at Jewish hands and procured for him a death by crucifixion at Roman hands, a death which this evangelist is able to describe as one, not of humiliation, but of glorification: a 'being lifted up'.

[24]Though the manner of execution, and the exact definition of the offence, changed in the course of time, the biblical list of capital crimes remained unchanged. The following are those which could conceivably have been committed by Jesus; sorcery, rebellious elder, profanation of sabbath, idolatry, blasphemy.

[25]For an example of this line of reasoning (which I now believe to be incorrect) see my *Jesus on Trial* (1976) 77-81.

[26]5.18; 7.30; 8.59; 10.31. Cf. Harvey, *Jesus on Trial* 46-66.

We therefore need to be circumspect if we wish to use this piece of information as the key which will explain an otherwise mysterious course of events. The other three gospels tell the story without any hint that any such key is necessary: either the legal incompetence of the Jewish court in capital cases was a fact so well known to all their readers that it was unnecessary to mention it (which is for various reasons unlikely[27]), or else they regarded the story as sufficiently intelligible and coherent without it (a hint we must follow up presently); and in John's gospel it is placed in the mouths of Jews who have on several previous occasions attempted to act without regard to any such legal restriction,[28] in a scene which is already loaded with irony,[29] and at a point in the narrative where a pretext, rather than an explanation, for the conduct of the Jewish authorities is called for. From this point of view, the continuing debate of historians[30] over the actual competence of the Sanhedrin at this period can be seen not greatly to affect the issue. It seems impossible to prove that the Sanhedrin either was or was not empowered to carry out the death penalty. The most that can be said is that there is no evidence to suggest that the author of John's gospel was certainly mistaken on the point; but even if his report is historically correct, its position in the narrative is such that it ought not to be used as the foundation of a historical reconstruction. We must take seriously the fact that three of our gospels tell the story without so much as a hint that this piece of information is necessary to understanding it.

However, there is a more serious objection to the whole reconstruction. A careful reading of the gospels shows that it is by no means unanimously supported by our witnesses. Mark,[31] it is true, followed by Matthew,[32] describes a session of the chief priests, scribes and elders which culminates in the placing of Jesus under condemnation of death, apparently on a charge of blasphemy. And in those gospels it is occasionally stated, in other contexts,[33] that Jesus was so condemned. But it is not sufficiently often noticed[34] that the author of Luke's gospel takes the opposite view. Not only does he omit all mention of a verdict from his account of the session

[27] The Jewish tradition alone (that the Sanhedrin had temporarily lost the power to try capital cases, ySanh. 1.1; bSanh. 41a, bA.Z.8b) shows that this could not be taken for granted. Moreover the political regime in Judaea changed several times in the course of the first century, and a reader of the gospels after the Jewish war of 70 (when all Jewish autonomy came to an end) could not be expected to recall without help precisely what type of administration prevailed between 25 and 35 A.D.

[28] See above, n.26.

[29] Especially 18.37, 'Are you a king?' etc.

[30] For a recent survey, see E. Schürer, *History of the Jewish People*[2] (ed. Vermes, Millar, Black) 2 (1979) 218–23, and for a clear exposition of the necessary limits to our knowledge, cf. E. Bammel in *JJS* 25 (1974) 35–49.

[31] 14. 55–64.

[32] 26. 59–66.

[33] Mk. 10.33, Mt. 20.18 (prediction); Mt. 27.3.

[34] E.g. V. Taylor, *The Gospel according to St. Mark* 570.

of the Sanhedrin[35] (and indeed from another passage taken from Mark which appears to allude to it) but in Acts he allows St. Peter to say explicitly that the Jews found no cause of death in Jesus.[36] Luke, that is to say, appears to offer evidence for a tradition according to which Jesus was *not* found guilty by any Jewish court; and even if it is argued that this may be due to his own bias, seeking to bring all possible blame upon the Jews, including that of having brought to his death a man whom they knew to be innocent,[37] Luke still remains an important witness, since he could hardly have presented the story in this way if it had been generally known and understood that Jesus was in fact convicted by the Sanhedrin on a capital charge. Nor is Luke the only discordant witness. John's gospel, though it contains a number of episodes in which Jesus is convicted and nearly executed by competent Jewish judges,[38] nevertheless notably does not include such an episode, where Mark and Matthew do, as the immediate prelude to, and explanation of, Jesus' appearance before Pilate. Most significant of all is the argument from silence. Apart from certain instances in Mark and Matthew, which are related to the particular presentation of the session of the Sanhedrin which we find in these gospels,[39] there is no single occasion in the New Testament where it is stated that Jesus was condemned to death by the Jews.

At this point we have to admit the possible influence of some highly charged theological considerations. Three New Testament writers (Luke, Paul and the author of 1 Peter) choose to refer to the crucifixion of Jesus – which was a penalty unknown to the Old Testament – in terms which make it possible to identify it as a fulfilment of scripture. They describe it, that is to say, as 'hanging upon wood'[40] and so relate it to that provision of the Jewish law under which a criminal who had been sentenced to death and executed should then, in certain circumstances, have his body publicly hung on a tree.[41] This further penalty, executed on the corpse of the offender, was normally carried out only in cases of blasphemy or idolatry.[42] Did these

---

[35] Luke writes (22.71): 'What further need have we of testimony? For we ourselves have heard from his own mouth.' He pointedly omits the reaction of the high priest, the mention of blasphemy, and the judgment that Jesus was worthy of death.

[36] This conclusion is resisted by the great majority of commentators and the point must be argued in detail. See Appendix I, pp.174-5.

[37] This bias is seen even in Luke's consistent use of παραδιδόναι only of the Jewish people as a whole; cf. W. Popkes, *Christus Traditus* (1967) 183.

[38] See above, n.26.

[39] See above, n.33.

[40] Acts 5.30; 10.39 κρεμάσαντες ἐπὶ ξύλον. Cf. 13.29; Gal. 3.13 πᾶς ὁ κρεμάμενος ἐπὶ ξύλου (= Dt. 21. 23 LXX) applied to Jesus; 1 Pet. 2.24 ἐπὶ τὸ ξύλον.

[41] Dt. 21.22-3. A similar adjustment (this time by altering the order of the words) of the scriptural text to fit the abnormal penalty of hanging occurs in the Temple Scroll 64; cf. G. Vermes, *DSSE* 250-1.

[42] Josephus *Ant.* 4. 202; M.Sanh. 6.4. Symmachus introduces blasphemy at Dt. 21.22, where LXX has simply κρίμα θανάτου. Philo *S.L.* 3. 151-2 apparently takes κρίμα θανάτου to mean 'conviction for murder'.

writers therefore believe that Jesus, having (in a sense) received the appropriate penalty, was actually found guilty on such a charge? Idolatry would hardly have come into question in the case of Jesus; but blasphemy was a charge to which he could well have been exposed.[43] Paul, at least, seems to have believed in Jesus' guilt under the Jewish law – indeed he made considerable theological capital out of it: since Jesus, in the eyes of God, was right, then the law was wrong. But the theology was hardly possible without some basis in history. Paul must have believed, either that Jesus was at some stage actually convicted by a Jewish court, or else at least that he was culpable according to Paul's own (Pharisaic) understanding of Jewish law, whether or not such a verdict had been reached in any actual court.[44] In either case not only the court itself, but the Jewish law altogether, had been shown to be totally discordant with the will of God. Mark, followed by Matthew, gives some historical content to this belief by reporting an apparent condemnation[45] in a Jewish court as the immediate prelude to the trial before Pilate. Luke, as we have seen, seems to take the opposite view: Jesus was not found guilty and was delivered to Pilate out of sheer ignorance[46] of his real nature; but the result of this 'handing over' was a form of death which *looked like* the penalty imposed on certain criminals by Jewish law, and made it possible to apply to Jesus the words of Isaiah 53.12, 'he was numbered with the transgressors' even though (like the Suffering Servant) he was innocent. The author of 1 Peter, who also stresses Jesus' innocence (indeed it is essential to the argument of 2.18-25), takes a similar view. John's gospel stands in the middle position: Jesus was indeed condemned under the law on several occasions; but in this version it was the judges, not the law, that were at fault. The reader is allowed to see what factors were overlooked, what statements misinterpreted, by Jesus' earthly judges.

In view of this diversity among New Testament writers regarding the question of Jesus' condemnation under the Jewish law, it is all the more

[43] For the view that this was a more general offence at the time of Jesus than it became in Rabbinic *halakha,* see the evidence adduced in my *Jesus on Trial* (1976) 77-81, and below, pp.170f.

[44] His readiness to apply Dt. 21.23 to Jesus is most easily explicable if he believed him to have been convicted in a Jewish court: crucifixion could be held to be sufficiently comparable to the biblical 'hanging of the corpse' for it to have appeared that Jesus' death was a fulfilment of the Old Testament text; from which it would follow that he must have been convicted of a capital offence (Dt. 21.22). But the same reasoning could presumably also have envisaged the possiblity that the court or courts before which Jesus appeared did not agree on the verdict which a Pharisee would have regarded as inevitable. That is to say, Paul as a Pharisee would have regarded Jesus as a 'sinner' on a number of grounds (particularly perhaps his conduct on the sabbath). He might then have regarded the crucifixion = hanging on a tree as the providential carrying out of a sentence which a properly constituted court *should* have imposed. In either case, Jesus' resurrection will have shown the law to have been wrong: since Jesus had been proved to be righteous, culpability under the law, and therefore also innocence under the law, could no longer serve as a criterion of 'righteousness'.

[45] Note the use of κατακρίνω at Mk. 10.33// Mt. 20.18; Mk. 14.64; Mt. 27.3 ἰδὼν Ἰούδας . . . ὅτι κατεκρίθη. Yet, as we shall see, in other respects the judgment is *not* described as a judicial verdict.

[46] A favourite theme of Luke: Lk. 6.11; Acts 3.17, 13.27.

striking that they all unite to describe the action of the Jews which led to Jesus' execution by Pilate as a handing over, a 'delivering up'. The Greek word *paradidonai,* like its Latin equivalent *tradere,* had a wide range of meanings, wider in fact than any comparable word in either Hebrew or English. At the one extreme is the perfectly neutral sense of handing over a person or an object to someone who has a right to receive it.[47] At the other end of the scale is that act of deliberate and deceitful handing over for which English has the word 'betray', Hebrew *matsar.*[48] Between these two lies a whole range of nuances according to the degree to which someone may have both the freedom and the moral choice whether or not to hand someone or something over as a reward or a penalty, a hostage or a ransom. Instances at either end of this range can be found in the New Testament. In a parable, a man 'handed over' his possessions to his servants before going on a journey (Mt. 25.14); at the other extreme, the same word used of Judas Iscariot clearly means, not just handing over, but *betraying.* Between these two extremes there are two usages which particularly interest us. There is first what may be regarded as a purely technical use. It is said again and again in the gospel narrative that Jesus is 'handed over' to the Jews, to Pilate, to execution. The word is appropriate, exact and to the point. It describes the physical transfer of Jesus from one authority to another. In these instances it may be regarded as a technical term.[49] But the same word was also capable of expressing a more mysterious and theologically significant aspect of the 'handing over' of Jesus. No Christian wished to suppose that Jesus, in his last hours on earth, was a merely passive agent, being handed over unwillingly to his death. His acquiescence was not merely to men, it was also to his heavenly father. And for this there lay to hand a scriptural model using the very same expression. In Isaiah 53, God 'handed over' (*paredōken*) the Servant for our sins, his soul was 'handed over to death' (*paredothē*) and he was 'handed over' (*paredothē*) because of our transgressions.[50] Used as a technical term, the statement that Jesus was handed over need mean no more than that he was passed on from one authority to another. But to anyone familiar with the scriptures in Greek, it would readily suggest that the real initiator of this handing over was God himself, and that it took place, not just as part of a judicial procedure, but on a wider stage of human destiny. Like the suffering servant of Isaiah, Jesus was 'handed over' for our sins. It was God who handed him over (Is. 53.6; Romans 8.32) or even (if one is to stress the active participation of Jesus in his own

---

[47] Frequent in papyrus documents; cf. MM s.v.
[48] Clearly the case when applied to Judas; cf. W. Popkes, *Christus Traditus* (1967) 19-21.
[49] Id. ib. 183.
[50] The influence of the LXX is apparent here: it has παραδιδόναι three times in Isaiah 53, none of which is demanded by the Hebrew text. The Targum has the equivalent *m-ts-r* only once at 53.12c; cf. Popkes, op. cit. 32.

self-offering) it was Jesus who 'handed himself over' (Gal. 2.20; Eph. 5.2).[51] The word, in short, is one of those which comes to express the mysterious self-giving of Jesus which is at the heart of the Christian understanding of redemption. It stands in close relation, both to the early formulation in Mark according to which the Son of Man gives his life as a ransom for many (10.45), and to the Johannine development of the figure of the Good Shepherd, who lays down his life for the sheep (10.11).

This very theological richness[52] of the word 'handed over' presents us with a delicate problem when we come to consider what is probably the earliest occurrence in the New Testament of the description of Jesus' passion as a 'handing over'. In Romans 4.25 Paul appears to be making use of a formula which already existed before his time[53] when he writes of Jesus that he was handed over because of our sins and raised for our justification. The first clause of this formula is clearly a reminiscence of Isaiah 53.12 where it is said of the Suffering Servant that 'he was handed over' (LXX) to death.[54] It is well known that this suffering servant passage was referred to at a very early stage in order to make sense of the sufferings endured by Jesus, and the question arises whether certain remembered historical details, such as Jesus' silence before his accusers,[55] were eagerly taken as corroboration of this interpretation, or whether, once Jesus had been identified as the innocent sufferer of Isaiah 53, the nature of his sufferings, in the absence of historical evidence, was read out of scripture and embodied in what purported to be eye-witness accounts. The same question is posed by the formula in Romans 4.25, and by those predictions of the passion in Mark's gospel which use the same expression, 'handed over' (9.31; 10.33), and of which one clearly betrays the influence of Isaiah 53.[56] Was Jesus in fact 'handed over' to the Sanhedrin, to Pilate, to execution, as the gospels record? Or was the actual course of events no longer known by the time the gospels were written, and subsequently reconstructed as a result of identifying Jesus with the Servant whom Scripture described as having been 'handed over' to death? The transfer of Jesus from one court to another, and the act of betrayal by Judas, would all follow from this one single word in the text of Isaiah.

[51] In 1 Pet. 2.23 παρεδίδου τῷ κρίνοντι δικαίως some object must be supplied. Most commentators suggest 'his cause'. The oddity of the expression may be due to the author's desire to formulate Jesus' *traditio* in such a way that it would provide a ὑπογραμμός for the conduct of Christian slaves or servants towards unrighteous masters.

[52] Cf. B. Lindars, *New Testament Apologetic* (1961) 80: 'a word used with peculiarly evocative overtones.'

[53] 'Confessional formula', J. Jeremias, *New Testament Theology* 1. (1971) 296 and n.5; H. Conzelmann, *An Outline of the Theology of the New Testament* (E.tr. 1969) 63; etc.

[54] B. Klappert, *NTS* 13 (1966-7) 170, notes the very close correspondence of Romans 4.25 with Tg Is. 53.5b.

[55] The formulation ὃς λοιδορούμενος οὐκ ἀντελοιδόρει (1 Pet. 2.23) appears to have no basis in scripture, and may well be derived from historical reminiscence.

[56] Cf. 10.34 μαστιγώσουσι with 'scourging' Is. 53.5 (Hebrew).

A certain answer to this question is perhaps not possible. It is hard for us today to get inside the minds of those who read scripture precisely to find such connections, and who were ready to regard a seven-hundred-year-old prophecy as a source of information about recent events as reliable as an eyewitness account; yet the very frequency of the occurrence of this word 'handed over' in contexts where (as we have seen) it is technically correct and appears to have no scriptural overtones of any kind suggests that the New Testament writers believed that 'handing over' was in fact the process which brought Jesus to his death, and that it was this physical circumstance, which, among others, suggested the identification of Jesus with the Servant of Isaiah who was also 'handed over' by God.[57] At the very least, their preference for this word over any other for summarising the events leading up to the crucifixion is evidence that they cannot have been aware of any historical information which contradicted it. Rather, therefore, than assume that Jesus was convicted on a capital charge by a Jewish court, and that his transference to Pilate's court was due to the Jews' inability to carry out the sentence they had passed, we should start from the unanimous evidence of the New Testament that Jesus appeared before Pilate as a result of a decision by the Jewish authority to 'hand him over'. The implications of such a handing over have not received the attention they deserve.[58] When a nation is fiercely preserving its own culture and religion against the pressures of an alien occupying power, one of the things which is most jealously guarded is the right to bring offenders to trial in local courts according to their ancestral laws. Even in the Diaspora it was felt to be a disgrace and a weakness to allow internal Jewish disputes to come to the notice of the gentile courts.[59] Handing a citizen over to the occupying power for justice was inevitably a serious and infrequent course of action. In subsequent centuries, when Jewish communities in Palestine or Babylonia no longer had the right to make use of their own courts to the extent that was possible in the time of Jesus, the issue was seriously debated whether it could ever be right to yield to a pagan demand for the extradition of a Jewish citizen.[60] Following the precedent established by 2 Sam. 20. 18–22 (Joab's demand for Sheba, son of Bichri), the view was accepted that a named individual might be surrendered to such a demand, but that a request for the extradition of any Jew merely to satisfy the desire of the occupying power to inflict punishment on the community should always be resisted. Moreover, the presumption was doubtless already present which subsequently passed into Jewish law,[61] that any Jew so handed

[57] W. Popkes, op. cit. 223, wisely observes that these allusions to Is. 53 should be regarded as not so much apologetic as 'Stilmittel' in early Christian writing.

[58] But see now J. D. M. Derrett, 'The Iscariot, Mesira, and the Redemption', *JSNT* 8 (1980), 2-23.

[59] 1 Cor. 6.1 ff.

[60] A full treatment of the rabbinic evidence may be found in D. Daube, *Collaboration with Tyranny in Jewish Law* (1971).

[61] Maimonides I,III, vi. 14 (9).

over for trial in a pagan court must be one who would in fact have been found guilty of a serious offence in a Jewish court. At the period when they were held, such discussions were somewhat academic; Jewish courts no longer had sanctions such that a claim to cope with their own offenders without recourse to pagan courts would carry much credibility. But in the time of Jesus the issue will have been a real one.[62] Jewish courts had full authority in a very wide range of criminal offences. Even if (as seems probable) the Roman governor reserved the right to impose or confirm a capital penalty, there is no evidence (apart from a significant exception which will be noted in its place) that the Jews felt seriously restricted in enforcing the rule of law in Judaea, and a deliberate reference by a Jewish court of a case to the Roman governor must always[63] have been a step taken infrequently and unwillingly. The fact that Jesus was 'handed over' – *traditus* – to Pilate suggests something altogether exceptional in the circumstances.

What these exceptional circumstances were is a question to which the synoptic gospels offer no direct answer. That is to say, though they have a number of explanations why the Jewish authorities took action against Jesus – out of envy (Mark)[64] or ignorance (Luke)[65] – they make no comment on the fact that they took the unusual course of handing Jesus over out of their own jurisdiction to Pilate. It is only John's gospel which comments on the point; and, as so often, its comments are worth attending to. In the first place, when Pilate asks the reason for the Jews' unusual action in submitting Jesus to his jurisdiction, they reply, 'If he had not been a malefactor we would not have handed him over to you' (18.30). This, as we have seen,[66] is a principle which ultimately entered the Jewish code of law and which is even more likely to have governed Jewish procedure at a time when the Jewish courts retained considerable competence alongside the Roman ones. The extradition of Jesus was unlikely to have taken place (so this evangelist was informed, or so indeed he could have reasoned it out for himself) unless the Jews had come to regard Jesus as a serious criminal. But this still leaves the question why Jesus' case was not dealt with sufficiently by a Jewish court. As we have seen, this evangelist reports – rightly or wrongly, and in a context where a touch of irony cannot be excluded – that the Jews did not have the power to carry out the death penalty. But this information is not offered as an explanation of why the *traditio* took place in the first instance, but only by way of a reason for

[62] G. Vermes, in conversation.
[63] C.D. 9.1 (on which J. D. M. Derrett, *Law in the New Testament* (1970) 423 and n.1 places great reliance) yields contrary evidence only in Lohse's rendering. Majority opinion appears to be against him; cf. G. Vermes, *DSSE* 110; L. Rabinowitz, *Rev. de Qum.* 6 (1968) 433ff. Z. W. Falk, ib. 569. Any form of 'handing over' by an individual to Gentiles was invariably illegal: M. Ter 8. 12; 11 Q Temple 64; cf. Derrett *JSNT* 8 (1980) 3-5.
[64] Mk. 15. 10 (usually regarded as redactional).
[65] See above, n.46.
[66] See above, n.61

the Jews not taking the case back into their own hands when invited to do so
by Pilate. More light on the original cause of their action is shed by the
famous passage at the end of ch.11, where Caiaphas advises the Sanhedrin
that it is expedient that one man should die for the people rather than the
whole race be destroyed. The threat which faced the Jewish leaders,
according to this evangelist, was that the Romans should come 'and take
away both the place and the nation'. We know from Josephus[67] that in the
year preceding the Jewish revolt of 66 A.D. this danger was a real one: reprisals
by the Romans for insurrectionary behaviour by the Jews were expected to
take the form of destruction of the temple and removal of those privileges
which enabled the Jews to secure the continuance of their exclusive religion
and customs within the Roman empire. Whether or not this warning reflects
the situation at the time when Jesus was active[68] is open to question; but the
evangelist is surely right in suggesting that only a serious political crisis
would have caused the Jews to take the exceptional step of handing over their
prisoner. The account goes on: 'From that day they resolved to put him to
death'. The words describe an executive, not a judicial, action.[69] It is not said
that they condemned Jesus to death *in absentia*. Rather, they took a decision to
secure Jesus' death in the only way open to them, namely by handing him
over to Pilate for execution.

It is in the light of this that we must now look at the one case of voluntary
'handing over' recorded by Josephus, a case which bears a remarkable
resemblance to that of Jesus. The instance occurs at *B.J.* 6.300-305, and is
worth quoting at length.

> Four years before the war . . . there came to the feast . . . one Jesus, son of Ananias, a
> rude peasant, who, standing in the temple, suddenly began to cry out, 'A voice
> from the east, a voice from the west, a voice from the four winds; a voice against
> Jerusalem and the sanctuary . . .' Day and night he went about all the alleys with this
> cry on his lips. Some of the leading citizens, incensed at these ill-omened words,
> arrested the fellow and severely chastised him. But he, without a word on his own
> behalf . . . only continued his cries as before. Thereupon, the magistrates, supposing,
> as was indeed the case, that the man was under some supernatural impulse, brought
> him before the Roman governor; there, although flayed to the bone with scourges, he
> neither sued for mercy nor shed a tear, but merely introducing the most mournful of
> variations into his ejaculation, responded to each stroke with 'Woe to Jerusalem!'
> When Albinus the governor asked him who and whence he was and why he uttered
> these cries, he answered him never a word, but unceasingly reiterated his dirge over
> the city until Albinus pronounced him mad and let him go.[69a]

The legal processes behind this episode are clear enough. The man gave
offence with his ceaseless cry of doom, and the Jewish magistrates, having

---

[67] *B.J.* 2. 397, 400, 421.

[68] Probably not: E. Bammel, 'Ex illa itaque Die . . .' in E. Bammel, ed., *The Trial of Jesus* (1970)
24-5.

[69] Id. ib. 29-30.

[69a] H. St. J. Thackeray's translation (Loeb 1928).

presumably found him guilty on a charge of insolent language,[70] imposed the appropriate[71] penalty of scourging. But this failed to silence him; and since there was no charge under Jewish law which could be brought against him which would carry a severer penalty (and since the obvious remedy, imprisonment, was not a normal sentence in a Jewish court except for cases of debt),[72] they saw no way of dealing with the case other than by handing him over to the court of the Roman governor. There he was subjected to torture, doubtless in the expectation that this would force him to declare his true motive in creating the disturbance. When this failed, the governor evidently had no option but to let him go free as a harmless lunatic. Josephus tells us that he continued his melancholy dirge for seven years and five months until he was accidentally killed by a flying missile in the siege of Jerusalem.

This episode is particularly instructive, in that it illustrates the possibility of the Jewish courts being unable, according to their own procedure, to cope effectively with a Jewish citizen who was regarded as a threat to public order, and as being prepared to take the exceptional step of referring such a case to the Roman authority. The charge originally brought against Ananias was similar to one of those brought against Jesus, that he had threatened the destruction of the temple.[73] There was of course precedent for proceeding against such an offence in the case of Jeremiah, whose prophecies against the temple and the city created a demand for his condemnation to death (Jer. 26.7–19). But in the event the demand was resisted: the episode would have afforded dubious support for a conviction by a Jewish court, and we can guess that one of the reasons, if not the main reason, for the Jews' decision to hand over Ananias to the Roman governor was their inability to agree on the man's culpability under the law. We must remember that such failures of a court to come to a common mind were a frequent occurence. The scribes of which the courts were largely composed had been trained in different schools, and took different views on the interpretation and applicability of the law (a vivid illustration is provided by Paul's success in playing the Pharisees off against the Sadducees in the course of a court hearing in Acts 23.7). A man who seemed clearly guilty to one school might seem innocent to another, and even though the first school might not have been able to secure a sufficient majority among the judges for a condemnation, it would continue to hand on its view of the case to successive generations of scholars, among whom the defendant would necessarily be remembered as guilty.[74]

[70] πρὸς τὸ κακόφημον. Spreading alarm and despondency was also an offence.

[71] That the list of offences punishable by scourging in M. Makk. 3 was by no means exhaustive (at least before 70 A.D.) is proved by Jos. *Ant.* 4. 238.

[72] Cf. R. de Vaux, *Ancient Israel* (1965) 160; Z. W. Falk, *Introduction to Jewish Law of the Second Commonwealth* 2 (1978) 162-3.

[73] Mk. 14.58; Mt. 26.61; John 2.19; Acts 6.14.

[74] M. Sanh 7.2 shows subsequent Pharisaic tradition in disagreement with the action of a court in an earlier period.

This feature of Jewish legal history offers us a clue by which we may be able to make sense of the apparent contradiction between different New Testament writers with regard to Jesus' culpability under the Jewish law. As we have seen, Luke explicitly denies that Jesus was found guilty by a Jewish court, and suggests that he was handed over to Pilate (as we might put it) on purely political grounds. Paul on the other hand (whose interpretation of the law was of course according to the Pharisaic school) certainly regarded Jesus as a person who had at some stage been convicted (or who would at least have been liable to conviction, if a Pharisaic interpretation had been applied) under the law of Moses. It is possible that Jesus' well-remembered transgressions of specifically Pharisaic applications of the law[75] would have been sufficient for Paul, a Pharisee, to have regarded Jesus as an inveterate law-breaker and therefore accursed under the law, whether or not any court had actually convicted him. Nevertheless, the fact that he was prepared to describe Jesus' crucifixion in terms of that 'hanging upon a tree' which the Jewish law prescribed as an addition to the death penalty imposed for certain specific crimes, in particular blasphemy,[76] suggests that he believed Jesus to have been in fact guilty of such an offence under the law. We have here, then, two sharply divided opinions. Our other witnesses come somewhere between them. Mark and Matthew, as we have already noted, report a tradition which is flatly contradicted by Luke and John, that Jesus was found guilty of blasphemy immediately before being handed over to Pilate; but even in their accounts the judges, instead of proceeding directly to sentence and execution, hold a further meeting[77] to decide on Jesus being handed over to Pilate. That is to say, their narratives, though they include what appears to be a condemnation by a Jewish court, are nevertheless primarily an account of the handing over, the *traditio*, which was the fundamental event in the whole story of the passion. John's gospel, again, though it gives a number of instances of the way in which Jesus may have been convicted by a Jewish court of a particular composition, nevertheless separates them altogether from the handing over, which according to this version was due to political motives.

It comes naturally to the modern western critic to assume that the difference between these reports stems from a greater or lesser degree of access to the original facts, and that our task is simply to determine which of these versions is closest to the historical truth. But in this case it may be more important to ask why we should have such divergent reports in the first place;

---

[75] see Chapter 3.

[76] see above, n.42.

[77] εὐθὺς πρωὶ συμβόυλιον ἑτοιμάσαντες (Mk. 15.1), which undoubtedly describes an executive, not a judicial, decision; cf. Mk. 3.6. The v.l. in each case (ἐποίησαν, ποιήσαντες) assimilates the phrase to a Latinism = *consilium capere* (Bl.-D.§5. 3(b)), which shows that this is how it was understood, whatever the original text may have been.

and the answer which suggests itself is that no Jewish court before which Jesus appeared was able to agree, either upon the exact nature of his offence, or upon the question of his legal guilt or innocence. Different traditions, stemming from different attitudes to the Jewish law held by Jews who had subsequently become Christians, may have taken divergent views on the legality of Jesus' words and actions and on the validity of any court judgment to which he was subjected. As we shall see later on, Jesus' conduct was precisely such as to raise such questions without actually resolving them, and is in this way closely related to the circumstances of his death. But for the present purpose the important point is that if, as our conflicting evidence suggests, it was in fact impossible to reach a verdict upon Jesus in any official court, and if nevertheless it seemed necessary to the Jewish authorities to have Jesus put out of the way, then the only course left open to them was to hand him over to the court of the Roman governor, in the hope that the rather more flexible jurisdiction which he exercised[78] would enable him to find Jesus guilty and execute him. As we have seen, it must have been some such expectation as this which led them to hand over Ananias some thirty years later. In that case they were unsuccessful; but in the case of Jesus they appear to have been able to exercise so much pressure on Pontius Pilate that they obtained their objective. Jesus was crucified.

Our reasoning so far has suggested that the immediate prelude to Jesus' appearance before Pilate was not (as is usually assumed) a previous conviction in a Jewish court; indeed if Jesus was brought to trial at all before the Sanhedrin, it seems more likely (in view of the conflict between the sources) that the court failed to agree on a verdict, though some of the judges certainly believed in his guilt. Instead the event we have to reconstruct is that which is implied by the standard New Testament phrase used to describe this stage of Jesus' passion, the decision taken by the Jewish authorities to 'hand over' Jesus to the Roman governor. This decision will have been, not a legal judgment, but a political action, a fact which immediately relieves one of the greatest strains which is placed upon our belief in the general reliability of the gospel accounts. It is well known that the narrative of the so-called trial before the Sanhedrin in Mark and Matthew (and to a slightly lesser extent in Luke)[79] violates almost every rule of procedure which according to the Mishnah should have been followed in a capital case. A night sitting and a verdict passed without an adjournment (to name the two most flagrant irregularities) are explicitly ruled out by the Rabbinic regulations.[80] It may of course be argued that these regulations were not in force in the time of Jesus,

[78] According to the procedure of *cognitio*; cf. A. N. Sherwin-White, *Roman Society and Roman Law in the New Testament* (1963) 17-23.

[79] Luke avoids the irregularities of a night sitting and the omission of a second sitting (cf. D. R. Catchpole in *The Trial of Jesus* (1976) ed. E. Bammel, 58-9) but this raises other difficulties; cf. A. N. Sherwin-White, op. cit. 45.

[80] M. Sanh. passim.

that the Mishnah represents an academic and idealised form of procedure rather than an account of what actually took place in the time of the Second Temple, and that in any case the situation was the kind of emergency in which a number of the normal regulations might well have been waived. It is in fact along these lines that the credit of the evangelists is usually saved by Christian scholars.[81] But if we now recognise that the intention of the evangelists was not to report a trial, but rather a meeting of the Jewish authorities to decide whether Jesus was to be handed over to Pilate, these difficulties disappear. Such a meeting could have been held at any time and was perhaps particularly urgent when Jerusalem was rapidly filling up with pilgrims for Passover,[82] whereas even on the assumption of a major emergency a night sitting of a court immediately before one of the great festivals is not easy to believe in.[83] Moreover, the account as it stands in Mark does not for the most part read like a formal trial. It is introduced by the statement that the high priests and the whole Sanhedrin sought testimony against Jesus in order to put him to death (Mk. 14.55). It is true that this statement would have sounded less shocking to Jewish readers of the time than it does to us today. We assume instinctively that the role of judge and prosecutor must be kept rigorously separate, but in the Jewish system the tasks of witness, judge and indeed executioner were by no means so carefully distinguished,[84] and it would have been open to the court to seek out testimony against the prisoner. But such a process would normally have been complete before the formal proceedings began. What we read in Mark appears to be an account of a preliminary hearing, in which an attempt was made to frame and support a charge against a suspect. The attempt failed, and it was only Jesus' reply to a direct question from the High Priest which caused the court to pronounce the judgment that Jesus was worthy of death. This expression could certainly represent the verdict of a court, but it need not do so,[85] and in fact what follows is not the normal preparation for the carrying out of the sentence but a scene of extremely un-judicial insult and mockery, followed in due course by a further session which took the decision to hand over Jesus to Pilate. Apart from one brief episode of Jesus' alleged blasphemy, to which we must return in a later chapter, there is nothing in this account to suggest that Jesus was on trial on a capital charge. The task of the Sanhedrin was a political, not a judicial, one:[86] to decide whether, and on what grounds, to hand Jesus over to Pilate.

[81] E.g. J. Blinzler, *The Trial of Jesus* (E.tr. 1959) 142-3.

[82] That Jesus was condemned around the time of the Passover is confirmed by subsequent Jewish tradition, bSanh. 43a.

[83] A point well made by H. Cohn, *The Trial and Death of Jesus* (1972), 94ff.

[84] See my *Jesus on Trial* (1976) 46-7.

[85] In Aboth. 1.13, 'he that learns not is worthy of death', there is a clear case of 'worthy of death', ἔνοχος θανάτου, representing a moral, not a legal, judgment; cf. B. Viviano, *Study as Worship* (1978) 25.

[86] Luke (23.51) actually calls it βουλὴ καὶ πρᾶξις.

We are now in a position to summarise what may be known with reasonable certainty of the last stages of Jesus' life on earth and to relate this knowledge to the material which we find in the gospel tradition. Starting from the established fact of Jesus' crucifixion, which implies a trial before Pilate and condemnation on a charge of sedition, we have had to ask how a person such as we believe Jesus to have been could have been the object of such an accusation, and we have seen reason to accept the unanimous testimony of the New Testament witnesses that Jesus was 'handed over' to Pilate by the Jewish authorities. This 'handing over' must have been resolved upon by a decision of the Sanhedrin. That a meeting was held to pass this resolution is certain;[87] that it took the form of a criminal trial we have seen to be unlikely. The meeting – or at any rate the last of such meetings, since there may have been previous ones – was held when Jesus had already been arrested: a final decision to hand him over to Pilate could have been taken only when Jesus was physically in their hands. Presumably they will' also have taken the opportunity to interrogate him.

Let us now suppose (as we did with regard to the trial before Pilate) that this bare outline of the facts was all that was known to the evangelists. They will have realised that in order to justify their action in handing Jesus over the Jewish authorities will have needed to present certain charges against him. If our argument is correct, they will have known also that these charges did not establish his guilt under any Jewish law, since as a matter of fact Jesus was not formally found guilty by the Jewish court. A generalising summary of such a situation is offered by Mark and Matthew,[88] who report that the high priests and the whole Sanhedrin sought testimony against Jesus which would make him liable to the death penalty, but failed to obtain it, since although witnesses were found who were prepared to give false evidence, it did not amount to a consistent case.[89] Nevertheless the evangelists will have been able to infer from their own accounts of the activity of Jesus that certain actions and sayings might well have formed the basis of accusations during such proceedings. In particular, there was a well-attested saying about destroying the temple and rebuilding it in three days which, whatever its original intention, could surely have been used against Jesus and is consequently included in Mark's and Matthew's account of the hearing, though again with the recognition that it was insufficient to establish Jesus' guilt.[90]

[87] This is granted even, e.g., by Hans Conzelmann, who regards the scene recorded by the synoptic gospels as 'Christological teaching scenically formed' (*Interpretation* 24 (1970) 178–97, at p.190).

[88] Mk. 14. 55–9; Mt. 26. 59–61.

[89] Mk. 14.56 ἴσαι αἱ μαρτυρίαι οὐκ ἦσαν.

[90] The differences between the different versions of this charge (n.73) are usually taken as indications of the embarrassment of the evangelists at having to record an apparently unfulfilled prophecy. Their embarrassment is a good indication of the authenticity of some saying of Jesus such as is recorded in Mk. 13.2.

There must however have been a presumption in the mind of these evangelists that it was a reason more powerful than any of these that caused the Jewish leaders to take the very serious step of handing Jesus over to Pilate, and which also enabled them to secure his conviction in a Roman court. A clue to their thinking may perhaps be found in Luke's gospel. This gospel is the only one to give any account of the charges pressed by the Jews against Jesus in the presence of the Roman governor. These charges are given (20.2) as 'misleading'the people', 'preventing the payment of taxes to Caesar', and 'giving himself out as an anointed king'. It is significant that none of these could have formed the substance of a serious charge in Jewish law.[91] Luke is therefore correct in principle, in that had Jesus been causing a threat to the peace and well-being of the nation by acting in these ways, the only way the Jewish authorities could have restrained him would have been by handing him over to be tried on such charges under Roman law. But for the present purpose our attention is caught by the last of the clauses, 'giving himself out as an anointed king'. Any reconstruction of the events leading to Jesus' execution must start, and must always have started, with the known charge on which he was crucified: king of the Jews. What was there in the life and teaching of Jesus which could have given colour to such a charge? Luke gives us the clue by linking 'king' with another word, *christos,* meaning 'anointed'. Jesus (we shall argue) was known by this name in his lifetime. What more likely, therefore, than that Jesus was interrogated about this very name by the Jewish authorities, and that his reply seemed threatening enough for them to proceed with the transfer of the case to Pilate? Indeed what more likely than that there was mention of that other mysterious expression which Jesus so often used of himself, 'Son of Man' – harmless enough, for the most part, but if invoked with all the associations of that one like a Son of Man who, in the Book of Daniel, was invested with supreme honour and dignity in heaven – then small wonder that the Jewish leaders would feel impelled by Jesus' implicit claims to authority to act decisively against him.[92] The rending of his garments by the high priest would be a further touch added by the narrator, aptly signifying[93] the alarm felt by responsible leaders at the possible consequences of such absolutist language. One way or another, a man who said such things was deserving of death if a dangerous and

[91] διαστρέφοντα τὸ ἔθνος is a very general statement with moral rather than legal implications. Claiming to be a king was not as such a criminal offence in Jewish law.

[92] Cf. J. R. Donahue, *Are You the Christ?* (1973) 96–8 for arguments and scholarly support for the view that both the reference to blasphemy and the apparent condemnation are Markan.

[93] Too much attention has been paid to the direction in the Mishnah (Sanh. 7.5) that on hearing a blasphemous utterance the judges (not just one of them, as in the gospels) must rend their garments. The gesture was widespread in antiquity (see the instances quoted by Wettstein on Mt. 26.65), particularly as an expression of grief; among the Jews it was also a means of expressing consternation (Jos. *B.J.* 2. 316; Acts 14.14). The rabbis were naturally concerned about the expense involved, and sought to limit the occasions on which the gesture was *de rigueur* by close exegesis of the biblical precedents at 2 Kings 2.12; 18.37f.

unwelcome popular movement were to be avoided.

In this way most of the details of the narrative are accounted for. If in addition we allow for the influence, here as later on, of the Servant figure in Second Isaiah, we need look for no further explanation of the only two incidents which remain unaccounted for:[94] the silence of Jesus before his accusers (based on Isaiah 53.7) and the somewhat unexpected (and historically implausible) scene of insult and mockery inserted at this point, which is a recasting[95] of the mockery and scourging endured by the Servant in Isaiah 50.6. Moreover we now have a satisfying explanation of the apparent contradictions in our sources. As we have seen, the high priest's rending of his garment, and the pronouncement that Jesus was deserving of death, do not necessarily amount to a formal verdict of guilty in a court of law; and Luke, in order to remove any possible doubt which might attach to his assertion that Jesus was not found guilty on any charge, but was brought to his death by the almost irrational intention and wilful ignorance of the Jewish race as a whole, carefully omits the words which might suggest that the Sanhedrin actually passed a judgment. The Fourth Gospel goes even further, in that it omits all reference to a sitting of the Sanhedrin at this point, the decision to hand over Jesus having been taken some time before (11.53); but this gospel also recognises that Jesus was in fact convicted on a number of occasions by ad hoc Jewish courts of more or less Pharisaic composition, though the reader is helped to see that in each case the verdict was reached without full knowledge of the facts about Jesus, and was therefore incorrect. What in effect this reconstruction has enabled us to do is to separate out two questions which have become deeply entangled in modern treatments of the subject but which are not so intimately connected in the gospel accounts. One question is that of the *traditio,* the handing over: what was the reason for this serious and unusual action on the part of the Jewish authorities, and by what steps was it accomplished? As we have seen, the evangelists' answer to this question contains nothing which could not have been inferred from the bare bones of the situation. The other question is that of Jesus' guilt or innocence according to Jewish law. It appears from Paul that it was possible to regard Jesus as unquestionably guilty; from Luke, that Jesus was certainly innocent. The other gospels (we might say) reserve their position, the Epistle to the Hebrews, implicitly at least,[96] comes down on the side of Luke. The

[94] So E. Haenchen, *Der Weg Jesu* (1966) 514–15.

[95] The only verbal link is ἐμπτυσμάτων - ἐμπτύειν, but the same motif is common to both passages. Some reminiscence must lie behind the gospel tradition as well as the scriptural allusion, but it has given rise to a number of different episodes, of which that before the Sanhedrin is perhaps the least plausible. For a judicious treatment of the material, see P. Benoit O.P., 'Les outrages à Jésus Prophète (Mk. 14.64 par.)', *Neotestamentica et Patristica* (Cullmann Festschrift, 1962) 92–110. For a structuralist study arguing for the consistency of the gospel accounts see Olivette Genest, *Le Christ de la Passion* (1978).

[96] Jesus was not merely χωρὶς ἁμαρτίας (4.14) but ὅσιος, ἄκακος, ἀμίαντος (7.26): could the author have written this if he had believed that Jesus had been actually convicted under the Jewish law?

historical question whether Jesus was in fact, on any occasion, found guilty by a Jewish court is probably unanswerable on the evidence we possess; but the fact that opinions were divided on the subject so early in the history of the church yields us a historical conclusion of very great importance. Jesus' words and actions must certainly have been such as to *raise the question* of legality. Differently constituted courts might have reached different verdicts on Jesus; scholars belonging to different schools might have instinctively regarded him as innocent or guilty. But one thing is certain: his teaching and his conduct were such that legal questions were raised by it, on which different views might be taken. With this precious conclusion in mind, we can now turn to other aspects of the available evidence about Jesus.

# 3
# The Constraint of Law

We began our enquiry by observing that, as a matter of indisputable historical fact, Jesus was condemned and executed as a result of certain political and judicial procedures. In the Roman court, he was undoubtedly found guilty on a charge of sedition (though this appears to have been a miscarriage of justice). But with regard to Jewish law, the situation seems to have been more complicated. His conduct was clearly such as to raise the question of legality; but the most likely explanation of the unusual course adopted by the Jewish authorities in 'handing over' Jesus to the Roman governor is that the Jewish court could not agree on his guilt. In the eyes of some, Jesus had committed an offence or offences which were plainly illegal and punishable by death. In the eyes of others his conduct, though provocative, did not amount to an actual breach of the law.

We are led by this route to a question which has long perplexed New Testament scholars and which is usually formulated as Jesus' 'attitude to the law'. The phrase has a strange sound to modern ears, for the law under which we live is not such that we have much opportunity of forming a personal 'attitude' to it. We have no choice but to keep it. We may of course criticise certain detailed provisions of it, such as the tax laws or the speed limits imposed on certain stretches of road. But with regard to the law in general we cannot (unless we deliberately opt for a criminal way of life) afford to have any 'attitude' other than the intention to remain safely within it. Even those who deliberately flout the law are not usually expressing a protest against the law itself so much as pursuing their ends (whether criminal or idealistic) with the deliberate risk of being caught and punished as offenders. Now it is true that, in Jesus' culture and environment, 'the law' meant something very different from what it does today. It stood, not just for a legal system, but for the entire practical side and much of the inner dynamic of the Jewish religion. As such, it was certainly permissible to have an 'attitude' towards it, in that (for example) one might take the view that an inner devotion to God was more important than outward observances (Mk. 12.33) or adopt a personal policy towards the regulations concerning ritual purity or tithing.[1] But we

[1] A good example is Peter's reluctance to eat 'unclean' food (Acts 10.14), which expresses, not a fear of legal sanctions, but a personal attitude.

must never forget that the Law of Moses was at the same time the law under which people actually lived, a law which was administered through the courts and which determined the limits of an individual's freedom to conduct himself as he pleased.[2] In this sense the law for the Jews, as for us, was not something towards which you could have an attitude. It contained legal prohibitions which you either obey and live in peace, or transgress and take the consequences.[3]

When therefore we ask questions about Jesus' response to the constraint of the law to which he was subjected, there is one aspect of the enquiry which is severely practical: did Jesus or did he not perform actions which constituted an offence under the law? We have seen that such an offence is not necessarily presupposed in the accounts of the events leading to his death; on the other hand there seems to have been a widely held tradition from very early times that Jesus was in fact culpable according to the Law of Moses, whether or not he had actually been convicted by a properly constituted Jewish court. Do the gospels allow us to fill in the charge on which he might have been held guilty? Apart from charges which may have arisen out of his total activity, to which we must return later (such as being a blasphemer, a rebellious elder or a false prophet), there are two issues on which legal action was possible and for which we have some significant evidence.

(i) *Transgressions of the sabbath.* In this as in all other matters of legal observance we have to distinguish between interpretations of the law which would have guided any actual court before which Jesus might have appeared and those further refinements which were regarded as binding by the Pharisees or by sectarian groups but which would not at this time have been enforceable upon all citizens. But in fact sabbath observance appears to be a matter on which there was very wide agreement in Jewish society. The prohibitions of work in the Old Testament are somewhat general; the detailed regulations which appear in the Mishnah, comprising thirty-nine prohibitions deduced from scripture, with the addition of others derived, *a fortiori,* from specific prohibitions on feast-days, are confirmed in a number of points by independent evidence of the first century A.D. or earlier.[4] That is to say: the sabbath in the time of Jesus was already such a distinctive and important Jewish observance that detailed rules were in existence that seem to be identical with those later codified by Pharisaic rabbis. We can therefore properly use these regulations as a standard by which to judge Jesus' activities on the sabbath and decide whether they transgressed any law which would

[2] Failure to do justice to this aspect mars much of contemporary writing on this subject. For an egregious example cf. S. Pancaro, *The Law in the Fourth Gospel* (1975), a massive study of 'Law' which nowhere shows any recognition of the law's practical aspect.

[3] Only in the diaspora could there have been that kind of sitting light to Jewish customs which Philo reprimands in *Migr.* 89-90.

[4] E. Schürer, *History of the Jewish People*[2] (1979) 467-75. Independent confirmation is found in Philo and Josephus. Similar, but slightly different, regulations appear in Jub. 50 and C.D. 10-11.

have been enforceable in the courts. Viewed from this angle, the evidence shows a remarkable inconsistency. Jesus undoubtedly created controversy by carrying out healings on the sabbath – there are so many instances of this in the gospel tradition that it would be unreasonable to doubt it. But were these healings illegal according to the regulations in the Mishnah? According to John's gospel they were. Two episodes are recorded in that gospel: in one Jesus makes a paste and anoints the blind man's eyes (9. 1-7), in the other he commands (and so takes responsibility for) the patient to carry his bed (5. 1-9). Both these actions were clearly illegal,[5] and the evangelist explicitly records that they gave rise to attempts to bring Jesus to court.[6] In the synoptic gospels on the other hand the situation is quite different. In every case of sabbath healing Jesus does no more than speak certain words or at most touch the sufferer. He does nothing which could be regarded as a transgression of any known regulation.[7] Nevertheless the gospels record these episodes as being highly provocative to the Pharisees. Subsequent rabbinic opinion perhaps allows us to see why. Healing itself, apart from any actions which it involved and which might be forbidden, was not explicitly excluded on the sabbath.[8] But it could be argued that, unless it was necessary to save life (a consideration which overrode a number of sabbath laws),[9] it was an action against the spirit of the sabbath; and some sages accordingly decided against it.[10] Though not transgressing any established law, Jesus' acts of healing on the sabbath could well have caused dismay and anger among those who felt instinctively that such actions ought not to be performed. We have therefore to decide whether the synoptics or the Fourth Gospel are more likely to be correct. Given the anxiety of the latter to represent Jesus' activity as constantly precipitating the threat of legal action,[11] it is reasonable to prefer the synoptic account. Moreover, that Jesus' conduct raised questions of legality without actually being the subject of a clear verdict is the provisional conclusion we have already reached from our study of his trial.

There is however one sabbath episode of a rather different character. Jesus, as master and teacher, was responsible[12] for the action of his disciples in walking through a cornfield and plucking ears of corn (Mark 2. 23-8). There is independent evidence (in Philo) that this, though permitted on a weekday,

[5] M. Shab. 10. 1-5; 7.2.

[6] 5.16; 9.16.

[7] This is recognised by Jewish writers, e.g. *JE* 10, 397. s.v. 'Sabbath'; H. Cohn, *The Trial and Death of Jesus* (1972) 42; D. Flusser, *Jesus* (E.tr. 1969) 49; G. Vermes, *Jesus the Jew* (1973) 25. It seems to be implied also by M. Shab, 22.6: healing which follows actions permitted on the sabbath is not illegal.

[8] It may not normally have seemed necessary to do so; any kind of medical activity normally involved treatments which infringed the sabbath laws.

[9] M. Yom. 8. 6-7, etc.

[10] bShab. 12a-b: even visiting the sick was discouraged.

[11] Cf. A. E. Harvey, *Jesus on Trial* (1976) passim.

[12] Cf. D. Daube, 'Responsibilities of Master and Disciples in the Gospels', *NTS* 19 (1972) 1-15, esp. 4-5.

was illegal on the sabbath.[13] Jesus' defence belongs to a type which we must study later on: he argued that circumstances were exceptional and that therefore the law could be set aside. But none of the gospel accounts suggests that the legal aspects of the matter were pursued; either the judges contented themselves with a warning,[14] or else for other reasons not disclosed they decided not to proceed with the case. Whatever the reason may have been for the preservation of this story, it seems unlikely to have originated in an actual confrontation between Jesus and a competent court, even though the action itself was clearly illegal.

(ii) *Food Laws*. There is attributed to Jesus a 'parable' (*parabolē*, Mk. 7.17; Mt. 15.15) – which in this case seems to stand for the Hebrew *mashal*, meaning something more like 'riddle' or 'enigmatic saying' – concerning the religious and moral significance of food that is eaten compared with words uttered and intentions entertained. 'Nothing that goes into a man from outside can defile him; but it is what goes out of a man that defiles him'. Mark adds, as a comment on this, that he said this 'declaring all foods clean' (7.19). If this was really Jesus' intention, it would have been a frontal attack on a taboo that was deeply entrenched in Jewish national life and was moreover explicitly sanctioned in scripture. Jesus would have been saying, in effect, that from now on it was acceptable for any Jew to eat any kind of food, even though most would have instinctively recoiled from doing so, and even though certain foods were clearly prohibited by law (Lev. 11; Dt. 14). That he should have done any such thing seems highly improbable; there is nothing else in the records about him which comes anywhere near such a forthright repudiation of a central feature of the culture in which he lived, nor is there any hint that when the church had to make a decision on the question whether these food taboos should apply to gentile converts they knew of any clear declaration on the subject by Jesus.[15] On the other hand, a problem which did crop up in churches where Gentiles had become Christians was that of (to put it crudely) which butcher could be patronised. Jews would go only to those who, being themselves Jews, would guarantee that their meat did not come from any animal which had been slaughtered as part of a pagan sacrifice.[16] Were Gentiles, as a result of becoming Christians, to have the same scruples? We know that Paul had to arbitrate on this question when he wrote to the church in Rome (Romans 14.14). Somewhat later the author of Mark's gospel may have had the same issue in mind when recording Jesus' teaching about defilement, and have drawn the moral for his readers (who may well have been in Rome) that Jesus did not wish them to adopt the Jews' scruples in

---

[13] Philo. *De vita Mosis* 2.22.
[14] Cf. A. E. Harvey, op. cit. 69–71; Z. W. Falk, *Introduction to Jewish Law of the Second Commonwealth* 1 (1972) 119–21.
[15] Cf. R. Banks, *Jesus and the Law in the Synoptic Tradition* (1975) 141.
[16] M. 'A,Z.2.3; 1 Cor. 10.25. Cf. H. Conzelmann, *1 Corinthians* (E.tr. 1975) 176 nn.13, 14.

this matter.[17] Shorn of this specific application, Jesus' 'parable' is of far too general and riddling a character to have constituted the basis of a legal charge, nor is there any hint in our sources that it ever did so.[18]

These two issues – the sabbath and forbidden foods – were (as they still are) central to the Jewish way of life and defined by law in such a way that the interpretation of the courts would not have been in doubt. Had Jesus in fact transgressed these rules there is no reason why he should not have been punished for doing so, and we would expect to hear at least an echo of the fact in the sources. But apart from what appears to be a deliberate heightening of the issue in John's gospel, no Christian document before the fourth century[19] suggests that an offence against the sabbath was a charge against Jesus at any trial. The situation is somewhat different if we consider among possible offences committed by Jesus certain charges of a more general nature. The later Jewish tradition, for example,[20] describes Jesus as a sorcerer, and had this been proved against him it would certainly have been regarded as a capital offence.[21] Similarly, charges could be laid in Jewish law of being a false prophet or a rebellious elder, and it is occasionally argued[22] that one of these is likely to have been the charge on which Jesus was in fact found guilty. But apart from the fact that the New Testament makes no explicit mention of such charges, and offers at most very faint hints of them, it is extraordinarily unlikely that any actual court in the time of Jesus would have been able to agree on a verdict in such a case. The only charge of this kind on which agreement might have been reached is that of blasphemy – and this charge does appear to be mentioned in Mark's and Matthew's accounts of Jesus' trial. There are good grounds for thinking that this offence was defined a good deal more broadly in the early first century than is the case in the Mishnah, and it is certainly possible that Jesus' sayings and actions could have been construed as an instance of blasphemy. I shall consider this charge in detail at the end of this book. Meanwhile, we have already seen that the New Testament witnesses are by no means united on the question, and it seems more likely that, even if Jesus raised the question of legality by uttering what some regarded as blasphemy, he was nevertheless not formally convicted of it in any Jewish court.

[17] There are of course numerous other possible explanations of Mk. 7.19. For an ingenious suggestion (which depends on reading the phonetically identical καθάριζον for καθαρίζων), cf. J. D. M. Derrett, *Studies in the New Testament* 1 (1977) 176–83.

[18] In Mk. 14.3, Mt. 26.6 Jesus is reported to have been in the house of Simon the Leper one day before Passover. To have celebrated the Passover in the resultant state of uncleanness would have amounted to a blatant flouting of the law. But the evangelists give no hint of this consequence. J. Neusner, in his discussion of the point (*The Idea of Purity*, 60-1), suggests that they assumed that Simon's leprosy had been cured, and that the pericope may in any case have originally had no connection with the events leading up to Passover.

[19] *Acts of Pilate*; cf. *N. T. Apocrypha I* (ed. R. McL. Wilson, 1963) 451.

[20] bSanh. 43a.

[21] Ex. 22. 18; Lev. 20. 27; M. Sanh. 7.11.

[22] E.g. J. Bowker, *Jesus and the Pharisees* (1973) 46–51. On the offence, cf. M. Sanh. 11.3; T. Sanh. 14.12.

It seems therefore that we can exclude from our investigation of Jesus' attitude to the law the possibility that he deliberately flouted it or laid himself open to charges of having transgressed it. But this in any case is not the ground on which the discussion of this question is usually carried on. The material which bears on our question is found, not so much in Jesus' actions, as in his teaching; indeed the question of Jesus' attitude to the law can be asked in a more theoretical way: how far, for example, did he believe that a true relationship with God can be achieved by means of the religious observances prescribed by the law? The materials for answering this question are more difficult to handle; but we have a firm point of departure in another of those general statements about Jesus which (I have suggested) it would be unreasonable to deny – namely, that he was a *teacher*.[23] When this statement is set in the context of the constraints imposed upon any teacher by the Law of Moses, we shall find that it yields some significant information about Jesus. For since all teaching in the society in which he lived was given within a framework imposed by the law, the number of options open to anyone whose teaching could attract large crowds of listeners was strictly limited. We must begin by trying to form an accurate picture of the place and function of the written law in the society in which Jesus lived. We may then be in a position to assess such evidence as we have which bears upon the question of Jesus' 'attitude to the law'.

We may best approach this complex subject by distinguishing between what was mandatory for every Jewish citizen and what was a matter of choice or inclination. A Jewish boy was instructed in the Law of Moses, normally by his parents, but in some cases also at an elementary school.[24] The entire object of this education was a thorough knowledge of the scriptures, particularly the Pentateuch; and acquiring this knowledge was an absolute necessity of life, for the reason that ignorance was never allowed as a defence at law: as Josephus put it,[25] 'evasion from punishment is impossible'. Every Jew, therefore, could be presumed to have a thorough familiarity with the main scriptural laws under which he lived. The observance of the sabbath and of festivals, the practice of circumcision and the study of the Torah – these things constituted a way of life which gave the Jewish people its identity over against the pagan world.[26]

Josephus[27] tells us that from the age of sixteen he determined to gain experience of the *haereseis,* the sects or schools, which existed in his country.

[23] Apart from the evidence from all parts of the gospel tradition, Jesus' role as a teacher is presupposed in the subsequent rabbinic attacks on him, and is explicit in the Testimonium Flavianum (σόφος ἀνήρ) which, if it is not independent evidence, at least shows how an early Christian writer would seek to present the person of Jesus to a non-Christian Roman reader. For a recent discussion, cf. P. Winter in E. Schürer, *History of the Jewish People*[2] 1 (1973) 428ff.

[24] For the evidence, cf. Schürer, op. cit. 2 (1979) 418-19.

[25] *C.Ap.* 2. 178.

[26] Aboth 1.1; Gal. 4.10, etc.

[27] *Vita* 10.

This conveniently illustrates the degree of choice which lay before a well-educated Jew after he had mastered the basic laws of his land and fashioned his life by the traditional observances of the Jewish religion. It was a choice which by no means everyone was interested in exploring. The great majority of the population was content (as we might expect) to live in such a way as to keep out of trouble with the law and to fulfil the basic demands of their national religion. These people were disparagingly referred to by more zealous souls as 'People of the Land'.[28] From the point of view of the 'sects' which Josephus refers to they were simply non-starters in the quest for righteousness, even though there is some evidence that a few of them lived lives of piety.[29] Consequently it is not surprising that a person of Josephus' gifts would look beyond the standards and conventions of this folk-religion (as we might call it). Among the sects which he explored he lists the Pharisees, the Sadducees and the Essenes. For the benefit of his Roman readers, he describes these three movements in terms appropriate to philosophical schools – as if the main differences between them were matters of doctrine. Though such a description may be more appropriate to Pharisaism than is usually thought,[30] it hardly does justice to the nature of these movements, each of which sought to devise and exemplify a way of life which, while remaining faithful to the scriptures and to fundamental Jewish customs, would offer satisfaction to those seeking a more profound and active expression of their religious aspirations than was afforded by mere conformity to the standards of the Jewish populace in matters of worship, social conduct and respect for the rule of law. There doubtless existed more of these movements than Josephus enumerates;[31] but the range of options they offered can be charted with reasonable distinctness. At one extreme lay the possibility of a way of life which we may properly call 'sectarian', and of which the Essenes (who are known to us from literary sources) and the closely related community of the Dead Sea Scrolls[32] offer a striking example. The essence of this reponse to the demands of the God of the Old Testament was to form a society quite separate from the normal run of national life, and within that society to observe a degree of asceticism, enthusiastic study and ritual purity which was possible only within a community which deliberately set such a standard for itself.[33] The adherents of such a movement were 'sectarian' in the sense that they had voluntarily accepted rules of conduct which, though they would doubtless have wished to see them imposed on the

[28] Cf. G. F. Moore, 'The *Am ha-areṣ*' in *Beginnings of Christianity* 1. 439-45; R. Meyer, 'Der Am-ha-'Areṣ', *Judaica* 3 (1947) 169-99, esp. 187.

[29] L. Finkelstein, *The Pharisees* (1963) 754-61.

[30] See below, p.49.

[31] The Dead Sea Scrolls alone are evidence for this.

[32] H. Braun, *Spätjüdisch-häretischer und frühchristlicher Radikalismus* (1957), is a study of the sect from this point of view.

[33] Braun op. cit. describes this as 'Toraverschärfung'.

entire Jewish people, were in practice binding on themselves alone and which constituted the distinguishing marks of their society. Whether they actually lived together in community (as at Qumran) or formed more loosely-knit fraternities in the towns of Palestine (such as Josephus describes), their way of life was exclusive to themselves and in no way applicable to those who were not members of their movement. In their own eyes, they were the only community which was attempting to carry out completely the demands made by God upon the Jewish people; they would therefore be rewarded with salvation when the final reckoning came, all other Jews being exposed to a severer judgment, except in so far as the very existence of such a community might influence some to join them and be saved before the final verdict was pronounced.[34] In the eyes of others they represented a somewhat idiosyncratic (though not necessarily illegitimate or heretical) deviation from the commonly accepted norms of Judaism.[35]

At the other end of the scale lay the option of expressing one's Jewish faith by involvement in the political life of the nation. Our knowledge of the Sadducees is extremely limited,[36] and is almost entirely confined to small matters of doctrine on which they differed from the Pharisees. It seems clear, nevertheless, that they constituted less a religious party than a social class. Though their influence was declining during the period in which we are interested, it was they who were in closest contact with the Roman government in matters affecting the administration of the province. In questions of religion they were conservative; and they firmly resisted the notion that a deeper knowledge of the will of God could be obtained by sophisticated methods of scriptural study. The place to work out their religion was the real world of politics, institutions and the cultic life of the temple (for which they held the main responsibility). The movement was essentially pragmatic, aristocratic and conservative; but it evidently offered certain opportunities and satisfactions to one who wished to give more active expression to his ancestral beliefs than was possible in the routine performance of duties in the world of commerce, agriculture or administration.[37]

The option which presented itself between these two extremes was that of pursuing a more elaborate pattern of religious observance and piety amid the normal pursuits of daily life. An opportunity for this seemed in fact to be furnished by the Old Testament itself. The law contained regulations with regard to ritual cleanness and the tithing of produce which, strictly speaking, were applicable only to the priests and to laymen when they entered the temple precincts.[38] Accordingly, one way of expressing a greater piety was to regard these regulations as appropriate to daily life; every household meal

[34] G. Vermes, *The Dead Sea Scrolls* (1977) 170.
[35] Jos. *Ant.* 18. 18–19.
[36] Cf. Schürer, op. cit. 2 (1979) 404–12.
[37] Cf. R. Meyer, *TWNT* 7. 46–51.
[38] Cf. Josephus (himself a priest), *C.Ap.* 2. 198.

would be deemed to require the same degree of ritual purity as a temple ceremony.[39] But the whole notion of ritual cleanness involved careful separation of the scrupulous observer from all who did not follow the same rules; it was a programme which could be followed only by an association of people who were all committed to the same observance.[40] Such associations existed in the time of Jesus; they were both vigorous and widespread. Clearly it was a way of life which responded to the desire for a more earnest practice of religion. But by following it these 'associates' (*haberim*) inevitably separated themselves from the majority of ordinary Jewish citizens, and indeed their anxiety to avoid ritual defilement through contact with persons who might be in a state of technical impurity (the 'People of the Land')[41] imposed severe limitations on social intercourse and made the fellowships themselves into somewhat exclusive and inward-looking societies. But we can understand how the fairly clear-cut way of life involved, though concerned entirely with outward observances, nevertheless had the attraction of a secure basis in scripture and served to meet the religious aspirations of many to whom the minimal observances of the 'People of the Land' seemed inadequate.

Related to this movement (though not identical with it)[42] was the third of the 'sects' mentioned by Josephus, and for our purposes the most important: the Pharisees. Though they too placed great emphasis on achieving the highest standard of ritual purity that could be inferred from the Old Testament, their 'zeal for the law' was a great deal more comprehensive.[43] It amounted to nothing less than demonstrating, both by their own techniques of exposition and also by the conduct of the fellowships to which individuals attached themselves, that the ancient law given by God through Moses was still applicable in every point to their own day, and that it was capable of regulating every aspect of their lives.[44] There was of course a theological motive accompanying such reverence for the law: faithful observance would surely be rewarded by God, and there was abundant evidence in the Old Testament itself that the sustained and systematic study of the inspired words of scripture, involving in particular its most practical aspects, was the surest road to the knowledge of God and joyful fellowship with him.[45] But if we follow the approach with which we started, we can readily imagine that the immense possibilities which this movement offered for both intellectual and moral effort were sufficient to account for its

[39] Cf. J. Neusner, *The Idea of Purity* (1973) 65-6.

[40] Cf. J. Neusner, 'The Fellowship (*haburah*) in the Second Jewish Commonwealth' *HThR* 53 (1960) 123-42.

[41] These were 'by definition a source of ritual defilement' id. ib.

[42] J. Neusner, op. cit. 125.

[43] Cf. C. Westerholm, *Jesus and Scribal Authority* (1978) 14-15.

[44] Cf. J. Z. Lauterbach, 'The Pharisees and their Teachings' (1929) in *Rabbinical Essays* (1951) 106, 119.

[45] Ps. 119. 24 and passim. Cf. Aboth 3.

growing success and prestige among those who sought a more faithful and adequate expression of their ancestral religion.

This very sketchy survey of the options which are known to have been available to those who had a 'zeal'[46] for their religion may be sufficient to give some content to the phrase 'attitude to the law', when applied to a person such as Jesus. There would be, first, the attitude of a member of the ordinary lower classes – the People of the Land – whose main interest in the law was in that which was administered by the courts and regulated matters of practical concern. Such a person would doubtless attend to synagogue sermons in which he was exhorted to greater religious effort and probity of life; but he would not be likely to respond to any invitation to adopt an altogether more demanding interpretation of the demands the law made upon him – indeed for no less than half the population (women!) any such option was closed in principle, and for anyone whose living depended on agriculture it was probably impracticable. There would then be what we might call the 'sectarian' attitude of one who had joined an exclusive religious group and accepted as law all the regulations which governed the life of that group. The remaining options were doubtless open only to those who enjoyed the advantages of a sophisticated urban life. They included the somewhat conservative and (as we might put it) secular attitude of one who felt the promotion of national and political life to be the most urgent form of expressing the ancestral faith. And there was the attitude of those who looked to a more elaborate pattern of religious observances to satisfy their religious zeal, and for whom these observances became 'law' in that they felt obliged to abide by them themselves and were ready to censure others for their lack of attention to them. It was within this range of 'attitudes to the law' that a teacher would be obliged to formulate his teaching. Those who were not content simply to abide by the minimum demands of their religion and to keep out of trouble with the courts would expect from him an indication of how best they might seek to go further in their quest for a righteous and pious life. 'Teacher, what must I do to gain eternal life?' (Mk. 10.17) is the characteristic question of such a seeker; characteristic too is the assumption that the minimum and basic demands of religion are already being fulfilled – 'All these have I done from my youth up' (Mk. 10.19). We must ask, What kinds of answers were available to a teacher in this situation?

One possible road which the teacher might follow was that of forming a sect. Here, it could be said, is a way of giving a new religious dimension to your life. Here is a set of demanding rules to follow, which you can voluntarily take upon yourself, but having taken them on you will be bound to

[46] Paul, in describing his own religious position before his conversion (Phil. 3.5-6), well illustrates these various options. By birth and upbringing he was a Jew; the option he chose in order to express greater piety towards the law was Pharisaism (κατὰ νόμον Φαρισαῖος); as an extra work of religious zeal (κατὰ ζῆλος) he persecuted the church; and to demonstrate his legal scrupulousness he was a blameless *haber* (κατὰ δικαιοσύνην τὴν ἐν νόμῳ γενόμενος ἄμεμπτος).

keep them on pain of being excluded from the sect.[47] In this context, the teacher becomes in effect the founder, or at least the father-figure, of a new sect – and there was good precedent in Palestine for a teacher of this kind to emerge: the Teacher of Righteousness at Qumran, the Intepreter of the Law at Damascus were both father-figures of this type.[48] It is of course arguable that certain early Christian communities had some of the characteristics of such a sect, and that they therefore presented Jesus in the guise of one whose main work had been the formation of such an exclusive society. The gospel of Mark in particular might be thought to have arisen in such a milieu, and consequently to have laid especial stress on the esoteric character of Jesus' teaching.[49] But one very well documented feature of Jesus' activity makes it impossible to believe that this was his purpose. Though propounding an extremely demanding ethic, he consistently addressed himself to those whose lives were such that they could not by any stretch of the imagination be incorporated within a sectarian community, governed by strict rules and observances.[50] Picturing Jesus as a sectarian teacher does as much violence to the consistent evidence of the gospels as does picturing Jesus as a revolutionary.

Even less plausible is any attempt to place Jesus among those who sought and taught a political expression of their ancestral faith. It is certain that he had no sympathy with the opportunist attitudes of the Sadducees;[51] but the suggestion that he adopted what Josephus calls the 'fourth philosophy',[52] which is often called that of the Zealots,[53] is one that has found a number of advocates. A precise reconstruction of this movement is not easy, not least because there is virtually no evidence for its character, or even its existence, during the years when Jesus might have been influenced by it.[54] Nevertheless, a certain consistency can be traced from the ideology of Judas, the movement's founder (as reported by Josephus), to the activities of the zealot party in the Jewish War of 66 A.D.[55] In broad terms it may be said that it was a movement of which the members believed they could faithfully follow the precepts of the law only in a state which was totally free from pagan control, and who were therefore dedicated primarily to the liberation of Palestine from Roman rule. The strongest argument for identifying Jesus with this movement is of course the crucifixion itself, and we have already observed

[47] 1 QS 5-8; G. Vermes, *The Dead Sea Scrolls* (1977) 92-3.

[48] Id. ib. 142-4.

[49] For a study of Mark from this point of view, cf. H. M. Kee, *Community of the New Age* (1977).

[50] Cf. G. Aulen, *Jesus* (1976) 22.

[51] Apart from the silence of the tradition about any such sympathies, note the scorn for εὐέργεται expressed in the saying at Lk. 22.25.

[52] *Ant.* 18. 23.

[53] Probably not correctly: Josephus does not do so, and there is no other instance of the word datable to this period except the doubtful one of Lk. 6.15. Cf. M. Borg, 'The Currency of the Term Zealot', *JTS* 22 (1971) 504-12.

[54] Cf. J. Giblet, 'Résistance armée au temps de Jésus' *RThLouv* 5 (1974) 409-26.

[55] This is the foundation of M. Hengel's argument in the *Nachtrag* to the second edition of his study, *Die Zeloten* (1976) 387-412.

that, though it is impossible to prove that Jesus was in fact innocent of involvement with it, all the evidence we have points in the opposite direction. But the question may now be asked in a different form – not so much, Was Jesus himself a 'Zealot'? as, Was his teaching such as to respond to the aspirations of those who were? Is his work as a teacher to be situated in the context of those who sought to see their religion in terms of the establishment (by violence or otherwise) of an autonomous and theocratic Jewish State? There are perhaps a few sayings which lend colour to this suggestion. 'He who is not with me is against me' (Mt. 12.30) might be regarded as a typical slogan of a revolutionary movement; 'Let the dead bury their dead' (Mt. 8.22) is an injunction which (as we shall see) seems to presuppose an exceptional degree of personal mobilisation such as would characterise the way of life of a resistance movement. But again, there is at most a very small number of instances to set against a large number of sayings which have the opposite tendency,[56] and the whole tenor of Jesus' work and character as conveyed by the gospels is in total contradiction to any ideology which involved violence or forceful political action. Jesus cannot credibly be described as one whose teaching was situated within the context of revolution and political reform.

If these somewhat marginal possibilities are eliminated, we are left with the third of our options, that is, a form of teaching which would enable people to achieve a greater degree of religious commitment and satisfaction in the midst of the routine activities of ordinary life. In this connection we think at once of the Pharisees, much of whose teaching and example was certainly aimed at a wide public.[57] But this was by no means the only possible form which such teaching might take. We have already observed that one of the objectives of Pharisaism was to demonstrate, through precept and example, that the law was applicable to every branch of life; a complementary principle, which was equally well established in Pharisaism, was that every scriptural law had some application, and all must be observed with equal reverence and scrupulousness. In this the Pharisees distinguished themselves sharply from another approach which was followed mainly outside Palestine among Jews of the dispersion, but for which we have a small amount of evidence from Palestinian sources,[58] and which seems indeed to be reflected in certain of Jesus' own sayings. It is not always noticed that the only person in Mark's gospel who is actually commended for grasping Jesus' meaning is a scribe (12.28), that is to say, one who was a scholar in the Law of Moses. But this same scribe is credited with the opinion that love of God and one's neighbour is *more important* (*perissoteron*) than all burnt offerings or sacrifices. Such an opinion in a Jewish community in Rome or Ephesus would cause no surprise: the temple

[56] Mt. 11.12; Mk. 12.17, etc.
[57] Cf. Jos. *Ant.* 13.288.
[58] See below, n.62.

was too far away to be visited more than once in a lifetime,[59] and the ritual ceremonies there necessarily took second place in most people's religious interest to those aspects of the faith which were directly relevant to the daily practice of their religion. But this conversation with Jesus (according to Mark) took place in the shadow of the temple itself (Mk. 11.27), within earshot of the very ceremonies which were being relegated by the scribe to a place of secondary importance. As such it would have offended not only the Pharisees, who held firmly to the importance of apparently marginal aspects of the law, but the Sadducees who were responsible for the maintenance of the temple worship, the priests whose dignity depended on it, and indeed any passer-by who might have overheard it while carrying his offering into the great courtyard of the temple. Yet this apparently shocking lack of respect for the temple institutions, in favour of the strictly moral and religious precepts of the Old Testament, is ascribed, not to Jesus, but to the scribe. That is to say, it expressed an attitude which Mark's readers must have known to be held by some Jewish scholars. In fact, we have evidence for such an attitude elsewhere. It was not uncommon to think of the Ten Commandments, or other great ethical and religious principles preserved in the Old Testament, as the fundamental expression of the demands made by God upon man, and to regard the more detailed precepts, particularly the cultic and ceremonial ones, as of lesser importance.[60] Indeed the view was even held, based on a text of Ezekiel (20.25: 'I imposed on them laws that were not good')[61] that much of the written law was a 'concession' by God for the regulation of the lives of those who had been unable to fashion their conduct according to the great principles enunciated at the outset.[62] This attitude at once offers a plausible milieu for what may otherwise seem to be one of Jesus' most surprising sayings. In his famous discussion of divorce, he contrasts that which was intended by God from the beginning with a provision (or 'concession', *epetrepsen*) which Moses had made in view of the hard-heartedness of the people. We may reasonably assume that attitudes of this kind were held by some of those with whom Jesus came in contact,[63] and that his teaching, on some occasions at least, was such as to appeal to them.

However, by far the most influential of the teachers of the Law in Jesus' time were the Pharisees. As we have seen, they offered a demanding and satisfying approach to religion, in that by their methods of interpretation,

---

[59] Cf. S. Safrai in S. Safrai and M. Stern, *The Jewish People in the First Century* 2 (1976) 899-900.

[60] Cf. Philo, *Dec.* 18-19; G. Vermes, *Post-biblical Jewish Studies* (1975) 169ff.

[61] Cf. W. Eichrodt, *Ezekiel* (1970) 270-2 for the original, and startling, meaning of this passage. But what concerns us here is the use made of the text some centuries later.

[62] The notion of 'concession' occurs in Philo (*Spec. leg.* 2.232, ἐπέτρεψεν ὁ νόμος) and Ps. Clem. (*Rec.* 1. 161, Moyses . . . concessit), but has its roots in the Old Testament. Cf. D. Daube, 'Concessions to Sinfulness in Jewish Law', *JJS* 10 (1959) 1-13. The evidence is discussed in Kl. Berger, *Die Gesetzesauslegung Jesu* 1 (1972) 27ff.

[63] K. Berger, op. cit. 21.

and on the basis of an oral tradition which they claimed to go back to Moses[64] and to be divinely authorised, they raised the written scripture to a level where it could be looked to as a guide to every detail of daily life as well as an inexhaustible store of clues to the nature of God himself. The practical demands of this movement were rigorous, and inevitably produced a distinct social and cultural exclusiveness in its members, but it would be a great mistake to think of it as a closed intellectual system. Josephus doubtless had the Pharisees mainly in mind when he described the various options open to him as 'philosophies'[65] and his description was accurate in so far as the history of Pharisaism before 70 A.D. is constituted almost entirely by recollections of discussions between different 'houses' of sages on disputed questions,[66] and the techniques of the interpretation of scripture, which formed a central part of the activity of the movement, were in part derived from logical principles going back ultimately to Aristotle.[67] A remarkably wide range of belief and practice could be contained within Pharisaism, particularly in the period before 70 A.D.;[68] and any teacher working from within the movement would have large opportunities for expressing original opinions and, through his followers, of forming an influential school.

What was Jesus' relationship to this movement? An answer to this question is made extremely difficult by the fact that, by the time the gospels were written, the Christian church had come into conflict with Judaism, and Judaism itself had come to be dominated by Pharisaism. Any dispute, therefore, which had originally taken place between Jesus and his adversaries came to be written up in the light of the controversies which were now raging between Christianity and Pharisaic Judaism.[69] This appears to be particularly the case in the gospel according to Matthew,[70] which also provides us with the largest number of episodes which purport to bear on our question. It is possible, therefore, that in reality Jesus had less points of contact, and also less sharp disagreements, with the Pharisees of his day than the gospels suggest. Nevertheless there are three features of Jesus' activity which are so constantly

[64] This claim is not certainly authenticated in rabbinic tradition before 70 A.D. and is not recognised by Josephus; it may therefore have come to be accepted only after the time of Jesus. Nevertheless the authoritative character of the *Torah al peh* was certainly established; cf. C. Westerholm, *Jesus and Scribal Authority* (1978) 15-20.

[65] *B.J.* 2. 119.

[66] Cf. J. Neusner, *Rabbinic Traditions about the Pharisees before 70* (1971) 3. 301-19.

[67] G. Mayer, *RAC* 6.1196f.; M. Hengel, *Judaism and Hellenism* (1974) 81. But cf. L. Jacobs in *JJS* 4 (1953) 158-75, who demonstrates that *qal-wahomer* is both different from and older than the Aristotelian syllogism.

[68] There were certainly more than the two schools or houses which constitute the main rabbinic tradition of pre-70 Pharisaism; cf. Westerholm, op. cit. p.15.

[69] This at least may be regarded as an 'assured result' of Form Criticism. For a balanced assessment, cf. J. Roloff, *Das Kerygma und der irdische Jesus* (1970).

[70] This is of course by no means certain, though it is in fact presupposed by most commentators. For a judicious statement, cf. W. D. Davies, *The Setting of the Sermon on the Mount* (1964) 315: 'The juxtaposition of (Matthew) with Jamnia is not a leap into the dark, but into the twilight of available sources'.

and consistently attested in the gospel narratives that they can confidently be used as evidence that Jesus, though sharing a number of the beliefs and assumptions of Pharisaism, cannot have been received as a teacher within the Pharisaic tradition.

(i) He was frequently accused of not maintaining the standards of religious behaviour which were to be expected of anyone who sought (as the Pharisees did) a demanding code of practice in the law. Why did Jesus not fast (Mk. 2.18)? Why did he not wash his hands before meals (Mk. 7.2)? These things were not enjoined by the law, and no court in Jesus' time would have enforced them; but they did constitute part of the way of life which the most notable teachers of his time had voluntarily adopted. The comments aroused by Jesus' failure to conform in these matters give us precious help in our attempt to place him in the context of religious teaching. On the one hand he was clearly expected to have a high regard for such observances; that is to say, his activity was sufficiently like that of his learned contemporaries for similar expectations to be aroused. On the other hand he constantly shocked them by conducting himself in a way more characteristic of those who had no such ideals. We have seen that it is extremely unlikely that he rejected those basic observances which were characteristic of Jewish national life; but he evidently did not share the Pharisees' ambition to elaborate a more comprehensive code of conduct, even though he shared their ability to deduce such a code from scripture.

(ii) An aspect of Jesus' life that was much commented on was the company he kept. Every religious movement we have been looking at in Palestine in the time of Jesus resulted in a degree of social exclusiveness. The Sadducees were in effect one of the upper social classes themselves; the sectarians formed highly exclusive societies of their own; the Zealots (if such existed at this period) were intolerant of any who were not committed to their own ideology;[71] the Pharisees belonged to fellowships which preserved their standards of personal ritual purity only by severely limiting their social contact with the generality of Jews. Jesus, by contrast, mingled freely with those whom other religious groups shunned – especially persons whose way of life or whose profession was regarded as immoral.[72] Again, the shock registered by his religious contemporaries is highly significant for our purpose. Had he been regarded from the outset as a mere popular agitator, the character of his following would have caused no surprise; but his evident learning and his primary concern with matters of religion aroused different expectations, and there was dismay when he failed to fulfil them.

(iii) The third feature is directly relevant to the study of Jesus as a teacher.

---

[71] Jos. *Ant.* 18.23. Mt. 12.30 ('Whoever is not with me is against me') is a proverbial-sounding phrase (Bultmann *HST* 103, 107) which doubtless belonged originally to such a movement. It occurs with this application in Cicero, *Pro Ligario* 11.33.

[72] Tax-collectors, prostitutes, 'sinners': cf. J. Jeremias, *Jerusalem in the Time of Jesus* (E.tr. 1969) 310–12.

As is well known, the authority of the entire Pharisaic tradition of the interpretation of the law rested on the fiction that every detail of it could be traced back through a succession of teachers to Moses himself,[73] and that this oral tradition was therefore of equal weight, and possessed the same divine authorisation, as the written law itself. If followed that every teacher, whatever brilliance and originality he brought to bear on the question in hand, believed himself nevertheless to be doing no more than discovering what was already potentially there in scripture, and the arguments advanced in support of any new intepretation would always be formulated with reference to the work of previous sages.[74] The Pharisaic teachers worked in schools (or 'houses'), and new teaching emerged, not from a new departure by an innovating individual, but from the consensus of an influential group of scholars. The contrast with the teaching of Jesus is apparent at once. No single occasion is recorded on which Jesus appealed for support to the work of any other sage. On the contrary, one of his most characteristic and best authenticated forms of utterance explicitly claimed full personal authority for his teaching – 'Verily I say unto you'. We shall see in a moment that Jesus seems to have more than held his own in rabbinic argument;[75] yet his own teaching could never have been mistaken for theirs.

These examples are sufficient to show that, of the options we have outlined, Jesus came closest to that represented by the Pharisees. Like them, he offered a way of life in which religion would seem relevant to every activity; like them, he based his teaching on the will of God as revealed in the law; like them, he addressed much of his teaching to a public far wider than his immediate followers. But at the same time the differences are striking. On three matters which were of central importance to the Pharisees – a detailed code of observances, a careful selectiveness in the company they kept, and a concern for the authority of the tradition in which they stood – Jesus adopted a radically different stance. In order to understand this stance, it is necessary to examine in more detail the complex relationship between Jesus and the Pharisees, and for this the gospels offer us information which can claim considerable historical reliability. A large number of Jesus' sayings[76] is handed down in the context of controversy. As we have noted already, the evangelists may have had an interest in adapting his teaching to the terms of the controversies in which their own churches were involved, and some of the controversial settings of the sayings may be contrived. But it is hardly conceivable that the whole picture of an on–going controversy between Jesus and the sages of his time is fictional. There must surely have been enough

[73] Aboth 1.1; cf. H. Danby, *The Mishnah* (1933) 446 n.2; but cf. above, n.64.
[74] Aboth 1.1; cf. G. F. Moore, *Judaism* 1.255.
[75] Cf. especially Mk. 2.25f; Lk. 13.15; Mk. 10.6-8; Bultmann, *HST* 41ff. But cf. the careful discussion by W. D. Davies, *The Setting of the Sermon on the Mount* (1964) 422-5: the evidence does not allow us to say that Jesus had the *technical* expertise of a rabbi.
[76] Twenty-four are counted by Bultmann, *HST* 12-27.

common ground between them for their differences to have come so sharply into focus and to have left such a mark on the gospel tradition. Moreover Jesus is recorded as having been approached to give legal decisions (Lk. 12.13-14) – that is, as having been popularly regarded as a person of authority; and it was clearly the opposition of this authority to that of other established scholars that caused so much animosity to be felt against him. In order to place Jesus more accurately on the scene of first-century religion and culture, we must try to give a more precise account of his relationship to the most influential religious and intellectual movement of his time.

A distinctive feature of the Pharisaic approach to Jewish religion was the store set by oral tradition: it was to the refinement and application of this tradition that the main energies of the Pharisees were devoted. For the Pharisees themselves, these two things – scripture and tradition – belonged of course so closely together that it would have been artificial to separate them. The precepts of scripture, without any guidance as to their precise application, were lifeless and irrelevant; the tradition of interpretation would have had no authority without constant reference back to its basis in scripture. But from the outside it was possible to distinguish. We are told that the Sadducees, while respecting the letter of the written law, absolutely rejected the tradition of interpretation which the Pharisees laid upon it.[77] In the same way, Jesus is recorded as having explicitly criticised what he called the 'tradition of men' when it appeared to obscure the plain intention of the words of scripture (Mk. 7.3ff.). As we have seen, a number of the points of tension in the gospels are caused by Jesus unexpectedly refusing to accept those standards of conduct (with respect to washing the hands, a stricter observance of the sabbath, a concern for ritual purity and select company) which, though not compulsory under the law, were taken for granted as obligatory by those of his contemporaries who were seeking a more com-prehensive form of their national religion and finding it in a particular method of the interpretation of scripture. By doing so, he clearly repudiated the authority of the tradition by which those additional observances were supported.

But in the case of Jesus such an attitude raises a further question. Did he content himself with rejecting a particular interpretation of the written law, or did he propose some alternative to, or revision of, the law itself? The question may be asked simply as a theoretical possibility: we are seeking to sharpen our picture of Jesus as a teacher by defining the options open to him, and that of proposing some altogether new standard of moral and religious conduct is one which we ought to be prepared to consider. But there is also one set of texts in particular which raise the question in a sharp form. In the so-called 'antitheses' in the Sermon on the Mount there appears to be actual opposition between Jesus' teaching and the Law of Moses. The phrase 'It was

[77] Jos. *Ant.* 13. 297-8.

said' introduces a direct quotation from scripture. 'But I say unto you' replaces it with a more radical and far-reaching formulation. Are we to infer from this that Jesus was proposing an actual rewriting of the law?

An answer to the question must follow a close examination of the text. But there are certain more general arguments which may be considered first. In favour of the view that Jesus attacked or criticised the written law is the fact, first, that his followers were accused of doing so (Acts 6.11; 21.21), and secondly that Paul describes Christ as the 'end of the law' (Romans 10.4) and bases his whole gospel for the Gentiles on the premise that the observance of the law is now superseded. The weakness of these two arguments is of course that they are derived from a period when an entirely new situation had arisen, that of the admission of Gentiles into the church, and the question of the validity of the law had become a real and pressing one. By contrast, the arguments on the other side are consistent and impressive.

(i) Jewish life in the time of Jesus already revolved around the synagogue. A contemporary synagogue inscription defines the purpose of a synagogue as that of providing for 'the reading of the law and the teaching of the commandments'[78] – a definition that is confirmed by literary sources.[79] That is to say: the whole of Jewish life was based on the assumption of the validity and importance of the written law. It is extremely unlikely that Jesus contemplated an attack on this basic institution; indeed, he was remembered to have been present in a synagogue himself on numerous occasions.

(ii) The law, as we have insisted several times already, was that which was administered in the courts and defined criminal offences. Having divine authorisation, it could not be altered or reformed.[80] It could only be interpreted in the light of new cirumstances and needs. But let us suppose that Jesus, conscious of his own supreme authority, had chosen to offer new legislation in its place. His teaching, to have this effect, would have needed to be couched in comprehensive and legislative terms. To take only one instance. It is sometimes thought that in his teaching on divorce he was actually repealing the clause in Deuteronomy relating to divorce procedures.[81] But had this been his intention, he would surely have had to support it with further legislation; in particular, it would have been illogical to eliminate divorce without also eliminating polygamy, which, though seldom practised, was still permissible under the Law of Moses.[82]

(iii) The texts which raise most sharply the question of Jesus' attitude to the law are all in Matthew's gospel. But it is also Matthew's gospel which

---

[78] εἰς ἀν[άγ]νωσιν νόμου καὶ εἰς [δ]ιδαχ[ὴ]ν ἐντολῶν *CIJ* 2. 1404. Cf. B. Lifshitz, *Donateurs et fondateurs dans les synagogues juifs* (1967) 70-1. The inscription is dated early first century A.D.

[79] Philo *Hypothetica* ap. Eus. *Praep. ev.* 8.7.13; cf. Jos. *Ant.* 16.43.

[80] J. D. M. Derrett, 'Gesù maestro della Legge', *Studies in the New Testament* 2 (1978) 81.

[81] E.g. J. Dupont, *Mariage et Divorce dans l'Évangile* (1959) 21-2, 32-4.

[82] Jos. *Ant.* 17.14; M.Ket. 10.5, etc. Cf. S. Lowy, 'The Extent of Jewish Polygamy in Talmudic Times' *JJS* 9 (1958) 115-38.

presents Jesus most consistently as one who, like the scribes, stressed the binding character of all the precepts of the law. Matthew avoids those instances of Jesus' teaching which seem to depart seriously from the Pharisaic principles of interpretation;[83] he includes a number of sayings which emphasise the necessity of scrupulous observance;[84] and Jesus' relationship with his disciples is modelled closely on that of a Rabbi with his students.[85] In this context, a deliberate rejection of, or attempt to reform, the Law of Moses would be totally anomalous. This is not to say, of course, that Matthew could never include material which set Jesus in opposition to the scholars of his day or which diverged sharply from their usual teaching. On the contrary, Jesus is presented as a teacher bitterly critical of the attitude of his contemporaries.[86] But, in Matthew at least, he shared with them an unquestioned assumption that the written law must continue to be enforced,[87] and if the antitheses were really intended to say the opposite we should have to ascribe to Matthew a singularly obtuse editorial technique in deliberately including material which was so at variance with the portrait of Jesus which he presents throughout the rest of his gospel.

With these general considerations in mind, we turn to the antitheses themselves. It is of course by no means certain that they go back to Jesus himself. It may have been the evangelist who found it appropriate to record six of Jesus' pronouncements in this antithetical form, only a small number of them having been originally expressed in this way.[88] But if this were so, given Matthew's concern elsewhere to emphasise Jesus' regard for the law, it would become even less likely that he understood this form of teaching as a deliberate repudiation of it. When we ask, is it really the case that these antitheses represent Jesus setting his own teaching authority over that of Moses, we have to remember that Matthew has made small changes in the tradition taken over from Mark which seem to exclude the possibility that Jesus was doing any such thing.[89] We are therefore bound to explore other ways of understanding these sayings. From the mass of suggestions that have been made by scholars I select the two considerations which seem to me the most cogent.

(i) *Form.* Each of the antitheses begins with the words 'You have heard' – except for the third, which has 'It was said', a phrase also included in all the others. There is therefore in all of them a pointed stress upon the receiving of the

---

[83] Cf. Mt. 22. 35–40 with Mk. 12 28–34; Mt. 15.20 with Mk. 7.19, etc.

[84] 5.19; 23.2.

[85] Note especially Mt. 28.20: Jesus' disciples receive 'commands'.

[86] 23.13ff.

[87] 5. 17–20.

[88] Bultmann regarded only the first, second and fourth antitheses as original. M. J. Suggs, in *Neotestamentica et Patristica* (Cullmann Festgabe 1962) 433–44 takes this argument to its logical conclusion, and regards all the antitheses as secondary, derived from Mt. 19.9.

[89] Mt. omits Mark's διδαχὴ καινή (Mk. 1.27); he introduces a quotation from the decalogue by θεὸς εἶπεν (15.4) instead of Mark's Μωϋσῆς εἶπεν (7.10).

precepts by word of mouth. But this is not the way in which it would be natural to refer to the written Law of Moses. 'Have you not read . . .' 'It is written' etc. are the normal ways of introducing something which is to be found in scripture. To refer to something specifically as heard and spoken can most naturally be taken as a reference to oral tradition[90] – that oral tradition, in fact, which was the foundation of the whole Pharisaic school of inter-pretation and which Jesus bitterly criticises on other occasions. The difficulty is, of course, that in each case Jesus appears to be quoting a text from the written law. However, in two of them he follows this quotation with further words which are not scriptural, but are the subject of his criticism ('. . . and whoever kills shall be subject to the judgment'; '. . . and hate your enemy'). That is to say, he is here setting his own authority, not over the law itself, but over the law with a certain interpretation attached to it. In the remaining four antitheses this interpretation is not explicitly given; but it is not difficult to reconstruct from Jesus' own commentary the interpretation which he would have had in mind – namely a limited one, which in effect makes the law of less wide application than its divine author originally intended.[91]

(ii) *Content*. If it were not for the form, which appears to (though, as we have seen, does not necessarily) place the speaker in opposition to the Law of Moses, it is unlikely that the content of the antitheses would have caused us so much trouble. In no case would the following of Jesus' precepts have placed a person actually outside the law. To refrain from anger rather than merely avoiding homicide; to refrain from lustful looks[92] rather than merely avoiding adultery; to renounce the option of divorce rather than to invoke the protection of the law when a divorce is desired; to refrain from swearing altogether rather than merely to be punctilious in the performance of an oath; to abjure any form of compensation for insult or injury rather than to seek damages at law; and to include your personal enemies among the neighbours to whom you are bidden to show love – all these injuctions can be regarded as an application, rather than a repeal, of the existing law, and in fact analogies are to be found in the work of teachers who would never have been suspected

---

[90] Cf. C. Westerholm, op. cit. 19-20. The implications of the distinction between τὰ γεγραμμένα and τὰ ἐκ παραδόσεως are spelt out clearly in Jos. *Ant.* 13.297.

[91] (a) adultery: rabbinic interpretation of Lev. 20.10 limited the offence to adultery committed with a married Israelite woman, Str.-B. 1. 275ff. Jesus endorses a long Jewish tradition criticising *any* adulterous behaviour, Job 31.1,9; Sir. 9.5; Jub. 20.4, etc. (b) divorce: Jesus criticises, not the provision, but the making use of it which is implicit (not explicit) in Dt. 24.1. (c) oaths: rabbinic expositions of the biblical laws on oaths took the form of specifying exactly what forms of words should be regarded as constituting a binding oath (cf. M. Sheb. 3ff., C. Westerholm op. cit. 105). Such an exposition would be the precise object of Jesus' antithesis. (d) lex talionis: the words quoted by Jesus (though not the immediately preceding ones, 'a life for a life') were used by the Rabbis as a basis for assessing pecuniary damages. Jesus' commentary is aimed against claiming for any damages at all. Cf. D. Daube, *The New Testament and Rabbinic Judaism* (1956) 254-65.

[92] Or from provoking lustful looks: K. Hacker, *BZ* 21/1 (1977) 113-16.

of any lack of reverence for the Law of Moses.[93]

Along such lines as these it is undoubtedly possible to bring the teaching expressed in the antitheses into line with the general character of Jesus' teaching as it is presented throughout Matthew's gospel[94] – that is, a form of teaching which took for granted the authority and abiding validity of the written law, and was entirely concerned with its interpretation and application. But we have also observed that Jesus' teaching was in certain respects profoundly different from that of his Pharisaic contemporaries. We can perhaps approach this difference by way of an expression which is found just a few verses earlier than the antitheses, and which purports to give a concise and comprehensive description of Jesus' attitude to the law. 'Do not think that I came to abolish the law or the prophets. I came not to abolish but to fulfil.' There is no difficulty about the word 'abolish' (*catalysai*). It is that used, notably in the books of Maccabees,[95] for allowing or causing the traditional observances of the Jewish religion to be disregarded. The more teasing word is that with which it is contrasted – 'fulfil' (*plēroun*). It has been suggested[96] that this represents a technical word to do with the establishment or consolidation of the law; but recently an interpretation has been gaining ground[97] that it was a word appropriately used of both the law and the prophets in the sense of 'fulfil, give definitive meaning to'. That is to say, a person who (just as he fulfilled Old Testament prophecies in the sense that he revealed their true meaning and acted that meaning out in his own destiny) also revealed the true meaning of the law and gave a personal demonstration of how that meaning might be carried out in daily living, could be said to 'fulfil' the law. The term, so understood, expressed both a claim to possess the true interpretation and a programme for demonstrating its credibility. It is in this claim and this programme that Jesus' distinctive work as a teacher can be understood.

We began our study with the proposal to examine the options which (so far as our knowledge allows) we can believe to have been open to anyone who was to establish himself as a teacher among the Jewish people in the time of Jesus. We have seen that, of these, the option which comes closest to what we know of his activity was that of the scribes whose main task was the elucidation of the

---

[93] Against anger: Aboth 2.10; 5.11; discouragement of divorce: C.D.4.19ff. 11 Q Temple 57.17–19 – all deriving from prophetic condemnation in Mal. 2.14–16; discouragement of oaths: Sir. 23. 9ff.; Jos. *B.J.* 2.135 (Essenes); Str.-B. 1.328ff.; restraint in retaliation: Prov. 20.22; Sir. 28.1–5. Only loving one's enemy seems to be unparalleled (Bultmann, *HST* 105). In effect, Jesus' teaching here and at other places is comparable to the Pharisaic principle of a 'fence around the law'.

[94] For a recent study along these lines, see C. Dietzfelbinger, 'Die Antithesen der Bergpredigt', *ZNW* 70 (1979) 1–14.

[95] 2 Macc. 2.22; 4 Macc. 5.33. Cf. Philo, *S.L.* 3.182.

[96] Cf. R. Banks, op. cit. 208 for references.

[97] C. F. D. Moule, 'Fulfilment-words in the New Testament: use and abuse', *NTS* 14 (1968) 293–308; R. Banks, op. cit. 209–13; B. S. Jackson, 'Legalism', *JJS* 30 (1979) 1–22 at p.4.

written law; at the same time it is clear that Jesus was utterly unlike these other teachers in many significant respects. But we still have not completely exhausted the list of possible options open to him, in that there were certain roles which might be played in the religious life of the Jewish people in which teaching, though important, was not the only or even the principal activity. We possess, for example, a quantity of so-called apocalyptic literature from both before and after the time of Jesus, and it is perfectly possible to think of Jesus as an 'apocalyptist', a seer whose main task was to enable his contemporaries to understand the signs of the times in which they were living, to appreciate the imminence of a radical reversal of historical processes (such that the forces of good would finally conquer those of darkness) and to inculcate the qualities of vigilance, endurance and steadfastness which were demanded by such a moment in history. One invariable feature of such teaching was that it was by definition esoteric. What the seer had to reveal was intended for the chosen few, and his teaching was therefore couched in highly enigmatic language such that only the initiated could fully grasp its purport. Was Jesus an esoteric teacher of this kind? Certainly there are sayings preserved which have a suitably mysterious and oracular quality,[98] and all the gospels record occasions when his teaching was given to small groups of privileged disciples.[99] It would be difficult to deny that the conventions of a somewhat esoteric manner of teaching are present, not only in the work of the evangelists but in the earliest traditions of Jesus' sayings. Yet this model is hardly a helpful one for the description of Jesus' activity as a whole. Quite apart from the fact that we can hardly eliminate from the record all of his teaching which was clearly intended for a wide public, apocalyptic, as far as the evidence goes, was a literary phenomenon. Its authors were not teachers who gathered disciples or started movements – indeed they hid their identity behind the pseudonyms under which their writings were circulated.[100] If we think of Jesus as an 'apocalyptist', we may be proposing for him a category which never existed.

However, a category which most certainly did exist and which is more obviously applicable to Jesus, is that of 'prophet'. From a formal point of view, what distinguishes prophecy from all other forms of moral and religious teaching is the fact that it is a word spoken out of, and addressed to, particular circumstances in history. It is possible, of course, to find timeless truths and completely general exhortations in the works of the Old Testament prophets; but it is never the case that it simply does not matter when and where a particular prophet was speaking: his message was intended for and conditioned by a specific situation, and possessed an urgency that could be effective only when it was grasped as a judgment on the present and

[98] Cf. Bo Reicke, *Supp. Nov. T.* (ed. D. Aune) 33 (1972) 121-34 for a survey of such sayings.
[99] Especially the 'apocalyptic' discourse, Mk. 13.3; Mt. 24.3. But Luke (21.5) makes this discourse public.
[100] The point is well made by E. Schillebeeckx, *Jesus,* 484.

future circumstances of its hearers. Even in this formal respect, it is clear that Jesus had much of the prophet about him. A great many of his sayings have meaning when they are grasped as direct and urgent challenges to the Jerusalem, the temple, the leaders of his day. But there is also another and more far-reaching feature of prophecy which is exemplified in Jesus. A prophet spoke with the immediate authority of God. His characteristic introduction was nothing less than 'thus saith the Lord'. Jesus does not use this phrase, but his teaching is equally intransigent and authoritative.[101] He likens his own authority to that of John the Baptist, whom he calls a prophet; and when he speaks of God, he does so with an assurance that is paralleled in the whole biblical tradition only by the utterances of those who claimed direct communication with God – the prophets. It is no surprise, therefore, that Jesus appears to have been widely acknowledged as a prophet in his lifetime;[102] nor that this claim should have been challenged by those whose own authority would have been threatened had such a claim been true. It is often stated in the textbooks used by students of the Bible that since the time of the Second Temple there had been no prophet in Israel. This statement, which sounds like one of fact, was of course no more than a dogma propounded by those who had everything to gain by assuming it to be true.[103] During the first century A.D. the Pharisaic party was intent upon drawing power into its own hands. This power was based on the assumption, which needed to be progressively validated by their influence in the courts, that all authority in the interpretation of the law was vested in a tradition to which they alone had sufficient access by reason of the continuity of their sages' teaching going back – so the legend was – to the time of Moses himself. Now any prophet would necessarily challenge this assumption. He would claim to make his pronouncements and offer his interpretations of scripture on the authority of his own direct inspiration by God. To resist such a radical threat to the very basis of scribal authority, it would be vital to show that authority was on the side of the courts and the scholars, and not on that of the alleged prophet. It would be necessary, that is to say, to show that the prophet was a false prophet. In this, it is probably true to say that the scribes had scripture on their side. It is easier to find passages supporting the authority of the courts and the elders[104] than it is to find passages which made it seem plausible that authority would pass to any single prophet. This confidence of victory in any particular case would then be expressed as an

[101] Cf. C. H. Dodd, 'Jesus as Teacher and Prophet', *Mysterium Christi,* ed. A. Deissmann and G. Bell (1930), 63-4.

[102] Mk. 6.15; 8.28; Mt. 21.11,46; Lk. 24.19 etc. That Jesus acknowledged prophetic status is proved by his use of the proverb about a prophet not being acceptable in his own country, Mk. 6.4 etc.

[103] Cf. R. Leivestad, 'Das Dogma der Prophetenlosen Zeit', *NTS* 19 (1973) 288-99; J. Bowker, *The Religious Imagination and the Sense of God* (1978) 123-4.

[104] E.g. Deut. 17.12.

article of faith relevant to any case whatsoever: there had not been, and could not be, a new prophet so long as the present age lasted. This dogma could of course be challenged; and the challenge was a serious matter. According to a text in Deuteronomy (which was by no means a dead letter in the time of Jesus)[105] there was a clear set of alternatives with no easy escape from the consequences. Either the prophet was from God, in which case he must be attended to (with a consequent loss of authority for the scribes), or he was a false prophet, in which case the law sentenced him to death. Looking back on the case of Jesus, there must have been many who would see it in this light. Jesus had won wide popular acclaim as a prophet, but had been put to death as the law required. It is unlikely, as we have seen, that this came to the point of a judicial conviction on this precise charge; but in retrospect this version of the facts would have seemed to make sense to those well-trained in the law, and the recollection of such a version seems to lie behind the later Jewish tradition that Jesus was condemned as a sorcerer or a deceiver: these were the standard opposites of the claim to be a prophet.[106]

We shall find that the description of Jesus as 'prophet' is in fact one of the most useful and suggestive of those which the New Testament offers us. But we can see at once that it is by no means adequate to describe his activity as a teacher; indeed it is now becoming clear – as a Christian student of these matters would in any case have expected – that Jesus fits into no existing category. Having charted the options normally available to a teacher, we need not be surprised that Jesus was not content to grasp only one of them. His distinctiveness lies precisely in the combination of gifts and vocations which we find in him. We can say of him without incongruity of any kind that he was the first and only Jewish teacher to have combined in a single style of teaching the roles of legal expert and prophet, with perhaps a touch of the esoteric seer thrown in. But before coming to this conclusion we need to be a little clearer on what this prophetic quality consists in – an enquiry that will help us to place Jesus, not just as a teacher among other teachers, but as a religious figure in his own right.

One of the most disconcerting of all Jesus' sayings is his reply to one who wished to become his disciple but asked leave first to fulfil what was universally regarded as a duty that overrode all others – to attend to the burial of his father. Jesus' reply was again couched in the form of a *mashal* or riddling enigmatic utterance – 'Let the dead bury their dead' (Mt. 8.22; Lk. 9.66).[107] But the enigmatic aspect concerns only the first half of the clause. Who are the dead who are to do the burying? Presumably those who remain figuratively

[105] Deut. 18. 18–20; T. Sanh. 14.13 (R. Shimeon, *c.* 150 A.D.); cf. also Acts 5. 38-9.

[106] bSanh. 43a. Cf. K. Berger in *NTS* 20 (1973) 10 n.38.

[107] The authenticity of the saying is virtually assured by the 'criterion of dissimilarity'. It is impossible to suggest a plausible reason for it to have been attributed to Jesus if it is not authentic.

dead despite the offer of new life by Jesus.[108] There can be no doubt about the implication of the second half: the would-be disciple is unquestionably being advised *not* to attend to his plain filial duty. What are we to make of this apparent flouting of a well-nigh sacred observance?

If we wish we can begin by mounting a technical defence for Jesus. The duty to attend to the burial of one's father is not explicitly laid down in scripture;[109] therefore it could be said that here again Jesus was attacking, not law, but tradition. Moreover the saying itself, in its riddling and enigmatic form, might be difficult to construe as an express prohibition to perform this act of filial piety, and would hardly sustain a formal charge in a court of law. But these points are no more than a quibble. The duty to provide for a parent's burial was taken for granted throughout the ancient world,[110] and any teacher who encouraged people to neglect it would be seen as attacking a fundamental article of social morality and instinctive religion. Our question must be rather, was Jesus' attitude to generally accepted customs and taboos as radical as this saying suggests? We have seen that in other basic questions of the Jewish way of life – the sabbath, the food-laws – it does not appear that Jesus deliberately flouted the conventions. Is the situation totally different here?

We must approach it by recalling that it was occasionally demanded of an Old Testament prophet that for a special reason he should abstain from fulfilling the usual conventions. Jeremiah is forbidden to take part in any mourning, as a sign that an age is coming when even the rites of burial will be neglected (Jer. 16.5-7); Ezekiel is commanded to observe none of the usual conventions when his wife dies, as a sign to the people of how they will react to the coming national calamities (24.15ff.). Clearly this is a very different matter from a teacher telling his followers to act in such a startling way, but it does reveal a recognition that in exceptional cases what would otherwise be illegal or outrageous behaviour could conceivably be a means by which God delivers a warning to his people. Closer to our theme is the precedent that is likely to have come to the minds of Jewish readers of the gospel. When Elisha became Elijah's disciple he asked permission to take leave of his parents (1 Kings 19.20). Elijah's answer, and Elisha's next actions, leave the reader in some doubt whether permission was granted.[111] Josephus thought that it was, and wrote it into his account of the episode (*Ant.* 8.354). But if Jesus' reply to a similar request was modelled on this episode, it would have been open to him, or the evangelist who recorded it, to interpret it as an example of the

---

[108] This was a widespread figure of speech; cf. Iambl. *Vita Pythag.* 17.73: those who refused to follow the Pythagorean precepts μνῆμα αὐτοῖς ὡς νεκροῖς ἐχώννυτο κτλ.

[109] It was merely inferred from the Fifth Commandment.

[110] Cf. Tobit 4.3-4; 6.14: 14.9ff.; Jos. *B.J.* 5.545; Str.-B. 1.487ff.; 4.578-92. Philostr. *Vit. Ap. Tyana* 1.13; cf. M. Hengel, *Nachfolge und Charisma, BZNW* 34 (1968) 10 n.28; E. Stommel, *RAC* 2.200.

[111] Commentators are divided, e.g. J. Gray, *I and II Kings* (1970): 'enigmatic'; cf. M. Hengel, op. cit. 18-20.

altogether exceptional demands which might be made by a prophet to meet the needs of the hour. It would be characteristic of Jesus to add a touch of almost grotesque exaggeration.[112] Not only does his demand supersede normal family obligations; it leaves no time even for the fundamental duty of burying the dead.

However this may be, these biblical precedents point us in a direction which helps us to understand this remarkable saying of Jesus. It could be the task of a prophet to announce, by word, gesture and symbolic action, that a critical moment of history had now dawned, a crisis which both demanded and justified exceptional breaches of the normal conventions. It could, of course, be the circumstances themselves which created the emergency, as when, at the beginning of Mattathias' revolt, 'he and his sons fled into the mountains and left all their possessions in the city, and many others went to live in the desert' (1 Macc. 2.28-9); it could be the dreaded final end-time before the judgment that would create unnatural division within families (Luke 12.51-53), an unexpected separation between partners in the field or in the mill (Mt. 24.40-1), and even the possibility of having to set aside the sabbath (Mt. 24.20). But equally it could be the herald and proclaimer of the critical time who would throw down the challenge. Jesus, as prophet, had many of the traits of a second Elijah. Elijah would come to 'restore all things' (Mal. 4.5), to reconcile the estranged members of families (Mal. 4.5 LXX) and restore the tribes of Israel (Sir. 48.10). But he would do this only as the messenger and agent of a critical moment in history. There was no time to lose: his followers must not even pause to exchange the customary greetings on the road (Lk. 10.4) – a social solecism almost as serious as failing to bury the dead,[113] but again authorised by the precedent of Gehazi sent urgently by Elisha to heal the Shunammite widow's son (2 Kings 4.29). The moment was exceptional. Jesus, as prophet, could set aside even fundamental duties in view of the urgency of the task.

This notion of an exceptional demand signalled by the arrival of a prophetic figure empowered to authorise even serious dispensations from the demands of law and custom is the key to understanding a number of episodes in the gospels. We have already referred to the one occasion on which Jesus might have been found in actual breach of the law as generally interpreted in the courts: the episode in which his disciples were found plucking corn on the sabbath (Mk. 2.23-8). Jesus' defence, namely that David had apparently been able to exempt his followers from the normal legal proscription which would prevent anyone who was not a priest from eating the sacred shew-bread, is one of which the logic has always seemed perplexing.[114] The analogy between Jesus authorising his disciples to satisfy their hunger at the expense of a

---

[112] Cf. C. H. Dodd, *The Founder of Christianity* (1971) 39.
[113] Cf. J. Jeremias, *The Parables of Jesus* (E.tr. 1963) 215 n.33
[114] Cf. R. Banks, op. cit. 115-26 for a survey of scholarly explanations.

transgression of the sabbath and David authorising his troops to make use of food reserved for cultic purposes seems too weak to support a formal defence against the charge. But if we start from the model of a prophetic figure waiving the strict provisions of law or custom in order to meet an emergency or to draw attention to the exceptional character of the moment, then the analogy becomes meaningful. David was in a quite exceptional situation which the high priest acknowledged as a sufficient reason for an exceptional exemption from the normal ban on laymen eating the sacred bread: the obligation to save life took precedence over the obligation to observe a cultic law. Jesus, similarly, introduced an exceptional situation which justified exemption from a sabbath prohibition – indeed may even have demanded it, in so far as it was a kind of sign which indicated the proper place of the sabbath in the religion of the Jews. Somewhat similar is the question raised in the immediately preceding section about the disciples' failure to fast. Admittedly this did not constitute a breach of the law; but it was a sufficiently unexpected departure from the kind of behaviour expected of the followers of a religious teacher to require some explanation.[115] Jesus' answer runs along the same lines: it was as if this moment in history were like a wedding (which in fact dispensed from certain observances even in Pharisaic tradition),[116] his own presence was like that of a bridegroom, and authorised exceptionally festive conduct. But it was a special moment. If normality returned, the usual observances would of course be binding. Similar again, if we may cast our net somewhat wider, is the passage in the fourth gospel where Jesus defends himself for doing a 'work' on the sabbath (5.17). He is acting (as a prophet might) with the direct authorisation of God. If God does not rest on the sabbath, no more should God's agent; but this does not mean that the sabbath regulations should not continue to obtain in the normal way.

We can now see a little more clearly the implications of describing Jesus as a teacher who was also a prophet. It introduces in the first place a notable difference between him and any rabbinic teacher. The records of the great rabbis make no reference to the moment at which any of them was teaching. They were sages who each made his own contribution to Israel's slow progress along the way of understanding God's will for men. Each was distinguished by his wisdom, his style of argument and his holiness of life; but the impact which he made was the result of these qualities and of these alone. There is no hint in the sources that the appearance of any one of them marked a decisive moment or stage in the religious history of the Jewish people. Jesus, by contrast, made constant reference to the significance of the present hour, and to the decisive stage marked by his own appearance. This sense of a particular moment in history is a vital element in our reconstruction of the person and work of Jesus, and must be the subject of the next part of

[115] Mk. 2.18; cf. G. F. Moore, *Judaism* 2.260.
[116] Str.-B. 1.500ff.

our enquiry. But in the meantime we need to consider the extent to which it bears directly on his work as a teacher. If Jesus was in certain respects a prophet, how will this have affected his teaching? Does the teaching as recorded by the gospels suggest that it was delivered in what we might call a prophetic tone of voice?

We have seen that on a number of occasions Jesus justified an apparently exceptional attitude to law and observances by pointing to the exceptional character of the time in which these directions were given. Can we go on from this point to say anything about his teaching in general? That is to say, was it a kind of teaching that was conditioned through and through by the particular circumstances in which it was given? One answer to this question has quite often been proposed as a solution to the problems presented by Jesus' more radical teaching. The Sermon on the Mount, in particular, contains a number of moral injunctions which demand such a radical freedom from the normal responsibilities of economic and domestic life that they can hardly be applicable (it is said) to normal circumstances. But Jesus proclaimed the imminent end of the world as we know it; therefore his teaching was intended, not as guidance for a normal settled existence, but as an 'interim ethic'[117] valid only for that very short period which he believed still to remain before the establishment by God of a completely new order. Unfortunately, Jesus was mistaken in this matter. The end did not come when he expected it, and his teaching, originally intended only for a brief and altogether exceptional period of mankind's existence, has to be fundamentally reinterpreted if it is to provide guidance for human beings living their lives in an era which shows every sign of going on (for practical purposes) indefinitely. This dismissive approach to the Sermon on the Mount has a certain logic; but the reason why it has not found acceptance is not just that (as we shall see) it greatly oversimplifies the question of Jesus' understanding of history, but rather that it does not do justice to the quality of the teaching itself, which seems to have an extraordinary power to capture the attention and inspire the behaviour of those who hear it, and which generations of Christians would therefore have been unwilling to consign to the limbo of great but occasional literature that was intelligible only in a particular period or circumstance and is too outdated for serious consideration today.[118]

Nevertheless this view of Jesus' teaching does point us in a useful direction. It reminds us that Jesus seems again and again to set his moral demands at a

---

[117]The phrase seems to have been coined by A. Schweitzer; cf. *The Quest of the Historical Jesus* (E.tr. 1910) 352.

[118]The interesting thesis of Gerd Theissen, presented in popular form in his book, *The First Followers of Jesus* (1978), and with closer argumentation in *ZThK* 70 (1973) 245-71; *Nov. T.* 19 (1977) 161-96, that a group of radical itinerant charismatics was responsible for preserving (and, by their life-style, giving credibility to) the challenging ethics of Jesus, also fails to account for the continuing appeal of his teaching to people living in settled communities. Cf. my review of Theissen in *JTS* 30 (1979) 279-83.

level which verges on the impossible. His challenge is to a degree of commitment, discipleship and dedication which lies just beyond the limit which is attainable by anyone caught up in the normal responsibilities and complexities of daily life. From a general point of view one may say that it is perhaps precisely this quality – this tantalising appearance of being just beyond one's reach – which has given Jesus' teaching its power, its enduring quality and its attraction. It is arguable that if he had not made demands that were beyond what men and women normally think themselves capable of his religion would not have lasted until the present day.[119] But from the particular perspective of our enquiry into the prophetic character of Jesus' teaching, the important point is that, though his demands may be assented to as a valid interpretation of the will of God as expressed in the Law of Moses, their implementation often seems difficult, if not well-nigh impossible, in the normal circumstances of life. The key to understanding them, and thence to understanding Jesus' manner of teaching, is that he does not regard the circumstances in which he gives it as normal. He comes as a prophet, announcing that a decisive stage of history has arrived. The response demanded is one which was always envisaged in the ancient law of Israel but can only now be realised. It is a response which also inevitably supersedes those traditional and systematic interpretations of the law which are based on the supposition that it is precisely the ordinary routine of ordinary life which needs regulation and slow and constant reform through the patient application of legal and moral norms. This prophetic character of Jesus' teaching allows us to move beyond those formal contrasts which are often invoked – sometimes even in the gospels themselves[120] – to characterise his method. It is said that he was concerned with the moral law rather than with ritual or cultic observances[121]; or that he stressed the spirit rather than the letter of the law.[122] But these judgments are not entirely satisfactory. It is true that, like some of the prophets, he seems to have shown little interest in the affairs of the temple or in encouraging the cult. But on no occasion does he actually attack the cult as Amos or Isaiah do; it is merely that his priorities are elsewhere. Again, though his interpretation of the law is based on the broad commandments (particularly the Decalogue and certain humanitarian provisions found in Deuteronomy) he is perfectly capable of taking a particular clause in its strict and literal sense.[123] The truth is that, unlike either the Pharisees on the one hand or the sectarians on the other, he refused to see the essence of God's will as something that could be expressed in detailed

---

[119]Cf. (for example) C. Montefiore, *The Synoptic Gospels* (1927) 2. 90, quoting Taylor, *Problems of Conduct* (1901): 'An end that is to be permanently felt as worth striving for must be infinite, and therefore infinitely remote . . .'

[120]Mt. 23.23; Mk. 12.33, etc.

[121]C. H. Dodd in *Mysterium Christi* (ed. Deissmann and Bell, 1930) 60–1.

[122]C. Montefiore, op. cit. 2. 126.

[123]Mk. 12.36; Mt. 19. 4–5.

outward observances. The Christian, as both Matthew (5.20, 48; 23.3) and Paul (Romans 13.8) were ready to agree, might well (if he were a Jew) find that this new understanding of the law would result in a punctilious observance of all its commonly accepted provisions, and would certainly ensure that the believer would not come near to committing a serious offence. But the urgency of Jesus' message, and the provisional character of the ordinary circumstances of life which was implied by it, made all attempts to give casuistic expression to the law – that is, to formulate the conduct required or permitted in a large number of foreseeable circumstances – not merely useless but damaging. The follower of Jesus will always be in a special situation; and only a fresh return to the basic commandments will enable him to discover the response which is demanded of him.

We have tried, so far as our knowledge permits us, to lay out the options which would have been open to anyone who acquired the reputation, as Jesus undoubtedly did, of being a teacher. The evidence of the gospels – taken once again as a whole, and therefore less vulnerable to the suspicion of fabrication by the early church – tells strongly against Jesus having adopted any of these options as he found them. Rather, his activity had features drawn from several of them, and indeed his record stands out from that of any other figure of his time and culture (with the possible exception of John the Baptist) in that he combined the learning and expertise of the scribes with the freedom and directness of a prophet. Moreover, unlike the sages of the Pharisaic schools, his teaching was inseparable from the particular circumstances which he invited people to believe now prevailed. If we ask, what circumstances? we find that our conclusion has a formal similarity with our previous one. All the evidence points to Jesus having been put to death as a rebel leader; but there was no rebellion. So here: all the evidence points to Jesus having put his teaching in the form of instructions appropriate to exceptional circumstances – just as, for example, the teaching (Josephus calls it the 'philosophy') of Judas of Galilee was appropriate to the emergence of a violent resistance movement in the early years of the first century. But in the case of Jesus there were no exceptional circumstances. History went on just as before. It was only by choosing the prophetic option that Jesus could invest the time in which he taught with such significance that it could justify exceptional responses. By so doing he may be said to have challenged the constraint of law; but only at the price of making himself highly vulnerable to the constraint of time. We shall see in the next chapter that his challenge to this further constraint resulted in a temporally conditioned form of utterance which has caused difficulty and dismay to his followers ever since, but which may in fact prove to be part of the secret of the continuing power of his message.

# 4

# Jesus and Time:
# the Constraint of an Ending

The time is fulfilled. The kingdom of heaven is at hand. They shall see the Son of Man coming on the clouds. It is language like this which, since attention was brutally drawn to it just over a hundred years ago,[1] has seemed to confront the student of the New Testament with a painful dilemma. If this was really the kind of language used by Jesus, then he is indeed a total stranger to the world in which we now live. Today, we take it for granted that the world will continue to exist for practical purposes indefinitely much as it is now. We are prepared to allow for certain changes taking place in our environment as a result of human manipulation of it or of such factors as a massive overall growth in population. But we do not envisage any sudden and cataclysmic intervention by the deity, we do not expect any dramatic reversal of those trends and problems which make so uncertain and elusive the path to a better world. But the promise of such a cataclysm and such a reversal lies at the heart of Jesus' teaching; in which case, if his message is to have any meaning for us now, we shall have to subject it to radical reinterpretation and reformulation, discarding the primitive and dated expectations with which it was originally associated, and eliciting from it an understanding of God and man that is set free from the crudely temporal outlook apparently possessed by Jesus and his contemporaries.[2] The only alternative is to assume that it was Jesus' own followers who cast his message in such an unwelcome mould, and that the essence of his teaching originally had the kind of timelessness which would make it still accessible and meaningful to us today.[3] But even if this were the case, the chances of recovering this universal and timeless message from the thoroughly time-conditioned records which are our only source for it would be well-nigh

[1] The story has been frequently told: cf., e.g., W. Kümmel, *The New Testament: The History of the Investigation of its Problems* (E.tr. 1973) 236ff.

[2] The classic formulation of this programme was in Bultmann's famous essay of 1941, *The New Testament and Mythology* (E.tr. 1953)

[3] Essentially the view of Harnack, worked out in detailed exposition of the gospels by E. Stauffer, *Jesus and his Story* (E.tr. 1960) 127ff.

impossible. Moreover, the study we have just made of Jesus' teaching has suggested the precise opposite, namely that it is only by allowing for its temporal setting – that is, its constant assumption of a particular view of time and history – that we can account for its apparent originality and power.

It seems, then, that we are forced back on to the first horn of our dilemma. The teaching of Jesus was totally conditioned by a particular attitude to time, and if we cannot share this attitude then we shall have to embark on a radical reformulation of his message if it is to be of use to us today. But before we accept this unwelcome conclusion, we should at least try out the method we have been using so far, and ask, in this respect as in others, what options would have been open, in this matter of an attitude to time and history, to a man who lived and taught in first-century Palestine. We might well look first for an answer to this question to the work of social anthropologists, who will tell us that the kind of beliefs that we are concerned with – beliefs in an imminent end to the present world order, the appearance of a messianic deliverer, and the ultimate vindication of those who have held steadfastly to their traditional faith – are found again and again in primitive peoples at a moment when the old order is threatened by the impact of an alien colonial power: those who remain faithful to their ancestral beliefs and values, seeing themselves inevitably on the losing side in the encounter with the more advanced culture of their conquerors, take refuge in millennial speculations, messianic dreams and cargo cults.[4] On the face of it, the cap fits perfectly. The Jews possessed a highly traditional and exclusive culture, which was threatened by Hellenistic colonisers in the early second century B.C. and then by incorporation into the Roman Empire after the conquest by Pompey in 60 B.C.. It was precisely at these moments that so-called apocalyptic literature found acceptance, with its emphasis upon an imminent supernatural deliverance; it was precisely under these conditions that messianic hopes were born.[5] The consequence for our understanding of Jesus is discouraging. He belonged to this well-documented phase in the development of primitive peoples, and his message was totally conditioned by the normal messianic expectations produced by the circumstances in which he lived. If we follow this sociological analysis, we shall feel more acutely than ever the need to subject Jesus' teaching to radical reformulation if it is to have anything to say to us today.

But before we accept this conclusion, we need to look more critically at the premises on which it is based. In particular, we must ask whether the fact that such beliefs can be shown to be held by 'primitive' peoples implies that

[4] K. Burridge, *New Heaven, New Earth* (1964). J. Gager, *Kingdom and Community* (1975) 20-37, effectively applies Burridge's sociological model of millenarian movements to early Christianity, but he obscures the fact that the culture from which it emerged itself had millenarian tendencies. In any case the model is far from having the force of a sociological law: there is also (as Gager admits) negative evidence; cf. B. Wilson, *Magic and the Millennium* (1973) 219-20.

[5] M. Hengel, *Judaism and Hellenism* (1974) 1. 194.

anyone who holds these beliefs must also be regarded as (in this respect at least) 'primitive' and therefore far removed from our own mentality. In point of fact, the evidence which we have for the culture in which Jesus lived – indeed for the whole intellectual and spiritual development of the ancient world – makes the adjective 'primitive' seem wholly out of place. We must start by ridding ourselves of the notion that it is a normal, or even necessarily correct, view of the world in which we live that it will continue to exist (as we tend to think) indefinitely. In antiquity this was certainly not the usual view. The great philosophies which dominated not only the brilliant intellects but also the general education and popular thinking[6] of the Roman Empire all assumed that the present age of the cosmos was strictly finite. From Plato's *Timaeus* (which has been called 'the Bible of Hellenistic cosmogony'[7]) it could be inferred that history moves in great cycles, each brought to an end by cosmic catastrophes.[8] The Stoics, whose view of things became the standard one for any sensible Roman gentleman,[9] adopted this doctrine enthusiastically, and imagined history to be moving towards the close of the Great Year, when the earth would return to its original state of fire before a new and identical cycle of history began to take its predestined course.[10] When would all this take place? Estimates naturally varied; but it was unusual to reckon in numbers of more than a few thousand years;[11] and since there was naturally no record of the date at which the cycle had begun, the possibility that they might now be nearing the end of it was never far from thinking people's minds.

There was therefore no fundamental difference in these matters between the Jews and their pagan neighbours.[12] Indeed the only factor which distinguished Jewish thinking on the subject[13] was the greater degree of

[6] This statement needs qualification: Epicureanism, Scepticism and Pythagoreanism were always somewhat élitist and specialised philosophies. But Stoicism was a truly 'popular' philosophy.

[7] W. L. Knox, *St. Paul and the Church of the Gentiles* (1939), 4.

[8] *Tim.* 22d; 39d. On the long history of this notion, from the pre-socratics onwards, cf. M. Eliade, *The Myth of the Eternal Return* (1955) 120ff.

[9] Cf. A. A. Long, *Hellenistic Philosophy* (1974) 107.

[10] Diog.L. 7. 142, 156-7; Philo *De aet. mund.* 8; Epict. *Diss.* 3. 13.4. The doctrine is clearly alluded to at 2 Pet. 3.7, and is closely bound up with astrological beliefs; cf. B. Sticker, *Saeculum* 4 (1953) 241-9.

[11] Aristarchus believed that the Great Year might be as little as 2,484 years (cf. Knox, op. cit. 7 n.3) possibly based on the statement of Hecataeus (Hdt. 2. 142) that there was evidence in Egypt for four such cataclysms in 11,340 years, but more probably (since Aristarchus was an astronomer) on planetary observations. Cf. Jos. *Ant.* 1. 106.

[12] They may indeed all have a common source in Babylonian or Iranian eschatology; cf. M. Hengel, op. cit. 1. 191-4, B. Sticker, art. cit. 244. For an interesting example of a Stoic thinker expressing this philosophical belief in the form of an exotic myth, cf. Dio Chr. 36. 42ff., on which see F. Cumont, *RHR* 103 (1931) 33ff. Others used the myths of Deucalion and Phaethon: Or. *Cels.* 1.19; Manil. 4.832ff., 1. 734ff.

[13] There was also of course the fundamental difference between Chaldeans and Stoics on the one hand and Jews and Mazdeans on the other that the former believed in an endless cycle of identical Great Years, the latter in a single Year leading to a final End (Cumont, art. cit. 56-7).

precision which their scriptures allowed them to bring to bear on it. God had created the world in six days. But it would have been naïve to assume that there was no significance in this figure. The clue to its meaning was there for all to read in Psalm 90: a thousand years in thy sight are as one day.[14] Each 'day' of the creation symbolised a thousand years.[15] The narrative in Genesis was a forecast as well as a historical report. The world was destined to last six thousand years before that new age, God's sabbath rest, the ultimate millennium should dawn.[16] But now consider the implications of this. It was widely agreed that the new age – the final thousand year period – would be preceded by an era that was itself radically different from the present.[17] This would be a time of greatly sharpened contrasts and simplified moral choices. The righteous would at last have right visibly on their side, the waverers would be subject to intensified tribulation – *peirasmos* – to determine their true allegiance,[18] the wicked would have a foretaste of their ultimate damnation – so might run a typical scenario of the messianic age.[19] Suppose, at any rate, that this penultimate phase were to last four hundred years – a supposition widely, if by no means universally, held.[20] That brings the course of ordinary, one-thing-after-another history down to five and a half thousand years. But it was widely believed that history had already gone on for some 5,000 years;[21] and if, as some thought, the penultimate or messianic age was to be, not 400 years, but a thousand[22] – then the time could well be up: it might be any moment now!

There is evidence that expectation of an imminent end to the present age reached particular intensity in the course of the first century A.D.[23] It

[14] A meaning extracted without difficulty from the LXX ψ 89.4 χίλια ἔτη ἐν ὀφθαλμοῖς σου ὡς ἡ ἡμέρα (ἡ ἐχθές κτλ). Cf. Barn. 15. 4.

[15] Jub. 4. 30; 2 En. 33.2; bSanh. 97a, 99a etc. Ir. *C.H.* 5. 28.3.

[16] This cosmic chronology was of course widely accepted, and the Hebrew version may ultimately have an astrological basis. Seven periods of a thousand years, each governed by a planet, is a Babylonian astrological doctrine: *Cat. Codd. Astrol. 4. 114-18; Bardesanes, Patr. Syr.* 2.612, Firmicius Mat. 3.1. 10ff.; 1 Enoch 52.

[17] Jub. 23. 13ff.; 2 Esdras 9. 3; 2 Bar. 70 etc.

[18] Or. Sib. 3.63ff.; Test. Iss. 6.1.

[19] This is not only typical apocalyptic language; the same postulates are found in rabbinic speculation, bSanh. 97b-98a.

[20] 2 Esdras 7.28; bSanh. 99a (R. Dosa 400; R. Jose 365).

[21] Jos. *C.Ap.* 1.1; *Ant.* 1.13; 2 Esdr. 14. 48 (syr). The creation was subsequently brought down to the traditional date of 3761 B.C. Cf. A. H. Silver, *A History of Messianic Speculation in Israel* (1927) 18, 26.

[22] Rev. 20.4.

[23] A. H. Silver, op. cit. 12-13, who argues (a) that there were no political events in the second quarter of the first century A.D. to warrant an upsurge of expectation; (b) that the movements of Theudas and others presuppose this expectation (Jos. *Ant.* 20. 97-9; 169-70. *B.J.* 2. 261-5); (c) that much significance was attached to the oracle which Josephus applied to Vespasian (Tac. *Hist.* 5.13; Suet. *Vesp.* 4 etc.); (d) that therefore the reason for interest was *chronological.* The convictions held by R. Eliezer ben Hyrkanos and R. Aqiba about the dawning of the messianic age must have seemed reasonable to their contemporaries.

provides, as we shall see, the essential context for understanding the predictions ascribed to Jesus. But our immediate concern is with the question whether those who entertained it were in any sense 'primitive' people whose outlook was necessarily far removed from our own. To this question our sources give an unambiguous answer: this urgent expectation, though it was shared also at a popular level, was typically held by men of the very highest sophistication and culture. Its literary expression in the form of what we call 'apocalyptic' was the product of minds steeped in the Old Testament and capable of a high degree of subtlety; and its public must always have been an élite and educated one.[24] Moreover at least one leading rabbi was the author of a kind of apocalyptic scenario,[25] and R. Aqiba himself was the person who was ready to identify Bar Kochba with the messianic inaugurator of a new age. For this there was doubtless good reason. The Jewish religion was not one which could easily be satisfied with a world which seemed so far removed from the intentions of its creator. God had seen to it that his creation should be good. But man had evidently failed to maintain that goodness. Wherever one looked there was sin and idolatry, bringing the inevitable nemesis of war, plague and famine. God could hardly be expected to tolerate indefinitely such a melancholy result of his creative work; indeed so settled was this conviction that the question was normally phrased, not in terms of whether, and if so how soon, the great restoration would come, but rather of what it could be that was making God hold his hand so long. And the answer which (by the time of Jesus) was usually given was that God could hardly be expected to act until there was evidence of greater faithfulness, and greater readiness to repent, among his chosen people.[26]

This climate of expectation, which provides the context necessary for understanding not only the teaching of Jesus but also the movement initiated by John the Baptist and the sectarian religion of the time, is one which was created and sustained by educated and intelligent men as well as by simple people. It would therefore be quite inappropriate to dismiss it as 'primitive', a stage of development which was soon to be grown out of. It was at most a variant of an attitude that was so widespread in the ancient world that exceptions to it were both rare and noteworthy.[27] But to say this does not necessarily help us to understand how sensible and intelligent people could have seriously believed such an improbable set of propositions as that the world might come to an end at any moment, that the righteous would be

[24] D. S. Russell, *The Method and Message of Jewish Apocalyptic* (1964) 28–9; M. Hengel, op. cit. 209 assumes popularity in 'the wider circles of the pious'.

[25] R. Eliezer ben Hyrkanos, M. Sotah 9.15.

[26] bSanh. 97b–98a – a tradition dated to the second half of the first century A.D.; cf. G. F. Moore, *Judaism* (1946) 2. 355.

[27] In philosophy, Panaetius attracted attention by denying the Stoic doctrine of *ekpyrosis* (frs. 64–9 van Straaten (1952)), and was alone among the Stoics to reject astrological determinism. Cf. Long, op. cit. 211. Even Philo allows for a supernatural age, *Praem.* 165.

visibly vindicated and that there would be (most miraculous of all) a general and pervasive change in the heart of man. Our minds are inevitably oppressed by the fact that none of this has ever come to pass. These people may have been sensible and sophisticated in their way, but their attitude to time and history is not merely difficult for us to enter into: it was wrong. Their predictions were never fulfilled. Surely there can be no virtue in twentieth-century people like ourselves committing ourselves to the same naïve attitudes and exposing ourselves to the certain consequence of being proved, as they were, utterly mistaken. Even if the Jews were by no means exceptional in their expectation of an imminent end to the present world order, and even if the whole of the ancient world shared something of this view, must we not be prepared to say that the ancient world itself was (in this respect) primitive, and that being more advanced ourselves we cannot now be expected to move back into a world of ideas so different from our own?

It would take me too far from my main theme to attempt a full answer to this question.[27a] But the objection is such an important one, and is so prominent in the work of theologians over the last half-century, that it is worth at least trying to suggest the lines along which it might be met. I would make just three observations, one literary, one empirical, and one philosophical.

First, then, an observation based on a study of literature. When one is puzzled (as it is only natural to be) by the Christian claim that the truth about God is contained in a collection of works as diverse, and as temporally conditioned, as the Bible, it may be useful to ask oneself the following question. Suppose one had a message for mankind which one wished to be attended to for several thousand years, in what form would one cause it to be written down?[28] Clearly, the Bible does not represent the only possible, or even the most plausible, answer to this question. But given the tendency of all literary forms to become dated and ultimately unintelligible, the answer to our question is likely to be some example of the medium which does in fact seem to have the power to survive the passage of time – that is, a story. The Bible of course is not all narrative; but not only does it include an enormous number of individual stories, it also makes an implicit claim to tell the complete story of the world, starting from the very beginning and looking forward to the very end. In this, it obeys a convention, or perhaps we should rather say a necessity, which lies on every story-teller. A story needs an ending. A point must be reached at which one can feel that certain issues are resolved, a certain finality has been achieved. In this respect a story departs from real life. In reality there never is an end. Life goes on, and what seemed like a critical or decisive moment at the time turns out to be just another phase of the endlessly varied pattern of human existence. Even death – which is most eagerly seized on by novelists as a genuine punctuation mark in the long

---

[27a] A helpful approach to it may be found in G. B. Caird, *The Language and Imagery of the Bible* (1980) ch.14.

[28] I owe this illuminating suggestion to Professor Basil Mitchell, who has developed it in his essay in *Believing in the Church* (Doctrine Commission of the Church of England, 1981).

and complicated sentences of life – turns out in our experience to be no end at all. New events spring from it immediately, there is no pause in the continual drama of life. But the story-teller cannot accept this. He cannot make his story meaningful unless, by giving it an end, he can show who wins and who loses, who is rewarded and who punished, who succeeds and who fails. The never-ending progress of real life leaves every question open; new events may alter the judgment passed on the old, unforeseen consequences may cause previous decisions to be seen in a new light. The story-teller needs finality, a closed sequence of events such that a judgment can be passed. He needs to impose something which does not exist in the real world: an ending. How necessary this is can be seen from the shock created by Tolstoy when, at the end of *War and Peace,* he deliberately flouts the convention and allows his narrative to wander aimlessly into the affairs of the generations which survive the deaths of his heroes. The reader is nonplussed. Of course life goes on – we don't need a novelist to tell us that. But the story ought to have come to an end.[29]

What I am describing is of course more than a literary convention. It is an essential device for making sense of our experience. Unless we postulate an end towards which our efforts are tending, or which will relieve us from our suffering, our life becomes meaningless and even unendurable. Let me take as an example the experience of one who endured many months of solitary confinement in a German prison during the last war. In his account of it the victim, one Christopher Burney, describes how, having been thrown into prison some time in the autumn, he consoles himself with the assurance that it is 'out of the question' that he will still be there at Christmas.[30] This enables him to introduce a kind of purpose into his days of confinement. After a necessary period of adjustment he can settle down into a regular routine. He can easily get through a couple of months like this – and then it will be nearly Christmas. Of course Christmas comes and he is still in prison. But it does not occur to him to abandon the fiction that he can calculate the date of his release. On the contrary, he simply revises his prediction. I was wrong about Christmas, he says, but it is inconceivable that I should still be here at Easter.[31] And so, once again, he structures the period ahead by reference to an almost arbitrary end. The fact that he is wrong about the timing – indeed that he has no way of ever being right about it – makes little difference. 'The essential', he writes, 'though I did not know it consciously at the time, was to have a boundary which would make time finite and comprehensible.'[32]

---

[29] I am much indebted in this paragraph to a valuable study by Frank Kermode, *The Sense of an Ending* (1967).

[30] Christopher Burney, *Solitary Confinement* (1961) 92.

[31] Cf. H. Focillon, *L'an Mil* (1952) 61: Those who expected the end of the world 1,000 years after the birth of Christ were able to adapt to its non-occurrence by revising their predictions: the end would come in 1033, 1,000 years after the Passion.

[32] Burney, op. cit. 102.

This need to postulate an ending in the near future in order to give meaning to the present is an important key to understanding the nature of biblical prophecy. The politicians of ancient Israel were doubtless primarily opportunists, seeking solutions to their immediate problems. If we could see it only through their eyes, their history would have little more interest than that of any other small nation in the ancient middle east. Significance was given to it by the perspective of the prophets, who invested the present with meaning by setting it under the judgment of an imminent future. God had chosen this people and set abundant opportunities before it. The coming invasion, conquest, plague (or whatever other event could be dimly foreseen) would mark the definitive end of God's patience. Therefore the present, instead of being just one stage of an endless series of minor political vicissitudes, sprang into focus as the last and decisive opportunity for the nation to reform itself before it was too late. After each crisis, history still went on. Each ending turned out not to be the end. But this did not rob the prophetic message of credibility. The timing might be wrong, but the sense of an imminent end remained. It was indeed this that gave meaning to the present.[33]

We shall see in a moment how this model illuminates also the teaching of Jesus. But our immediate concern is to argue that the model itself, far from being dated and archaic, still underlies much of our thinking today. When we follow the course of events through which we are living, we know only too well that one problem is solved only to produce another, and that the causes of any significant change in our fortunes are far too complex for us ever to be able to say that one event in particular was a unique and decisive turning point. Yet, as we try to find our way through the turmoil, we impose a pattern on it all by picking out a certain conjunction of circumstances and calling it 'a crisis'. By so doing we imply that it is a turning point, a moment in history at which an issue comes to a head and must be resolved. In fact, of course, it is nothing of the kind. The 'crisis' ceases to appear as such in the newspapers, not because it brought a promised resolution to the issue, but because the sequence of events in that quarter has slowed down again and something else is occupying our attention. Things continue to go on and on, with all their habitual indecisive complexity. We impose a momentary significance upon them by suggesting that one particular complex is moving towards an end, a crisis. The moment passes: it was not an end at all, nothing

[33] This is of course somewhat simplified. It is by no means certain that the pre-exilic prophets envisaged more than a particularly severe national crisis; cf. J. Lindblom, *Prophecy in Ancient Israel* (1963) 360ff.; C. F. Whitley, *The Prophetic Achievement* (1963) 218; and it may be a mistake to talk about an *eschatological* end before post-exilic prophecy. Nevertheless, it was by interpreting the impending political, military or natural disaster as more than an ordinary crisis, i.e. as being final and decisive for the history of Israel or Judah, that the eighth century prophets gave meaning to the times in which they lived. A somewhat different explanation of the persistence of the prophets' credibility despite disconfirmation is offered on the basis of 'dissonance' theory in social psychology by J. P. Carroll, *When Prophecy Failed* (1979). Carroll well analyses the hermeneutical problems involved in the judgment that any particular prophecy 'failed'.

is resolved. But the approach does not lose credibility. The word 'crisis' appears in the newspapers in another context the very next day. Rather similarly: we know perfectly well that no great change is likely to take place between December 31st 1999 and January 1st 2000; but we shall still feel that something has happened, one century has ended and another begun, one era is closed and a new one opened. We recognise that all these divisions are completely artificial. History runs on in an unbroken continuum. But in order to give meaning to it we divide it into epochs, and look forward to the end of one in order to start afresh at the beginning of another.

This necessity of imposing an ending on our stories and our experience offers us a means of approaching that expectation of an imminent cosmic cataclysm which initially looked so strange to us. The notion of giving meaning to the present by viewing it in the light of an imminent and decisive future is not totally alien to us; indeed we make use of it ourselves in a modified form to make sense of our own lives and of our contemporary history. But (it will be said) the form in which we do so is indeed so modified that it hardly amounts to an attitude towards time and history which has much in common with that of the ancient world. It is one thing to assume that the present will hardly go on quite unchanged indefinitely, and that we can look forward to some turning point in the near future; it is quite another to believe seriously that the world will come altogether to an end and that mankind will then receive its due judgment at the hands of God – and all this within a mere generation or two. We may still have a psychological need to impose a pattern on our destiny that is expressed both in our literature and in our ways of speech; but this does not mean that we are ready to entertain quaint and improbable notions about imminent cataclysms and messianic ages. Yet it would be fair to say (and this is my second observation) that such notions do not now seem nearly so quaint and improbable as they did even thirty years ago. We now live in an age when our future has two threats hanging over it. One is that of nuclear war or accident, which could actually lead to the extinction of large parts, if not all, of the human race. The other is that of such accumulated and ruthless contamination of our environment that life could cease to be possible in the form which we know today. The significance of these threats is that they affect us on a very short time-scale. It has been known for a long time that the earth cannot sustain life indefinitely. The cooling down of the sun, the effects of the second law of thermodynamics, set a limit to our existence of some 200,000 years. But this prospect is so far removed from our human time-scale that it can have no influence on the choices and policies which we adopt in our day to day life. On the other hand, a nuclear catastrophe or a malignant level of pollution are possibilities that could be upon us in the lifetime of ourselves, our children or our grandchildren. Moreover they will not come to pass by pure accident or inexorable natural laws. They will occur, if at all, through the decisions and errors of men;

indeed many competent observers would say that they can be averted only by a significant change of heart in our leaders and their constituencies. But this, of course, is precisely what was being said in the time of Jesus. Only repentance on a national scale would avert God's judgment in the form of a cataclysmic end to civilisation. The time scale was short: but the issue would depend on the moral choices of men.[34]

This new change of perspective can be tested by considering the interpretation of a puzzling text from Paul. In Romans 8.19 he writes that 'creation awaits the manifestation of the sons of God . . . for it was subjected to frustration, not of its own will, but because of (the nature of) man who had enslaved it, in the hope of being liberated from the slavery of corruption into the freedom of the glory of the sons of God. Meanwhile the whole creation has been groaning and travailing together until now.' Throughout the middle ages, and until very recently, these verses have been constantly misunderstood.[35] The world was thought of as of indefinite duration, the unchanging arena in which souls are trained for better things hereafter. Paul's words which implied a destiny for the natural order dependent upon a new moral and religious order among men could obtain no purchase on such presuppositions. But the recognition that our world is after all threatened, and that its destiny is ultimately in our own hands, enables us at last to join hands with those early exegetes[36] who found Paul's words full of significance and hope.

My third, more philosophical, observation may best be put in the form of a question. May it not be precisely its emphasis on a radically different state of affairs promised in the near future which has given Christianity its power and appeal through the centuries? I have already suggested that it is the tantalising unattainability of Jesus' moral demands which has given them their attraction and their capacity to inspire again and again a radical approach to ethics. May it not also be the case that it is the promise of a new order in personal relationships, and a new acquiescence of the free human spirit to the sovereignty of God, that has continually given appeal and immediacy to the Christian proclamation, and this because the promise has seemed, even though incapable of fulfilment by human effort alone, yet to be on the very point of being realised through the gracious intervention of God? It is surely significant that the only movement which has had an impact on the western world comparable with that of Christianity is Marxism, and that Marxism contains the same emphasis on a new world order which is already almost

[34] Somewhat similar arguments for the renewed relevance of apocalyptic ideas are worked out by P. D. Hanson, *The Dawn of Apocalyptic* 1-3; D. S. Russell, *Apocalyptic, Ancient and Modern* (1978).

[35] The demonstrably erroneous solution of taking κτίσις to mean 'humanity' runs through the commentaries from Origen to Karl Barth.

[36] John Chrysostom, *Hom. 14.5 in Rom.* and others.

within reach but which can be brought about only through a violent disturbance of existing institutions such as is created by revolution. The power of this philosophy is that it promises a new and desirable form of society, not as a distant and unattainable utopia, nor as a kind˜of pragmatic socialism which may be realised through slow and patient political action,[37] but as a radical innovation which must be preceded by a major social upheaval, but of which the signs are already present, the possibility close enough to inspire purposeful action. Very similar in tone (if not in content) is Jesus' proclamation of the kingdom of God. It is a state of affairs which cannot be fully established without such a fundamental change in human attitudes and institutions that only God can bring it about. Yet there are already such signs of its dawning, such experiences of its possibility, such a foretaste of its enjoyment, that the striving for it which is laid upon us must itself hasten the radical processes of change which are the content of Jesus' promise. Christianity, like Marxism, has always been indifferent to that concern for an uneventful stability and security which Marxist observers see to be characteristic of bourgeois society.[38] Far from being a primitive element to be eliminated or demythologised, Jesus' concern for a pattern of human conduct that is dominated by the prospect of imminent and radical change may turn out to be one of the most powerful and enduring elements in his message.[39]

It seems, then, that the conditioning of Jesus' teaching by a certain attitude to time and history does not necessarily isolate him in a remote backwater of civilisation; in fact it brings him into relation with a widespread human instinct of which we are by no means innocent ourselves. But though this may make him seem a less alien figure than is sometimes thought, it does not help us to sharpen our image of him when seen against his own background. We still have to ask in more detail what options were open to him as a prophetic teacher casting his message in the form of an urgent summons to action in the face of imminent judgment and change. We need to consider the kind of expectations which his contemporaries held, and the influence these may have had both on his own proclamation and on the ability of his followers to understand and to put into practice the teaching he gave. The necessity for doing this has of course been recognised for a long time. The titles given to Jesus (whether or not claimed by him himself) – Christ, Son of Man, Son of

[37] Cf. Ernst Bloch, *Das Prinzip Hoffnung* (1959) 165: 'The point of contact between dream and real life, without which the dream-world results only in abstract utopia, and real life only in triviality, is given in the utopian capacity which is within reach and therefore related to what is actually possible.' Bloch goes on to illustrate this insight by the undoubted appeal of Marxism.

[38] Ernst Bloch, op. cit. 335: 'Periods in which nothing happens have almost lost all sense of the new . . .'

[39] This is felt strongly by Marxist writers. Cf. M. Machoveč, *A Marxist looks at Jesus* (E.tr. 1976) 86-9: 'What Jesus proclaimed was the demand which the "future age" makes on men in the present . . . There can be no doubt that Jesus here touches on one of the key problems for the genuinely human character of our life.'

God – are by no means self-explanatory. Let us see – so the usual proposal runs – what they would have meant to Jesus' contemporaries: we can then get a clearer idea of the place in history which was claimed either by Jesus himself or on behalf of Jesus by his followers. So begins an arduous investigation into every instance of these titles in the surviving literature, in an attempt to define the functions and status of any person who might hold them. The picture is then drawn of Palestinian Jews eagerly expecting a particular kind of Messiah (for example); and the question about Jesus becomes the question whether in fact this was the kind of Messiah he claimed or was believed to be.

But this may not be the right way to approach the matter. When people entertain expectations of an imminent and radical reversal of the normal run of history, they are not usually so precise about it that you can read off from what they say a detailed scenario of future events. There may of course be individual seers who communicate complex and circumstantial visions; but these (in the Jewish culture at least) are essentially literary phenomena: we must not assume that the populace as a whole held beliefs about the future of anything like such distinctness. In particular, it is extremely unlikely that they had any clear or standard notion about a coming Messiah. As sociologists would be quick to tell us, it would be rare for beliefs about a coming deliverer to be anything but secondary to a general belief in the coming deliverance. It may of course happen that a particular individual, by the performance of notable exploits, comes to be recognised as a messianic figure. But this will be the case only if there is already a powerful expectation of a new age to come; moreover the individual is unlikely to be identified because he conforms to a pre-conceived type. Rather, the very unexpectedness and unfamiliarity of his words and deeds may be the catalyst of a situation already highly charged with eager expectation. These observations, drawn from social anthropology and history,[40] do not of course necessarily hold for the Jews in the time of Christ. But they gain in significance when we find that Jewish expectations, even when spelt out in detail by apocalyptic writers, conform obediently to the same general pattern. It is always the coming new age which is the primary concern; the human agent of its inauguration is secondary.[41] Often, indeed, the change is imagined as taking place without the help of any such personage at all; on the other hand, when an individual Messiah is envisaged, his role and character remain vague and undefined.[42] That is not to say (of course) that there was no speculation about him. It was taken for granted that the new age, when it came, would be more than a mere

---

[40] Cf. Henri Desroche, *Dieux d'hommes* (1969) 19; G. Scholem, *Sabbatai Sevi* (1973) 252, 'the Messiah functioned as a slogan or image rather than as a living personality'; W. D. Davies, 'Reflections on Sabbatai Svi', *JBL* 95 (1976) 529-58, esp. 542: 'The one decisive factor was that the Messiah had come. Who he was, or what he was like, was for many unimportant.'

[41] D. S. Russell, op. cit. 9; J. Klausner, *The Messianic Idea in Israel* (E.tr. 1956) 458-9.

[42] G. Scholem, *The Messianic Idea in Judaism* (E.tr. 1971) 17: 'The figure of the Messiah . . . remains peculiarly vague, and this, I think, for good reason.'

change in the natural environment: it would presuppose that most
demanding of all conditions, a change in the heart of man. And how would
that change be effected? Clearly it would be the work of God himself; but
God might be expected to make use of an inspired leader who would help to
bring it about. What would this leader be like? The only place to look for an
answer was in the Old Testament. He would surely have the qualities of the
greatest figures of Israel's past. He would have something of Moses, of
Elijah, of David, of Solomon. When this line of thinking became standard-
ised in rabbinic writing, at least a century after the time of Christ, the
description adopted was 'Son of David'. This embraced the power of a
military leader, the charisma of a king, and the wisdom of him who had been
David's greatest son in the past, King Solomon.[43] But even then, and
throughout Jewish history, the new age itself remained the prime concern. It
would make no sense to look for a Messiah until there were signs that the
promised age was dawning.[44]

We must therefore beware of the supposition which is held without
discussion in most of the books about the New Testament, namely that the
populace as a whole was expecting a particular kind of Messiah, and that the
question raised by the appearance of Jesus was the question whether he
corresponded to this expectation.[45] Jesus may well have been the kind of
person who, by his remarkable acts of healing and by the urgent tone of his
preaching, alerted people to the possibility that a new age was dawning, of
which he himself was in some sense (under God) the inaugurator or Messiah.
But it is highly unlikely that those who encountered him had a ready-made
description of a Messiah in their minds that they would attempt to fix upon
him (though those who were anxious to resist his message would naturally
attempt to discredit it by showing that its bearer did not conform to the type
of anyone who would normally be recognised as being authorised by God);[46]
and in any case they would have been more concerned to discern signs of the
dawning of the new age than to argue about the claims of a certain individual
to be Messiah. To describe Jesus, as is so often done, as a Messianic
Pretender[47] – that is, as one whose words and deeds were such as to lay claim

[43] On the range of attributes suggested by a 'kingly' Messiah-title, cf. Kl. Berger, 'Die
königlichen Messiastraditionen des N.T.', *NTS* 20 (1973) 1-44.

[44] Cf. the following Jewish writers: L. Baeck, *The Essence of Judaism* (1931) 250; J. Petuchowski,
*Concilium* n.s. vols. 7/8, no. 10 (1974) 150-5; L. Jacobs, *Jewish Theology* (1973) 292.

[45] This, of course, did become the question a century later, as is clear, e.g., from Justin Martyr;
indeed it was always the inevitable question raised by an established messianic movement, cf. W.
D. Davies, art. cit. 540. But it is significant that Paul's controversy with Judaism does *not* turn on
the question whether Jesus was the Messiah.

[46] The charge of being 'out of his mind' is particularly well authenticated; likewise that of
casting out devils by Beelzebub. The implications of such charges are drawn out with particular
clarity in the Fourth Gospel: Jn. 8. 48-9; 10.20f.

[47] For a recent example, cf. I. H. Marshall, *The Gospel of Luke* (1978) 849: 'Jesus was clearly sent
to Pilate as a Messianic pretender.'

to a title and a role that was there for the taking in people's expectations – is to make an assumption which can be shown on general grounds to be highly unlikely. But there is also more detailed evidence which points in the same direction. It is easy, when reading the gospels, to form the impression that the title 'the Christ' was one which was widely understood and used. 'Art thou the Christ?' is a question asked of Jesus, apparently as if everyone at that time knew what the term meant, and was indeed expecting a personage to appear to whom it could be applied. But in fact the extant literature of the period gives no support to such a widespread usage of 'the anointed one' as a familiar technical term. It is well known that 'Messiah' is not yet established in the Old Testament as a title for a future deliverer; but it is not always sufficiently noticed that it appears only rarely in inter-testamental literature,[48] and when it does so it hardly ever has that appearance of a self-explanatory designation which it appears to have in the New Testament. The Qumran texts, for example, though they are evidence for a vigorous and explicit faith in a messianic age which will be inaugurated by a Messiah (or even two Messiahs), nevertheless never[49] use the term 'the Messiah' without qualification: he is always 'the Messiah of Israel', 'the Messiah of Aaron' etc.. And so it is throughout the intertestamental period until at least the second century A.D.: we find 'the Lord's Anointed', but never 'The Anointed One' (the Messiah or Christ) *tout court*.[50]

Against this strange hesitancy of the Jewish writings immediately previous to or contemporary with the New Testament to make use of 'Messiah' as a self-explanatory term, we have of course to set all those instances in the New Testament itself where 'the Christ' (meaning the Messiah and not simply a reference to Jesus) is used without any further qualification or description. These prove that, at least in Christian circles at the time the gospels were written, this expression must have been readily intelligible as a technical term

---

[48] The instances are conveniently collected by N. Perrin, *Jesus and the Language of the Kingdom* (1975), and discussed by M. de Jonge, 'The use of the word "anointed" in the time of Jesus', *Nov. T.* 8 (1966) 132–48. Cf. also F. Hahn, *The Titles of Jesus in Christology* (E.tr. 1969) 148: 'as a generalised title Messiah was just not in use at that period.'

[49] Apart from one very uncertain text, 1QSa 2. 12, cf. G. Vermes, *Jesus the Jew* (1973) 198 and n.31.

[50] The facts are as follows: In the Psalms of Solomon, where the noun χριστός occurs for the first time in Greek (in LXX it is always adjectival) it appears four times: 17.36 χριστὸς κυρίου (as amended by Rahlfs from the unlikely – perhaps Christianised – reading χριστὸς κύριος; 18 tit. χριστοῦ κυρίου; 18.6 χριστοῦ αὐτοῦ; 18.8 χριστοῦ κυρίου (De Jonge, art. cit. 134f. suggests that Ps. Sol. 18 is a conventional composition added when the collection was complete, and revealing a somewhat later use of χριστὸς κυρίου). In Parables of Enoch it occurs only twice (48.10; 52.4), and each time in the form 'his anointed'. This exhausts the occurrence of the title in any extant literature which may be held to have been written before 70 A.D., unless one dates the 14th of the 18 Benedictions to this period; but in any case the word 'anointed' there describes the historical David (De Jonge, art. cit. 145). No single reference to a Messiah is attributed to any sage before 70 A.D. (J. Klausner, *The Messianic Idea in Israel* (E.tr. 1956) 392–3), and even in the Mishnah the title occurs only twice, Ber. 1.5; Sotah 9.15 (a later addition; cf. H. Danby, *The Mishnah* 306 n.5). After 70 there is a very small number of instances of 'Messiah' used absolutely: Syr. Bar. 29.3; 2 Esdr. 12.32; but it still appears more frequently as 'my Messiah' or 'my son the Messiah' (Syr. Bar. 39.7; 70.9; 72.2; 2 Esdr. 7.28) and still stands alongside other designations of the one who was to come. It is only in the Talmud and Targums that the title, 'the Messiah', becomes frequent used absolutely, though the Talmud reports sayings which use the term attributed to Rabbis who taught from the time of the destruction of the temple onwards. But even here, the alternative title, Son of David, is just as common.

for the promised redeemer of Jewish expectation. Now it may well be that in this case as in many others the New Testament is the best evidence that we have for the linguistic usage and conceptual framework of the time, and that it is just an accident that we have no supporting evidence from other sources. It may still be true that if, in Jesus' time, someone said 'the Messiah', everyone knew at once what was meant. Nevertheless there are certain expressions in the gospels themselves which indicate a different solution.

(a) Alone among the New Testament writers (with the exception of the author of the Apocalypse) Luke preserves the kind of idiom we have found in the inter-testamental literature. In Luke 9.20, in his version of the reply to Jesus at Caesarea Philippi, and also in the mockery of the rulers in 23.35, Luke offers us the expression 'You are the Christ of God', i.e. God's anointed one. Similarly in 2.26 we have 'until he should see the Lord's Christ'. In 23.2 we have the accusation against Jesus in the curious form that he proclaimed himself *christon basilea,* which should perhaps be rendered, not 'christ and king' but 'an anointed king'. And in Acts 3.18 we have 'his anointed'. Apart from the first example ('God's anointed', which is an Old Testament phrase) none of these appears in the Septuagint, and they cannot be put down to Luke's fondness for using scriptural language; but they reproduce exactly idioms which are found in inter-testamental Jewish literature. It is possible therefore that they indicate his sensitivity to an environment in which it was usual to add some explanatory word to the designation, 'Messiah'.

(b) On three occasions, once at the end of his genealogy, and twice on the lips of Pilate, Matthew's gospel refers to Jesus as 'Jesus who was called Christ'. This phrase does not usually excite comment; in the minds of most readers it probably signifies no more than that Jesus was not yet widely acknowledged as being truly the Christ (he was only 'called' Christ). But a pointer in a different direction is supplied by the reading in Mt. 27.16, supported only by a minority of manuscripts, but adopted, for example, by the New English Bible, of 'Jesus Barabbas' (instead of simply 'Barabbas'). If this were correct,[51] and if in fact Barabbas was also called Jesus, the phrase 'who was called Christ' would be a means of distinguishing Jesus of Nazareth from Jesus Bar-Abbas. But in any case Jesus was one of the commonest names at the time – Josephus mentions no less than 21 men of this name, of whom 16 belong to the first century A.D. (By way of comparison, Josephus has 18 Josephs, 11 Johns.) In the case of a name as common as this it was often necessary to add, either the father's name (Simon Bar Jonas) or else some other name by which the person was usually known. In Josephus there are two idioms which are used for this. One (the more common) is *epikaloumenos* – literally 'surnamed'.[52] The other is *ho legomenos*[53] – 'called' or 'known as' –

[51] Strong reasons for accepting it are advanced by A. Deissmann, *Mysterium Christi* (ed. Bell and Deissman, 1930) 19-21. Cf. R. G. V. Tasker, *The Greek New Testament* (1964) 413.
[52] E.g. *Ant.* 19. 297; 20. 196.
[53] *Ant.* 13. 370. For parallels from papyri to New Testament usage, cf. MM s.v. λέγω.

which is also the standard idiom in the New Testament. So we find Simon 'who is called Peter' (Mt. 10.2), Thomas 'who is called Twin' (Jn. 20.24; 21.2) and (significantly) Jesus 'who is called Justus' (Col. 4.11). In each of these cases the additional name is something approaching what we could call a nickname – Rock, Twin, the Just One – that is to say, a name given by others to a person in view of a particular quality, characteristic or accident of birth, distinguishing him from other men of the same official or family name.

Could this have been the way in which Jesus acquired the title 'Christ'? It is stated as an axiom in all the textbooks that it was only after the resurrection that Jesus was recognised by his followers as being truly the Christ, and that their description of him as Jesus the Christ rapidly turned into the proper name, Jesus Christ, or Christ *tout simple*. But this is not the only possible explanation. If Jesus had come, in his lifetime, to be distinguished from other persons of the same name by the additional name 'Anointed', just as his disciple Simon was distinguished by the name 'Zealot', it would have been entirely natural for this name to have stuck to him subsequently, particularly in view of the scriptural associations it aroused, and the theological weight which it carried. We must consider in a later chapter whether this supposition is likely, and, if so, for what reasons Jesus would have attracted such a designation. But meanwhile there is a third pointer to consider.

(c) Alongside the numerous instances in the gospels in which 'the Christ' is used absolutely, there are certain occasions on which other expressions are added. 'Thou art the Christ, the son of the living God' (Mt. 16.16). 'Art thou the Christ, the Son of God?' (Mt. 26.63) or 'the son of the blessed one' (Mk. 14.61). 'Let him save himself, if he is the Christ of God, the chosen one' (Luke 23.35). The usual explanation of these additions is that they are in the manner of glosses added by the evangelist or his source in order that the reader unfamiliar with the implications of the Jewish title 'Messiah' might be helped to grasp what it was that Jesus was claiming or of which he was accused. But again this is not the only possible explanation. If Messiah was not so readily intelligible a title as we normally assume, then some sort of definition, especially in a court of law, might have been necessary in the time of Jesus himself. In effect, the judges could have been putting their question as follows. 'Jesus, you come before us known as "Anointed". Do you mean that you are that Anointed One, the Messiah, who is the Son of God?'

These pointers, significant though they may turn out to be, do not of course account for more than a small number of instances of the word *christos*. It is perfectly clear that in the great majority of instances in the gospels in which there is any reference to the Messiah, the phrase 'the Christ' occurs without any explanation or qualification, and the reader is evidently expected to know that it denotes the person whom the Jews awaited as an agent in bringing about a new age. But we must not forget that these writings were by Christians and (in the main) for Christians. That is to say, they were written by and for people who had come to recognise in Jesus the person expected by the Jews as the inaugurator of a new age. It is possible, therefore, that they had learnt to use the specific title 'Messiah', or 'Christ', first for Jesus himself, and then for that figure of popular expectation with whom they identified Jesus. In other words, instead of assuming (as is usually done, despite the virtual absence of any such usage elsewhere) that the title existed already in popular speech and was simply claimed by or assigned to Jesus, we should perhaps allow for the possibility that there was something about Jesus which caused him to be distinguished from other men called Jesus by this additional name, and that this name then became the determinative title both for Jesus himself and for that person of Jewish expectation whom his followers believed him to be, for whom 'Messiah' (though usually with some further qualification) was already emerging as a possible title.

This argument will be carried a stage further in a later chapter. Meanwhile, we can work with the provisional hypothesis that the occasional instances which we find in the gospels of 'the Christ', 'the anointed one', being used as a self-explanatory title are the result, not of the application to Jesus of a title which already had wide currency, but of the identification made by Christians of Jesus 'who was called Christ' with that Coming One who was occasionally described as 'anointed'. We have seen that the primary expectation is likely to have been, not so much of the Messiah, as of the new age promised by God to his people; but that many expected this age to be brought about with the help of an individual appointed and authorised by God. If (as I have argued) this individual was not generally described as 'Messiah', how would he have been referred to? We would expect a vague and general designation; and sure enough, traces of this remain in the gospels. 'Art thou he that should come?' 'Many will come in my name saying "I am he".' The appearance of Jesus was such as to raise the question whether the new age was dawning and a person emerging as its principal architect; 'the coming one' expressed as much about this person as anyone dared to predict. The greater precision afforded by the title, 'the Anointed One', may have been possible only after the event.

There has been long and vigorous debate among scholars over the two occasions in the synoptic gospels (Mk. 8.29; 14.61 and parallels) on which Jesus is reported to have claimed, or at least acquiesced in, the title 'Messiah'. The question whether these go back to Jesus is still not resolved, though the majority opinion is now against it.[54] The drift of our argument so far would suggest that, in their present form at least, they are the creations of the early church. But the whole debate has tended to divert attention from a much more significant feature of Jesus' teaching as a whole, namely that it is not

[54] For a representative British view, cf. C. K. Barrett, *Jesus and the Gospel Tradition* (1967) 23: 'I do not see how the gospel material, critically evaluated, can lead to the conclusion that Jesus publicly stated the claim, "I am the Messiah"; or even that he thought privately in these terms.'

primarily about himself at all. In this respect, indeed, it offers further confirmation of the view I have been putting forward. If the primary object of expectation in Jesus' time was (as it always has been in the Jewish tradition, and normally is in any such popular movement) a new age, a radical change, a reversal of present values, then we would expect a teacher who responded to such expectations to speak primarily about this age and its imminence, and only to a much lesser extent about his own status and role in respect of it. And this is exactly what we find in the case of Jesus. Characteristically, his message is not concerned with himself, his function and his nature. It is concerned with the kingdom,[55] that is to say, with the state of affairs which can be discerned even now in the world around, and especially under his own influence and in his own vicinity. His challenge is not that men should acknowledge him, but that they should respond to the hour, be ready for the crisis. His teaching directs attention away from himself to the world of experience and to the action of God in that world. When the question of his own status with regard to these events arises (as it was bound to) he uses the evasive and ambiguous self-designation, Son of Man.[56] We have already noted that the question 'Art thou he that should come?' has an authentic ring. This is how we would expect it to be formulated, not in terms of a somewhat technical and literary title such as 'Messiah', but as generally as possible: 'he that should come'. The same is true of Jesus' reply.[57] The blind see, the lame walk. In other words, look around and see what is happening. Only then need you consider whether someone has appeared on the scene who may be instrumental in bringing about the change. There is an instance of the same sense of priorities even in the fourth gospel. Nicodemus approaches Jesus with a direct comment on his status. 'Rabbi, we know that you are a teacher come from God'. But Jesus refuses to take the cue. Characteristically, he replies with teaching on the manner of entering the Kingdom of God (Jn. 3.2-3).

It is thus not only probable on general grounds, but a conclusion suggested by a wide range of New Testament evidence, that in so far as Jesus lived and preached in the context of popular expectations of a coming new age, his

[55] Cf. the famous remark of Albert Schweitzer: 'Jesus proclaimed the Kingdom, and the Church proclaimed – Him.'

[56] Opinion seems once again to be shifting towards the view that ὁ υἱὸς τοῦ ἀνθρώπου is to be understood primarily as an oblique and idiomatic self-designation; cf. B. Lindars, 'Re-enter the Apocalyptic Son of Man', *NTS* 22 (1975) 53 n.1: Vermes' argument is 'unlikely to be over-thrown'. It would be premature to use this shift of opinion as confirmation of my argument; but there seems now to be a fairly wide consensus among specialists that it was at least possible to use the Aramaic idiom as an oblique and enigmatic way of referring to oneself, and this would accord perfectly with the characteristic reticence of Jesus to make claims for himself. For a recent survey of the discussion, cf. G. Vermes, *JJS* 29 (1978), 123-34, and for criticism of Vermes' argument, M. Casey, *Son of Man* (1979).

[57] Mt. 11.4-6; Lk. 7.22. The authenticity of both question and answer (though not their present setting in the gospel) is strongly defended by W. Kümmel, *Promise and Fulfilment* (E.tr. 1957) 109-11.

main concern was not the promotion of any claims of his own to special status and recognition, but the alerting of his contemporaries to the state of affairs which was already (by virtue of his own presence and activity) radically different from what had gone before, but which was also no more than a foretaste of the full realisation to come. His message, that is to say, was not about himself so much as about the kingdom of God, already partly present but to be fully realised and experienced in the future. This observation has consequences for our understanding of his life and purpose which must be explored later. In particular, it bears on the significance of the name Christ which it seems may have been attached to him at an early stage. But in the meantime it is necessary to give it further precision. More than one option was open to someone who had a message of this kind. To put it in another way: if you were going to cast your teaching in the form of a summons to readiness and action in view of an imminent change in the world order, there was more than one tone of voice in which you could do so. You could announce that circumstances had now become so critical that all normal preoccupations must be laid aside and exceptional measures taken to hasten the kingdom; or you could merely encourage people to continue to believe that a new age would ultimately come, but that meanwhile one must get on with one's ordinary concerns with just a somewhat heightened degree of alertness in view of the dénouement which must one day be brought about. Within the range marked out by these two extremes there existed a number of options. Only when we have considered them can we be sure that we are correctly describing the stance taken up by Jesus towards the so-called 'eschatological' temper of his time.

One of these options figures so largely in the textbooks which are written on the background to the New Testament that it is necessary to consider it in some detail. This is the option of violent rebellion against the Roman occupying power with the purpose of bringing about a new freedom for the Jewish people to serve and worship the true God. We have already considered such a movement in its secular aspect, as a possible explanation for Jesus' crucifixion. We have found that it is extremely unlikely that he was involved in anything of the kind, or even that his teaching was such as would have had an appeal for such people. But we must now ask the somewhat different question, whether such a movement might nevertheless have presented a serious option to one who was concerned to alert his contemporaries to imminent and radical change. The point is important, since it is often stated that there were in first-century Palestine a number of 'pseudo-messiahs' or messianic pretenders who attempted to institute an entirely new regime; and even if Jesus was fundamentally different from these, yet he could, almost by accident, have aroused similar expectations and have been in danger of being misunderstood. In fact, however, this whole construction goes considerably beyond the evidence. Two points in particular need to be borne in mind.

(i) Although there were undoubtedly attempted risings immediately after the imposition of direct Roman rule and in the years preceding the war of 66 A.D. there is a notable lack of information about any such movement in the period that interests us, that is, in the twenties and thirties of the century. It is true of course that what Josephus calls the 'philosophy' of the rebel party[58] – above all a concern for political liberty – may have been in existence[59] throughout the years between the death of its founder, Judas of Galilee, and the resurgence of the movement in which his sons were involved some forty years later.[60] But the awkward fact remains that we have no other evidence of actual disturbances during Jesus' lifetime.[61] There is still no reason to dispute Tacitus' succinct report on Judaea in this period: *sub Tiberio quies*.

(ii) That rebel leaders should have arisen from time to time in an attempt to gain liberation from Roman rule need cause no surprise; but it is another matter to claim that they had a religious programme such that it would be appropriate to call them 'messianic pretenders'. Josephus never uses such language about them and indeed, by representing them as violent men mainly concerned to secure a throne for themselves,[62] makes it clear that they could not have belonged to what came to be known as the 'zealot' movement, which, in the view at least of its founder Judas, was utterly opposed to 'calling any man master'.[63] It can be argued that it was to be expected of an historian with Josephus' bias that he would have deliberately suppressed any reference to a religious dimension in these rebellions, and emphasised the personal and worldly ambition of their leaders. But Josephus not merely omits any reference to messianic pretensions; he gives a perfectly plausible explanation of their motives.[64] To attribute deeper religious aspirations to them is neither demanded by the evidence[65] nor justified by our general understanding of the nature of messianism.

It is far from certain therefore that active resistance to the Romans was seen as more than a political or terrorist programme. Doubtless it was a movement which, like many others of its kind, contained its thinkers and

---

[58] *Ant.* 18.9, 23–5.

[59] Cf. above, p.46 n.55.

[60] *Ant.* 20.102.

[61] Cf. P. W. Barnett, 'Under Tiberius All was Quiet', *NTS* 21 (1975), 564–71; J. Giblet, 'Résistance armée au temps de Jésus', *RThLouv* 5 (1974), 409–26. The silence of Philo (*Leg.* 298–305) on any armed resistance under Tiberius is significant. This leaves the στάσις referred to in Mk. 15.7, Lk. 23.19 as the only evidence for an armed uprising; but this is too slight and general a clue on which to base a whole scenario of violence. For a recent discussion of the evidence in the light of a sociological study of 'brigandage', cf. R. A. Horsley, 'Jesus and the Bandits', *IJS* 10 (1979), 37–63.

[62] *Ant.* 17. 285.

[63] *Ant.* 18.23

[64] 'Making themselves king', *Ant.* 17. 285

[65] On the rebel leaders who are often claimed to have been 'messianic pretenders' in this period, see Appendix II, p.175.

idealists. Doubtless also its members, in the tradition of the Maccabaean revolt, often showed qualities of courage and devotion which enabled them to present a moral and spiritual challenge to their less militant contemporaries. But this is not to say that the prospect of liberation they held out, however different from the oppression of the time, corresponded to the yearning for and expectation of a radically new and divinely ordered age which we have seen to have seized people's imagination. Not only, therefore, is it historically unlikely that Jesus sympathised actively with any such movement; he is unlikely to have regarded it as an expression of that alertness towards a new order on earth which we have seen to lie at the heart of his message.

A genuinely religious, but no less radical, response to the prospect of imminent judgment and renewal was that offered by the sects. If the time was short and judgment strictly by the Law, then the appropriate course was to withdraw as far as possible from the contamination of the world and prepare oneself by asceticism, study and discipline. This response, as we have seen, was not favoured by Jesus; but nor did he adopt the alternative proposed by the Pharisees, namely a gradual and piecemeal improvement in the general standard of obedience to the law of God stimulated by the example of exclusive fellowships, and all constituting a preparation for, even a hastening of, the promised new age. Jesus' teaching had an altogether more urgent tone, and indeed is sharply distinguished from that of the rabbis by its emphasis on the critical importance of the present moment in the light of an impending change. In this respect the only precedent for the style Jesus adopted is to be found in the prophets, or (in times closer to his own) in John the Baptist. But we still need to get this style into sharper focus by asking in what time-scale Jesus was setting these expectations. The kingdom was at hand; but precisely how soon might it be expected – tomorrow, or only in the imaginable future?

Perhaps we may begin by somewhat sharpening the contrast between the teaching of Jesus and that of the sages. It is possible to find in rabbinic sources both instruction about what we call 'the last things' and exhortations to a certain style or standard of living in the light of such instruction.[66] But with Jesus there is a significant difference. True, he taught about the judgment to come and about life after death; true also, that he exhorted his hearers to be prepared. But the centre of his teaching did not lie in either of these things. Jesus did not speak about the possibility of better things. He proclaimed them, their imminence and their actuality. It is not merely that 'the Kingdom' is a concept which appears far more frequently in his message than in any other Jewish literature. The idioms in which he refers to it – that it is near, that it has come upon us, entering into it, seeking it and so forth – are completely without parallel in any extant writings.[67] It is perhaps dangerous to claim (as

[66] M. Sotah 9.15; bYoma 86b, Cf. G. F. Moore, *Judaism* (1946) 2. 350-1.
[67] J. Jeremias, *N. T. Theology* 1 (1971) 32-4.

is sometimes done) that because these expressions were, so far as we know, completely original, they must be due to the inventive genius of Jesus himself;[68] their absence from all other literature of his period may be due to the accident of survival; they may have occurred in abundance in other writings now lost to us, or at least have been common enough in ordinary colloquial speech of which the gospels happen to be our only record. At the same time it is exceedingly unlikely that such an apparently unusual set of idioms should have been foisted upon the records of Jesus by subsequent writers if nothing in his teaching had given rise to them. We may take it as established that Jesus not merely used the word 'Kingdom' as a way of talking about the eternal sovereignty of God, but proclaimed it as an imminent reality.

But exactly how imminent? It is in seeking to answer this question that we can best sharpen our image of Jesus as a preacher and teacher. Was the change to be expected literally at any moment, in which case the appropriate response would have been total mobilisation, a preparedness unencumbered by family, possessions and the routine of a working life? Or was it no more than an ever-present possibility, allowing one to continue with one's normal commitments and preoccupations, but with a heightened sense of reponsibility in view of a possible confrontation, at some unpredictable time, with a greater reality? We have already seen that there are general reasons for thinking that Jesus' proclamation fell somewhere between these two extremes. The same conclusion is reached if we examine certain individual sayings which have a strong claim to authenticity and which give a further degree of precision to Jesus' prophetic utterances. The most important and troublesome of these is the prediction (Mk. 9.1) that the Kingdom would come with power within the lifetime of some of those who were present when Jesus spoke. This is a singularly precise forecast. It does not say that the Kingdom would come the very next day, for in this case it would have been virtually all, and not only some, of those present who would live to see it. Moreover, as we have seen, Jesus' teaching as a whole does not appear to demand the total mobilisation and suspension of all normal activity which would be the appropriate response to such an urgent summons. But nor could the coming of the Kingdom be more than about fifty years away if some of those present were going to witness it. Within this fifty-year span there could be no further precision. On a number of occasions Jesus emphasised that the exact time was known to no one, perhaps not even to himself (Mk. 13.34; Mt. 25.13; Lk. 12.40, 46). But this indeterminacy was itself a challenge to further vigilance. Certain events might be read as signs of the imminence of the great change (Lk. 12.55-6; Mk. 13.28-9), and some might even be necessary conditions of its coming about (Mk. 13.10 etc.). But the primary and constant feature of it would be its suddenness. Fifty years is quite a long

[68] Id. ib. 34, 103.

time; one can go to sleep and forget all about it if it may not happen until one is an old man. Hence Jesus' constantly repeated summons to be alert and prepared (Lk. 12.37; Mk. 13.35,37 etc.). The time might seem long to some, but it was strictly limited to the span of a human life, which from one point of view is very little time at all.

Our embarrassment when we read this saying is caused by the fact that it was not fulfilled. Nothing that could reasonably be described as 'the Kingdom of God come with power' took place in the period prescribed. It would seem to follow that Jesus was either mistaken or misunderstood: and either conclusion is exceedingly difficult to reconcile with any reconstruction of Jesus as a teacher who might still be authoritative for us today. Scholars have naturally tried to find a way round the difficulty. It has been argued[69] that the words do not go back to Jesus at all, but were attributed to him in the early years of the church when tribulations had become severe and all hope was set on a speedy divine intervention. But apart from the fact that there is no evidence for this degree of persecution within the first generation of Christianity,[70] it seems highly unlikely that a prediction so precise and so vulnerable to falsification within a few years would have been fastened on Jesus had he said nothing of the kind himself.[71] Alternatively, it can be suggested that the phrase, 'the Kingdom of God come with power' means something less than a radical reversal of normal conditions and values, and was intended to describe the new possibilities for human existence which were opened up by the resurrection, the outpouring of the Spirit and the existence of the church,[72] or even a permanent and ever-present dimension of experience which becomes accessible to anyone who attends seriously to the teaching of Jesus.[73] But if our analysis of the situation in which Jesus offered his message is anywhere near correct – if, that is to say, there was a generally held expectation of an imminent and radical change in the circumstances of life – then Jesus could not have expressed himself in terms as urgent as these without leading people to believe that he was endorsing this expectation and encouraging his hearers to be prepared for its fulfilment in the near future.[74] Moreover it does not appear as if the early church felt it necessary to introduce

---

[69] Particularly by Bultmann (*HST* 121) and his followers.

[70] Modern scholars' references to 'persecution' in the New Testament period are usually due to a circular argument. Some passages in the New Testament (e.g. 1 Pet. 4.12) would be particularly appropriate if persecution was severe. The only time such persecution could have taken place is in the reign of Domitian. Therefore these writings are dated to the 80s of the first century. It is *then* inferred from these that there *was* persecution in this period. The point is well exposed by J. A. T. Robinson, *Redating the New Testament* (1976) 155, 231.

[71] Cf. O. Cullmann, *Salvation in History* (E.tr. 1967) 211-13.

[72] For a long list of those who have advocated this view (which can be traced back to Clement of Alexandria, Exc. Theodoti ap. Clem. Al. 4.24), cf. W. Kümmel, *Promise and Fulfilment* (1957) 26-7.

[73] Cf. C. H. Dodd, *The Parables of the Kingdom* (1961) 37 n.1.

[74] 1 Th. 4.15 is important evidence that this is in fact the effect his words achieved.

any fundamental reinterpretation.[75] The plain meaning of the words is the one which best fits the circumstances in which they were spoken and the history of the tradition in which they were preserved.

We have therefore to try to come to terms with an element in the teaching of Jesus which, though fitting well into the religious and cultural environment in which he lived and worked, seems nevertheless to involve him in a mistaken view of his own time, and so to undermine the general authority and credibility of his message. The point is of critical importance. For even if we have succeeded in showing that a general sense of an impending end to the present world–order does not separate his world from ours as much as is usually thought, we shall still feel a very strong sense of alienation from one who apparently believed that he could predict the date of this end within certain limits and whom we now know to have been totally mistaken in his prediction. Oracles, prophecies and apocalyptic scenarios are normally expressed in ambiguous terms: if the promised event fails to materialise, you can always say that this is not quite what was meant, you have given the wrong interpretation of the number of the beast. But Jesus was so specific that no mistake is possible. 'There are some of those standing here who shall not taste death until the kingdom of God be come with power' (Mark 9.1). It is the very precision of the prophecy, laying itself wide open to early falsification, which forces us to face the question in all its starkness. In trying to answer it, we can proceed a certain distance with one of the categories which we have already found to be to some extent appropriate to Jesus: that of the prophet. Old Testament prophecy was (among other things) an interpretation of contemporary events as significant of the judgment of God upon his people. A combination of events in the near future might have such catastrophic consequences that it could be thought of as God's final judgment on his people and the end of human history as ordinarily understood.[76] In the light of such a prospect, a radical change of outlook was required. Only repentance, a new social order, a new concern for justice would avert the final catastrophe. The present time must be understood as one in which all priorities were determined by the imminent threat of judgment. There would be no second chance: the present was a critical moment in the working out of God's purpose for his people. It is obvious that the very precision of these predictions made them highly vulnerable to falsification; and indeed, they could be proved wrong. The dénouement, like the recurring 'crises' in our newspapers, brought no final

[75] Luke, it is true, eased the difficulty of the prediction by omitting ἐν δυνάμει (9.27). But H. Conzelmann's view (*The Theology of St. Luke* (E.tr. 1961) passim) that Luke was responsible for a fundamental reinterpretation of early Christian eschatology has had to be considerably modified. Cf. R. H. Hiers, 'The Problem of the Delay of the Parousia in Luke-Acts', *NTS* 20 (1974) 145-55; E. Franklin *Christ the Lord* (1975).

[76] So, e.g., W. Eichrodt, *Theology of the Old Testament* 1 (1961) 383. But there are important qualifications to be made with regard to the pre-exilic prophets. Cf. above n.33.

solution or irrevocable judgment; even the fall of Jerusalem and the exile were events which were found to be, not just an end, but a new beginning. Yet – and this is the important thing – these successive modifications of the prophets' predictions appear never to have brought prophecy itself into disrepute. The credibility of the prophet's message depended, not on the timing of its future fulfilment, but on the validity of its interpretation of the present in the light of an imminent end. What sociologists of religion call the 'disconfirmation' of prophecies of judgment or deliverance does not greatly affect the credibility of the prophets themselves. Indeed, there is abundant evidence from messianic sects in modern times that (paradoxical though it may seem) fervour and faith may actually increase when a particular prediction fails to be fulfilled on time.[77] The time-table may have to be modified, and the application of the prophecy reinterpreted in the light of changed circumstances.[78] But the sense that the prospect of an imminent change makes best sense of life and history at this particular moment will sustain a religious movement through many apparent failures of prophecy to be punctually fulfilled.

Set in this tradition, Jesus' predictions certainly become more comprehensible. It is not, after all, as if they were totally unfulfilled, but that what might have been expected to be the final and decisive turning-point in human affairs turned out, as 'crises' always do, not to be final and decisive at all: history has continued to run its inexorable course, after as before. Just as some part of what the Old Testament prophets predicted, with their sensitive eye on the trends of their time, did in fact come to pass, only without bringing with it that ultimate resolution which they had prophesied, so Jesus' proclamation of events of extreme significance was partially fulfilled. On the negative side, Jerusalem was destroyed and the Jewish nation effectively dispersed; on the positive side, a new factor of immense significance for the future progress of mankind came into existence, namely the church. As we have seen, it would be wrong to assume that it was these events, and these only, that Jesus was referring to by the phrase 'the Kingdom of God come with power'. But the precedent set by the Old Testament prophets does help us to see why, when the radical change and final solution prophesied by Jesus took the form of events which were then taken up and absorbed into the on–going course of history, this did not rob his teaching of its credibility and its urgency.

However, even if this feature of the prophetic tradition helps us to understand the element of unfulfilled prediction in Jesus' message, it by no means takes us the whole way in our attempt to grasp its distinctive quality over against its background in contemporary Jewish expectation. When we

[77] Cf. Festinger, Riecken and Schachter, *When Prophecy Fails* (1956) ch.1.
[78] Cf. B. Wilson, *Magic and the Millennium* (1973) 493 n.14: 'Of course millennialists adjust their claims when prophecy fails – reset dates' etc.

were studying the teaching of Jesus in relation to the law, we observed that although it had elements of the prophetic it had much in common also with the work of scribes and lawyers; indeed the distinctiveness of Jesus consists precisely in this combination of more than one style of utterance: he mingled judgments which seem to presuppose a continuing faithful regard for the law with injunctions justified only by the existence of exceptional circumstances. And so it is here. Jesus' proclamation of the Kingdom is by no means exclusively prophetic. New Testament scholars, who seem agreed at last that Jesus' Kingdom-sayings contain statements that are both irreducibly future and irreducibly present,[79] tend to speak at this point of a tension between the 'already' and the 'not yet'; and indeed some tension of this kind is inevitable whenever the phrase 'the Kingdom of God' is used. For it is in reality nothing more than the abstract noun corresponding to the factual statement that God is king, which itself carries the same tension between present and future. That God is king, here and now, no believer would dream of denying. To say the opposite would be blasphemy. But if asked whether God is yet fully king, whether the world as we know it now is the perfect paradigm of his kingship, the believer who stands in the tradition of the Bible would be bound to say that there is a sense in which God is not yet king. His kingdom is not yet universally acknowledged by his creatures.[80] The perfect establishment of it still lies in the future. It is possible to argue from this tension, which is particularly prominent in Jesus' teaching (where the kingdom is referred to so often) that Jesus saw himself as standing at a true turning point. With his appearance a new epoch had begun. Things were still outwardly the same, but the present was necessarily transformed by the new light thrown upon it by the imminent realisation of God's kingdom. The difficulty with this argument is that it places a still greater weight on the concept of 'epoch' – a concept which, as we have seen, is artificial in the sense that history itself continues without a break: it is only our need to make it intelligible that makes us indulge in the fiction that one 'time' is any different from another.[81] The tension between the already and the not-yet is an academic tension to which nothing real corresponds, either in the experience of life or in the teaching of Jesus. To make sense of this apparent contradiction in one part of Jesus' teaching we need to widen our enquiry and look for a moment at his ethical teaching as a whole.

After thinking of Jesus as in certain respects a prophet one cannot but feel a sense of surprise[82] that a large number of his ethical sayings can be exactly

[79] W. Kümmel, *Promise and Fulfilment* (1957); O. Cullmann, *Salvation in History* (1967) 193-209.
[80] Cf. the Rabbinic saying, 'God is enthroned on the praises of his creatures'.
[81] Cf. K. Koch, *The Rediscovery of Apocalyptic* (E.tr. 1972) 70-1 for a just criticism of theologians' 'tension' language.
[82] Cf. O. Cullmann, op. cit. 221: 'Again and again people have marvelled (*hat man sich gewundert*) that wisdom teachings are to be found in Jesus . . .'. Such teachings, it is true, are not found in all parts of the tradition: they are notably absent from Mark. But their prominence in Q cannot be entirely due to subsequent tradition. Cf. J. Dunn, *Jesus and the Spirit* (1975) 369 n.108.

paralleled in the so-called wisdom literature of the Old Testament. Wisdom is in many ways the antithesis of prophecy. It shows no concern for any change in the normal progress of history; indeed it works on the assumption that human nature and human society will go on being the same, and that by acute observation a man may avoid the errors and temptations of the common run of mankind and bring his life into conformity with the nobler ideals set before him by God.[83] Its typical paradigm is pragmatic; if you do this, certain consequences will follow. Therefore you must either get into the way of doing it or of not doing it as the case may be. Jesus used this paradigm frequently. If you do not agree with your adversary quickly, you will end up in jail; therefore do not stand on your rights but be ready to reach a quick compromise. If you love only those who love you, you are no better than your basest neighbours; therefore love those who are not well disposed to you. But this paradigm will operate only if things are going on normally. In emergencies men may act quite differently, indeed unpredictably. And other parts of Jesus' teaching speak as if it is indeed an emergency in which we are involved. What we have to give an account of is not a kind of metaphysical tension between present and future, but an extraordinary ability of Jesus to give teaching which is sometimes appropriate to normal routine, sometimes to the exceptional demands of an emergency.

It may help to keep this phenomenon in perspective if we remember that those whom Jesus addressed were accustomed to hearing both tones of voice, both kinds of teaching, in the synagogue. Moreover, both kinds were thought of as serving the same purpose – that of enabling people to understand and adhere to the law of Moses.[84] The prophets, it is true, spoke out of their own time to people of their own time;[85] but the tone of urgency in their message was by no means extinguished by the passage of the centuries. The sense of the present being determined by an imminent future, holding a promise of either reward or judgment, continued to be felt. When the eighth-century prophets referred to events in the near future, they were speaking of political or military developments which they were able to discern as in any case probable, but which they also related to the broad sweep of Israel's history up to that time, and interpreted as expressions of the judgment and the restorative power of God. Only after the exile[86] did some more general and distant expectations, taking the form of a new epoch of peace and blessedness, begin to appear; and these expectations in particular

[83] This generalisation obscures the fact that there was of course more than one meaning of 'wisdom' and the *hakam* in the Old Testament. Cf. W. McKane, *Prophets and Wise Men* (1965) 48ff. But in the time of Christ all the Writings were assumed to be of divine origin and intimately related to the Law of Moses. Cf. Str.-B. 4. 446-60.

[84] Str.-B. loc. cit.

[85] Cf. S. Mowinckel, *He that Cometh* (1959) 131.

[86] So C. F. Whitley, *The Prophetic Achievement* (1963) 218, as against the older view of Volz, Gressmann, Eichrodt, etc.

were seized on by subsequent apocalyptic writers who, in the darker times in which they lived, constructed a more immediate time-scale in which these prophecies seemed to be on the brink of fulfilment, and to regain their power of giving consolation and hope. But it would have been utterly strange to the contemporaries of Jesus to approach the prophetic literature in the spirit of modern historical criticism. For them, the important thing about the prophets was that they spoke with the authority of God, and that their predictions must at some time or other (if they had not done so already) come true.[87] In the time of Jesus there were those who diligently kept watch for the signs of the times and 'searched the scriptures' – particularly the prophets – for indications that the divinely ordained drama was moving into its final stage. To people who were accustomed (as we have seen) to find significance in the present by seeing it as the prelude to an imminent and radically different future, the tense threats and promises of the prophets, their call for a change of heart in view of impending catastrophe, were heard as a relevant and challenging summons. Yet at the same time there was the daily business of life to attend to, children to be brought up, bargains to be negotiated, litigation to be carried through. These routine concerns had a moral as well as a legal or conventional dimension; and the wisdom writers offered a guide as to how one might bring them into relation, not just with the law as administered in the courts, but with the will of God as revealed in that law. They provided, in effect, for the fact that however earnestly one may look to an imminent and revolutionary change in the circumstances of life, one has still to attend to everyday matters, and the conduct of these will itself be a challenge to those who seek to bring their lives into conformity with the will of God.

This last observation helps us finally to situate the message of Jesus within the range of options which we may believe to have been open to him. Its uniqueness consists precisely in the fact that it combines – in a way for which there is no precedent in the Jewish culture[88] – all the main strands which contribute to the ethical teaching of the Old Testament. Like all Jewish teachers, Jesus took as his point of departure the Law, and showed a zeal to interpret

---

[87] Explicitly stated by Josephus, *Ant.* 10.35 πᾶν εἴτε ἀγαθὸν εἴτε φαῦλον γίνεται παρ᾽ ἡμῖν κατὰ τὴν ἐκείνων ἀποβαίνει προφήτειαν. Cf. Philo, *Quis rer. div. haer.* 261.

[88] It is sometimes argued that there were some among the sages who showed prophetic powers – e.g. a group of Pharisees in Herod's court (Jos. *Ant.* 17.43), Josephus himself (*B.J.* 3. 351ff.), Johanan ben Zakkai (bGittin 56a-b) and several Tannaites. But these accounts refer to feats of foresight or of particularly zealous matching of scriptural texts to present events. They were exceptional, not characteristic, and do not earn for their bearers the title 'prophet'. Again, Jesus may indeed have had much in common with the charismatic Hasidim of the first century A.D. (cf. G. Vermes, *Jesus the Jew* (1973) 58ff.), but they, unlike him, seem to have had no interest in legal matters: 'The tradition . . . contains no legal materials' (J. Neusner, *Rabbinic Traditions about the Pharisees before 70* 1. 395), nor in eschatology. It is doubtless true that the Pharisees owed much to the prophetic tradition (Lauterbach, *Rabbinical Essays* (1951) 122-4, 138ff.), but this does not mean thay they now spoke in a prophetic manner.

and apply it equal to that of the professional scribes, with whom indeed he shared some of the traditional techniques of interpretation. He also gave general moral instruction, in the fashion of the wisdom literature, which was relevant to the ordinary concerns of life and which presupposed (though without actually referring to it) the Law of Moses.[89] But in addition to this, Jesus spoke as a prophet: that is to say, he gave significance to the present time by relating it, through both word and deed, to a future world-order in which the power of evil is overcome and the social priorities are reversed. The time-scale in which he made these predictions was that of his own generation or (at most) their children; and to our question, why precisely this was the period of time he envisaged before the end, and why therefore he laid himself open to such early and inevitable falsification, the answer must be that this was the only time-scale available to him. If, as we have argued, the purpose of the prophet's message was to challenge his contemporaries to a change of heart in view of an imminent crisis, then the options offered by the time-table were extremely limited. The end could not be prophesied as if it were certainly upon them in the next few days: a suspension of all routine activity was not what the prophet aimed at; at the other extreme, it could not be proclaimed as something which might take place only in a subsequent and distant generation, for it would then cease to have any influence on the motives of those alive at the time. It could be preached only as something far enough away in the future to allow for purposeful and responsible action to continue, but near enough to invest the present with meaning and urgency. In other words, the only option for a prophet was to warn his contemporaries of an end occurring at a still unknown moment roughly within his own generation.

I am not of course intending to imply that this option ever presented itself as a matter of deliberate and conscious choice. A prophet is not a cynical manipulator of opinion. But I do suggest that, in a culture where prophecy was a credible and respected form of the interpretation of the divine will, this option was the only one which could have presented itself to one who had a serious message and who intended to stimulate moral and religious conduct in the light of a future reality. To see that this is so, we need only take a simple example from our own time. An entirely appropriate use of the word 'prophecy' today is in relation to the threat of nuclear war. The public on the whole is lulled into a sense of security by the assurances given of the effectiveness of a policy of 'nuclear deterrence'. If the major powers (so the argument runs) possess more or less equivalent nuclear armaments, the result is a kind of stalemate. It is in no one's interest to begin a major war, so peace is preserved and the threat of nuclear warfare averted. In the face of this comfortable doctrine the contemporary prophet alerts us to the inevitable

[89] Cf. R. Banks, *Jesus and the Law in the Synoptic Tradition* (1975) 26–7 and the literature cited at 26 n.2

precariousness of such a policy. Not only does it offer no protection against precipitate or careless action by one of the great powers, but it can at most be a holding operation until nuclear weapons are possessed and developed by a large number of smaller nations, to whom the same restraints may not apply. Far from offering us security, the present apparent equilibrium yields us only a breathing space in which to solve the problem at a deeper level. Such prophetic voices are indeed raised, and even respectfully listened to; but my point is that the option of a time-scale open to them is exactly the same as in the case of a biblical prophet. They do not wish their prophecies to be taken as an invitation to panic, as if the whole population should immediately take refuge underground; but equally they cannot speak of the threat as if it lay a century away in the future; for that would rob it of its power to stimulate urgent action in the present. Their message is necessarily of a catastrophic event which will take place in this very generation unless strenuous measures are taken to avert it – indeed unless (as they may well put it) there is a fundamental change of heart. They may be wrong. This generation may (we pray it will) pass without bringing destruction on itself. But such a delay would by no means discredit the prophets. For we can all see the truth of a message which interprets the present time in terms of a highly probable future, instead of regarding it merely as a series of opportunist steps in a direction which cannot be certainly charted.

I would urge, then, that the saying of Jesus which has given us so much trouble is in fact a singularly precise expression of the constraint involved in the prophetic option. Jesus did not intend his message to cause panic, paralysis or anarchy. The change would not come so soon that all normal activity must now be suspended; only some of those present would live to see it, and meanwhile life went on as usual, and Jesus had plenty to say about the way it should be lived. But equally it would not be so far in the future that anyone could afford to forget about it. Fifty years may seem a long time, and one might be forgiven for putting off preparations for a year or two. But no, it could be any time, one must be constantly vigilant and alert. So speaks the prophet. It will be within this generation. No other time-scale is available to him. The possibility – with hindsight we may prefer to say the probability – of disconfirmation is far less of a threat to his credibility than would be any relaxation in the urgency of his summons. Live joyfully, responsibly, to the full; but never lose sight of that crisis, that dénouement, that ending which alone makes sense of the present, and which affects your living precisely because it is a possibility every day of your life. Such was Jesus' message; such his respect for, and exploitation of, the constraint of time to which he exposed himself by choosing the option, not of a teacher only, but also of a prophet.

We started from the observation that there is in the teaching of Jesus an irreducible element of concentration upon an imminent and radically different future. We found this to be something which responded to the hopes and expectations of the people of his time, and which in fact is related to the manner in which we continue to make sense of our own lives and our own history. And we have seen finally that the time-scale in which this element of threat and promise is set – that of a single generation – is the only option available to one who has a prophetic message, and the failure of events to manifest that ultimate finality which was prophesied nevertheless does not rob the original message of its credibility, since the programme which gives meaning to the present by relating it to an imminent future is one which we continue to find a source of inspiration however often the details of the predictions are falsified by events. But this is to put the argument in a somewhat negative form. I have talked as if the temporally conditioned and irreducibly predictive component of the teaching of Jesus were a difficulty or an obstacle which must somehow be circumvented or made harmless before one can reach the abiding significance of his teaching. But it is possible to put the matter in a more positive way. If we ask, once again, what it is that has given the message of Jesus its power and attraction down the centuries, we must certainly allow for certain respects in which it stands comparison with any other body of religious teaching in the world. We may mention the vivid and poetic form in which most of it is cast; the extreme purity of motive which is demanded; the constant appeal to what is best in human beings. Doubtless there have been and always will be people who give their allegiance to Jesus because of these qualities. But it is doubtful whether his message and achievement would have had their astonishing career in world history had it not been for the conspicuous element of hope and promise with which these qualities are allied. It is once again to Marxist students of Christianity that we must turn for an appreciation of the importance of this temporal dimension. It is a basic element of the Marxist message that a future fully socialist state is not a distant utopian ideal which may one day be brought to fulfilment, but is something that can be realised even within a generation if it can be preceded by a sufficiently violent overthrow of the existing structures of society. Those who are disillusioned and discontented with things as they are can be affected with enthusiam for things as they might be, not – or not only – by the sheer attractiveness of that vision, but by the exhilarating sensation of having its realisation in their own hands. If the essential condition for change is a revolutionary overthrow of the present social and economic system, then this is something which lies within the bounds of possibility. To become a convinced Marxist is to take the future into one's own hands, and to understand the present as important only in so far as it prepares for the future. In the words of Marx's famous eleventh thesis on Feuerbach: 'The philosophers have interpreted the world in different ways; but our task is now to change it.'

There can be no doubt that it is this orientation towards a future state of affairs set in the time-scale of at most a few generations which has made Marxism the most powerful intellectual and spiritual movement in the west after Christianity. But it is surely significant that Marxist thinkers themselves find in the teaching of Jesus that same power to transform the present through concentration upon a future, the realisation of which depends (wholly for Marxists, only in part for Christians who see the necessity of a decisive intervention by God) upon the ability of men to take hold of it through a deliberate reversal of the usual privileges and priorities.[90] Thus one Marxist writer sees the heart of Jesus' teaching as 'The decision must be reached *today*. The choice must be made *today* . . . The man who makes the choice chooses at a single stroke the whole of the future'.[91] Another calls it 'the demand which the future age makes on the present' . . . 'the recognition that the future is *your concern* here and now'.[92] It is a challenge which fundamentally affects one's attitude to the world around. In the words of Ernst Bloch: 'The Cosmos is not thought of with disdain, or as a negative component that can be left out of consideration, but as something which by its very collapse becomes the instrument, indeed the arena, of the Kingdom.'[93] These writers are of course tempted to envisage radical change in social and economic terms; but they recognise that the thrust of Jesus' teaching was not towards social reform, but towards a future in which man becomes more fully himself, more authentically human. We may express the matter in more personal terms by making the trite observation that any strong conviction that the future will be different from the present is sufficient to give a new meaning and purpose to the present itself. Indeed we can go further: it enables us to discover possibilities in the present which were not there before. I have already suggested that the lasting power of Jesus' ethical teaching consists in its location at the very edge of what we usually believe to be possible. We have now reached a similar conclusion by another route. Jesus' message has power, not in spite of, but because of its promise of a future which is not ideal or utopian, nor a mere variation for the better on what we know already, but is both radically new and able to be envisaged on a human time-scale, 'in our generation'. Faithful and eager attention to such a future introduces a new dimension into the present; for the present becomes, not a mere working out of the consequences of the past, but a transition to an altogether different future. The present is transformed by the discovery of possibilities which were not apparent until it was seen in the light of the future. It is this proleptic transformation of the present in the light of an imminent future which is the key to understanding another fact about Jesus which is established beyond any reasonable historical doubt: that he performed acts which were regarded as 'miracles', that is (in the normal way) impossible. This side of his activity must be the next object of our attention.

[90] Cf. F. Lochman, *Encountering Marx* (Belfast, 1977) 118: 'Among the most important things that Christianity and Marxism have in common is that both are consciously orientated towards the future.' Lochman goes on to observe that Marxism in fact owes this future orientation to the influence of the Bible.

[91] V. Gardavsky, *God is Not Yet Dead* (E.tr. 1973) 42.

[92] M. Machoveč, *A Marxist Looks at Jesus* (E.tr. 1976) 88.

[93] *Das Prinzip Hoffnung* (1959) 1453.

# 5
# The Intelligibility of Miracle

There is a famous paragraph in Josephus which purports to offer a brief account of the life and death of Jesus of Nazareth. Whether this paragraph was written by Josephus, or by a subsequent Christian interpolator who piously supplied what he felt Josephus ought to have written, is a much debated question[1] which, for my present purpose, has no importance. What concerns me about the passage is that in either case it offers to the kind of readers to whom Jospehus' work is addressed – that is, educated Roman pagans – a brief characterisation of Jesus in language they could be expected to understand. It contains two statements about him which are particularly relevant to my purpose: Jesus was 'a wise man', and he was 'a doer of paradoxical works'.[2] Expressed in terms that would have been readily intelligible throughout the Greek-speaking world, these are two of those general statements about Jesus which, as I have argued, are known with a high degree of historical certainty and are capable of yielding significant information about him. That he was a 'wise man', that is, a teacher, is a fact whose implications I have been exploring in the last two chapters. That he was a 'doer of paradoxical works' – for which our word is miracle-worker – is equally well attested: it is basic to the whole gospel tradition about him and is implied by subsequent Jewish attacks on him, which represent him as a sorcerer.[2a] It is instructive to note the place given to this aspect of Jesus' work by the author of the paragraph in Josephus. He evidently did not think that miracle-working was the most important thing about Jesus: it is just one in a series of his notable attributes, mentioned alongside others. At the same time there is no hint of apology or reticence. The story of Jesus could hardly be told without reference to miraculous works; indeed in the synoptic gospels such episodes make up a good proportion of the material they preserve. We know from the epistles that it was possible to speak and write about Jesus without any mention of his miraculous power;[3] and indeed it is a possible implication of the early hymn

[1] For a recent survey of scholarly opinion on the Testimonium Flavianum, cf. P. Winter in E. Schürer, *History of the Jewish People*[2] (1973) 428–41.

[2] παραδόξων ἔργων ποιήτης. παράδοξον is a common term for 'miracle' in Hellenistic Judaism; cf. G. MacRae in *Miracles* (ed. C. F. D. Moule, 1965) 143.

[2a] See above, p.59 n.106.

[3] Though not without reference to miraculous events in the church: Romans 15. 18–19; 1 Cor. 12. 9–10; 2 Cor. 12.12; Hebr. 2.4. Cf. G. Delling, *Studiem zum N. T.* (1970) 146–59.

preserved in Phil. 2. 5-11 that one who 'took the form of a servant' could hardly at the same time have been capable of performing supernatural feats.[4] But just as we have seen that the virtual silence of the epistles with regard to Jesus as a teacher cannot be set against the overwhelming evidence of the gospels that he was one, so we can reasonably accept the impression given by the synoptics of one who was believed to have performed notable miracles as a firm historical datum. Jesus was a man who was, or was believed to be, a doer of miraculous works.

In this modern age it may be necessary to offer some apology for regarding reports of allegedly miraculous feats as part of the available historical evidence about Jesus. It is possible to take the view that since these apparently supernatural events could not in fact have happened, the reports of them cannot offer any purchase to the serious historian; they must simply be left out of account.[5] I would not wish to meet this objection by disagreeing totally with its premise. It is certainly true that various miraculous feats are attributed to Jesus in the gospels which a great many modern readers find it impossible to believe. But I would want to argue that there are at least three reasons why this aspect of Jesus' activity cannot be disposed of so simply.

(i) I begin with the obvious point that what seemed inexplicable or miraculous to the ancients does not necessarily seem so to us. Our modern knowledge of the manifold and subtle connections between mental states and symptoms of physical disease makes it seem perfectly comprehensible that the influence of an authoritative and (as we say) charismatic personality may cause a dramatic improvement in what appears outwardly to be a physical condition but has in fact a nervous or emotional cause. In particular, those symptoms which the contemporaries of Jesus believed to be due to demon-possession would often have been amenable to such 'treatment'.[6] Along these lines, a substantial number of incidents reported as healing miracles in the gospels may be accounted for as natural phenomena and considered as possible additions to the stock of historical knowledge about Jesus.

(ii) My second point is a consequence of the particular character of the miracles attributed to Jesus. It is often said that it was inevitable that legendary feats of this kind would have clustered around the memory of one such as Jesus; that we have similar stories told of countless other persons of antiquity, be they sages or charlatans; and that indeed it would have been more surprising if the story of Jesus had been told without these inevitable accretions. It is true that Jesus by no means stands alone in his time and his culture as a doer of miraculous works: one of his own sayings acknowledges that there were other exorcists at work (Mt. 12.27), and stories are told of rabbis and charismatic teachers in Palestine, as well as of pagan wonder-

---

[4] R. Bultmann, *Theology of the New Testament* 1 (E.tr. 1952) 27.
[5] Cf. (for example) Michael Grant, *Jesus* (1977) 39 and passim.
[6] Cf. S. McCasland, *By the Finger of God* (1951) passim.

workers in other lands, which are no less sensational than those told of Jesus. But the collections which have been made of this comparative material[7] reveal differences as well as similarities. The most common miracle attributed to holy men of his time and culture was that of procuring rainfall[8] – an important and welcome feat in a country absolutely dependent on seasonal rain. But this is something never credited to Jesus. Again, Jewish miracle-workers certainly succeeded in curing diseases,[9] but there is a notable absence of reports of the curing of any kind of lameness or paralysis;[10] by contrast, many pagan healing shrines (like Christian ones in modern times) testify to the occurrence of precisely this kind of cure.[11] Above all, Jesus is credited with three instances of a very notable miracle indeed: that of raising a dead person to life. The frequently alleged parallels to this are highly questionable. The Jewish tradition knows of no actual instances of such a feat: it merely suggests that a rabbi of exceptional holiness might in theory be capable of it.[12] Two stories sometimes cited from Lucian are told with the characteristic cynicism of that writer, and were clearly not intended to be taken too seriously;[13] and the one close parallel, which occurs in the Life of Apollonius of Tyana,[14] is accompanied by a comment of Philostratus to the effect that he is not sure himself whether it is to be believed. In all these respects the tradition of Jesus' miracles has too many unusual features to be conveniently ascribed to conventional legend-mongering. Moreover many of them contain details of precise reporting which is quite unlike the usual run of legends and is difficult to explain unless it derives from some historical recollection; and the gospels themselves (as we shall see) show a remarkable restraint in their narratives which contrasts strangely with that delight in the miraculous for its own sake which normally characterises the growth of legend.

(iii) This is not to say, of course, that all the miracle-stories in the gospels must be given equal weight. We have to allow for some having grown in the telling, some being mis-recollections of sayings or symbolic actions, and some (in particular the so-called nature miracles) being even entirely legendary. But even when a number has been excluded for these reasons, we shall be left with a substantial body of material which belongs peculiarly to Jesus, which has no close parallel in the ancient world, and which at the very

[7] Cf. especially P. Fiebig, *Jüdische Wundergeschichten* (1911); O. Weinreich, *Antike Heiligungswunder* (1909); Bultmann, *HST* 231ff.

[8] Rainmaking is attributed to Honi and Nakdimon; cf. P. Fiebig, op. cit. 16ff

[9] Hanina b. Dosa, bBer. 34b; Rab, bHag. 3a.

[10] Morton Smith, *Tannaitic Parallels to the Gospels* (*JBL* Mon. Series 6, 1951) 81ff. shows (against P. Fiebig) the extreme paucity of rabbinic parallels to any of Jesus' miracles.

[11] *IG* 4. 951-2; A. J. Festugière, *L'Histoire générale des religions. Grèce-Rome* (1944) 132-6. Cf. below n.70.

[12] Str.-B. 1. 557-60, which even Bultmann, *HST* 233 calls 'highly artificial stories'.

[13] *Philops.* 26; *Alex.* 24.

[14] 4.45.

least testifies to the surprise and wonder which he evoked on many occasions. That this reaction to him may be regarded as historical becomes even more probable when we observe that it is by no means always the main element in the narratives. The evangelists seem to have a larger stock of miracles to record than any of them actually makes use of (Mk. 3.10; Jn. 20.30). But their criterion of selection does not seem to have been the sensational quality of each episode. As we shall see, Mark's selection and presentation was determined by a number of concerns, such as using the miracles as lessons in faith. John's gospel, by contrast, has a quite different selection, in which the implicit challenge to sabbath observance is made explicit, and the evidential value of the miracles as 'signs' authenticating Jesus' authority is strongly emphasised. There is a seriousness and a restraint in these reports which compels us to take them seriously as a source of historical information.[15]

Even if it is granted, however, that reports of miraculous activity can be reckoned among the firm historical data available to us about Jesus, it can still be said that they provide us with nothing which is of value for determining his religious significance. A sociologist of religion, for example, will expect to find thaumaturgy among the attributes of any messianic figure. As Bryan Wilson puts it:

> Messiahs must be capable of wonder-working, even if this is not what is primarily stressed in their mission. For the living claimant to Messiahship this is the touchstone of legitimacy. Since he cannot, without coming into direct contact with the civil authorities, claim political or military power, since he must eschew the spheres of rational economic activity, since he claims a unique quality and thus does not teach others to emulate him but rather only to serve him and rely on him, he has few styles of action other than wonder-working.[16]

It might seem tempting to infer from this that the reports which we have of Jesus performing miracles simply serve to classify him among the many messianic deliverers known to social anthropologists. If, as we have seen, these reports are not the result of an inevitable accumulation of legend around the memory of a notable figure, but go back to an impression made on his contemporaries, then we may say that this impression is one which Jesus would have intended to create, in so far as this was the only option open to him as a person who saw himself in a messianic role. It was only in this way that he could command attention for his teaching and his message.

We must return to this observation later. But first we need to be somewhat more precise about the kind of environment in which this thaumaturgic activity of Jesus took place. There is, for example, no justification for assuming that his contemporaries were a great deal more credulous than

---

[15] The synoptic miracle-narratives also stand up well to the criteria of authenticity currently applied by New Testament scholars; cf. R. Latourelle, 'Authenticité historique des miracles de Jésus', *Gregorianum* 54 (1973) 225-62.

[16] *Magic and the Millennium* (1973) 134.

ourselves.[17] Josephus, when reporting miraculous events from the Old Testament more than once expresses reserve over whether they can be believed.[18] Philostratus himself shows a certain scepticism about some of the feats attributed to his hero Apollonius;[19] and Eusebius, in his reply to Philostratus, explicitly denies that reports of miracles can strengthen the probability that the doer of them possesses divine power.[20] This critical attitude, which only takes an extreme form in the satirising of Lucian, suggests that the situation was not in principle very different from what it is today.[21] Then, as now, there will have been a considerable difference between the sophisticated and the simple with respect to credulity.[22] Indeed there were many of the former for whom religion itself might make it difficult to believe in miracles, inasmuch as they doubted whether the god whom they believed to be responsible for the inherent order and rationality of the universe would tolerate, let alone inspire, the irregularity involved in so-called signs and wonders.[23] As for the simple and uneducated, Lucian's caricature of the charlatan doubtless rests on an element of fact. In an age when it was widely believed that all terrestrial events depend on the influence of the stars, which themselves move in unalterable and predetermined courses, the surest means of gaining a reputation for extraordinary powers was to read the signs in advance, either by respectable astrological methods, or else by intuition, magic or occult practices. Many of the so-called 'miracles' of the ancient world belong to this category: their authors, through

[17] The assumption is at least as old as David Hume's dictum, 'Miracles abound chiefly among primitive and barbarous nations'. But reserve or scepticism towards miracles is often found in ancient historians: Herodotus 2.55-7, 73, 156; 4. 95-6, 105; Thucydides 5.26. 3-4; 1. 126. 4-6; Polybius 2.17.6; 2.56.10; 16.12.6f.; 3.47.6ff.; Plut. *Camill.* 6.1-4; *Coriol.* 37.3ff.; *Marius* 36.5f.; *Pericles* 35.2; Dion. Hal. *Ant. Rom.* 2.56. 2-3. Cf. G. Petzke in *N. T. und Christliche Existenz* (H. Braun Festshrift, 1973), 369: 'Scientific arguments took place already in antiquity . . . miracles were by no means accepted without question.'

[18] *Ant.* 1. 104-8; 4. 158; 17. 354 – though his scepticism is of course tempered by his belief in divine intervention in Jewish history; cf. S. Légasse, *Les Miracles de Jésus* (ed. X. Léon-Dufour, 1977) 112.

[19] E.g. *V.A.* 4.45; 5. 13-16. Such feats were not characteristic of the Pythagorean 'wise man', and laid him open to the imputation of sorcery, 1.2. Cf. G. Petzke, *Die Traditionen über Apollonius von Tyana und das N. T.* (1970) 156.

[20] *Contra Hier.* 6.

[21] It is important not to over-simplify: R. M. Grant, for example, in his article 'Miracle and Mythology' *ZRGG* 3 (1951) 123-33, argues that the first century A.D. was marked by an increase in credulity; but some of his evidence is questionable: the miraculous promises made by messianic prophets shortly before the Jewish revolt (Jos. *Ant.* 20. 167-70) were surely not characteristic of the age as a whole, and the note by Pliny *N.H.* 31. 18. 24, 'in Judaea rivus sabbatis omnibus siccatus', is probably no more than a slightly fanciful report of the well-known phenomenon of an intermittent spring, of which Jerusalem afforded a notable example.

[22] But we should not forget that a belief in the occult, and in the significance of dreams, was widespread among intellectuals; cf. G. Bowersock, *Greek Sophists in the Roman Empire* (1969) 71ff.

[23] Philo *Vit. Mos.* 1. 155-6; Aristobulus ap. Euseb. *Praep. Ev.* 8.10. Cf. D. Georgi, *Die Gagner des Paulus im 2 Korintherbrief* (1964) 152ff. The argument was used (somewhat inconsistently) by Eusebius in his attack on Philostratus' *Apollonius, Contra Hier.* 6.

dreams, premonitions, careful observation or simple hunches correctly foretold an event lying in the near future: having gained this reputation, it was not difficult to formulate further prophecies in such ambiguous language that they could hardly be proved wrong.[24] Such knowledge of the future seemed in principle possible of attainment in view of the predetermination of all terrestrial events by the movements of the heavenly bodies, and it was comprehensible that certain kinds of esoteric wisdom might procure these results. But feats which we would call more strictly 'miraculous' present a more difficult problem. Then, as now, the witnesses of a supernatural feat would need some context in which to place it.[25] Philostratus, when writing of Apollonius' feat of bringing a dead girl back to life (which incidentally is the only well-attested example of such a feat in pagan or Jewish antiquity) confesses to doubt whether such a thing could really have happened: it did not fit his Pythagorean portrait of Apollonius, and seemed something of a freak. At the other end of the scale is the raising of Lazarus in the Fourth Gospel, where it is the climactic expression of a power over life and death which is true and characteristic of Jesus throughout his activity: according to this evangelist, to disbelieve it would be to disbelieve in Jesus altogether. It was presumably a frame of reference of this kind, rather than a credulity greater than our own, which enabled sophisticated minds to accept the miracles of Jesus. Presented simply as remarkable stories, there is no reason to think that they would have gained any more credence then than they would today.

It is in this light that we must judge the accounts we possess of other miracle-workers in Jesus' period and culture. We have already observed that the list of such occurrences is very much shorter than is often supposed. If we take the period of four hundred years stretching from two hundred years before to two hundred years after the birth of Christ, the number of miracles recorded which are remotely comparable with those of Jesus is astonishingly small. On the pagan side, there is little to report[26] apart from the records of cures at healing shrines, which were certainly quite frequent, but are a rather different phenomenon from cures performed by an individual healer. Indeed it is significant that later Christian fathers, when seeking miracle workers with whom to compare or contrast Jesus, had to have recourse to remote and by now almost legendary figures of the past such as Pythagoras or Empedocles.[27] In the period nearer the time of Jesus we know of only one man, Apollonius of Tyana, who had comparable feats to his name; and there

---

[24] This is the progress cynically sketched out by Lucian in his *Alexander*.

[25] Such a context is implicit in the New Testament nomenclature τέρας, σημεῖον, δυνάμεις. Cf. G. Delling, *Studien* 148-50.

[26] O. Weinreich, *Antike Heiligungswunder,* can adduce only a handful of miracles attributed to certain kings or emperors, apart from those of Apollonius of Tyana.

[27] Clem. Alex. *Strom.* 3.6.28ff. Empedocles performed weather miracles, brought people back from the dead, and was γοητεύων (Satyrus, ap. Diog. L. 8.58-9); cf. E. R. Dodds, *The Greeks and the Irrational* (1951) 145-6, who calls him the last of the Greek Shamans.

is also the rather special case of the emperor Vespasian, who is reliably reported to have performed two notable cures. We shall come back to both of these. Meanwhile, on the Jewish side, stories of miraculous deeds are mainly confined to a small group of men whom it has become customary to call 'charismatics' and whom the rabbinic sources themselves call, significantly, 'men of deed'. These men – Honi the Rain-maker and Hanina ben Dosa are the only two of whom we have any detailed knowledge[28] – have a very clear frame of reference for their miraculous feats. They were men of prayer; and the degree of intimacy which they gained with their heavenly father afforded them an almost physical guarantee that their prayers would be answered.[29] The sheer intensity and concentration involved would make the man of prayer impervious, not only to interruption, but to physical harm.[30] There is nothing here to stretch our credulity even today: the extraordinary psychic power of persons capable of prolonged and concentrated prayer are too well authenticated to be completely disbelieved. To accept the stories about them is to accept that they were indeed exceptional men of prayer. To deny them would be to call into question, not just their (as we would put it) psychic power, but their whole claim on our attention which is based on an alleged intensity of spiritual life. Of this spiritual life these 'miracles' were an eloquent expression; but there is a notable humourousness – almost a flippancy – about the way they were narrated which suggests that these 'deeds' were by no means regarded as the most significant thing about them.

By contrast with these revered and holy men, there undoubtedly existed practitioners of more dubious arts – magicians, sorcerers, necromancers and all those other possessors of psychic powers who inevitably plied their trade in a society which took seriously the forces of evil. That such people were not uncommon is proved by the frequency with which the charge of sorcery is referred to in Jewish legal writings[31] and to the appearance of Jewish names and spells in the magical papyri.[32] Here again we should not draw too sharp a line between their civilisation and ours. That human beings can harm each other by manipulating dimly understood psychic forces was strongly felt in antiquity and is vaguely believed by many people even now (the recent spate of criminal offences in connection with 'exorcism' is a case in point). The difference is rather one between social classes: a greater fear of the black arts will have been evinced by those who had not the education or the intelligence to see through the charlatans. But no one doubted that a genuine sorcerer was a serious menace to society, and that he derived his power to cause damage,

---

[28] Cf. S. Safrai, 'The teaching of Pietists in Mishnaic Literature', *JJS* 16 (1965), G. Vermes, *Post-biblical Jewish Studies* (1975) 178ff.; *Jesus the Jew* (1973) 69-79.

[29] 'If my prayer is fluent in my mouth, I know that he is favoured' (Hanina ben Dosa, bBer. 34b).

[30] M. Ber. 5.1. Hanina was unharmed by a poisonous snake while praying, bBer. 33a.

[31] Deut. 18.10; M. Sanh. 7.11, etc.

[32] E.g. *PGM* 22b; 35.14; cf. J. M. Hull, *Hellenistic Magic and the Synoptic Tradition* (1974) 31ff.

not just from his own unscrupulous determination to exploit fear and credulity, but from his ability to harness supernatural forces to his purpose.

It follows that anyone who deliberately performed miracles was taking a serious risk, the risk of being taken for a sorcerer or magician;[33] and that this risk seriously curtailed the options open to him. Clearly, to speak of 'options' in this context is to use the concept in a slightly different sense from that in which I have used it up to now. A person who knows himself to possess supernatural powers is not quite so free to decide whether or not to use them as a man who has knowledge is free to decide whether or not to teach. Such powers tend to impel their owners into action. Nevertheless it remains within the discretion of the individual to choose and adhere to a particular style of miracle-working. Recognition of this freedom is reflected in the temptation narrative of Matthew and Luke, and in the secrecy motif which is particularly prominent in Mark but present also in the other synoptics. One question on which a choice not merely can but must be made is that of the degree of publicity which is invited. A sorcerer or magician is essentially a discreet and private operator.[34] His techniques are esoteric and mysterious, not to be communicated to the uninitiated; and his activity may have social consequences such that he does well to keep out of the public eye – the severe laws against sorcery in the Jewish code are an indication of how seriously this danger was taken. By contrast the miracle worker normally seeks an audience and performs his feats in the clear light of day: only a large number of witnesses to the event will confirm its authenticity and protect him from the charge of sorcery. Even on this simple analysis, it is clear that the miracles of Jesus have unusual features, in that they include examples of both styles. Sometimes he works openly before a great crowd, sometimes he deliberately seeks privacy. We know from Jewish sources that he attracted the accusation of sorcery, and the gospels confirm that he was not as careful as he might have been to avoid the charge by performing all his miracles in public. At the same time we can appreciate that there were dangers involved in too much publicity. A crowd may react unpredictably to an apparently supernatural feat: it may fear the consequences of further such actions and seek to drive the miracle-worker away; or it may seek to adopt him as a leader, thereby risking reprisals from the legal government. The gospels report that Jesus experienced both these dangers (Mk. 5.17; Jn. 6.15), and a natural anxiety to avoid them may be at least a partial explanation of the reticence he showed towards allowing his miracles to be widely known or even always publicly witnessed.

Another, less theoretical, way of defining the options open to one who possessed psychic or supernatural powers is to review the kinds of activity which persons with similar gifts undertook. We have noticed already that by

[33] Id. op. cit. 52-3. The risk was certainly incurred by Apollonius of Tyana: Lucian *Alex*, 4; Dio C. 78.18.4.
[34] Cf. G. Theissen, *Urchristliche Wundergeschichten* (1974) 237.

far the commonest manifestation of allegedly miraculous gifts was the ability to foretell the future from a close observation of present phenomena. The advantage of this was that it could be represented as a rationally explicable, if not actually scientific, procedure,[35] and therefore virtually immune from the charge of being associated with demonic powers. In a previous age it had depended on the skill and knowledge of a professional class of priests and augurers, who inherited specific techniques of divination from omens, dreams, the entrails of sacrificial victims and so forth. But in the hellenistic period this expertise passed to people of a more philosophical training, in that once astrology had taken a firm hold on people's minds and with it the conviction that events are in principle determined in advance, then it became a matter almost of scientific observation to predict the future course of events. Philostratus, when presenting the character of Apollonius to the empress who was his distinguished patron, makes much of this aspect of his hero's gifts, and is correspondingly reserved about other examples of miraculous powers;[36] for it was in such knowledge that the true Pythagorean was expected to excel,[37] and it went indeed with what we would recognise as a well-attested psychic ability to know what is happening in another place or what is being thought by another person. If one can work out from skilful observation what is going to happen in the future, it is surely no more difficult to work out what is happening in the present even if one cannot observe it by normal means. The ability to make such observations was the mark of an abnormally wise and divinely gifted man.[38]

It is a striking fact about the records of Jesus that they nowhere credit him with gifts of this kind. In John's gospel, it is true, it is said that Jesus 'knew what was in man' (2.25) and that he had a kind of second sight with regard to Nathanael (1.48) and the woman of Samaria (4.18). Similarly, in the synoptics, Jesus is frequently said to know what people are thinking (Mk. 2.8 etc.). These are the anticipated traits of a seer; similarly in John's gospel as well as in the synoptics Jesus shows foreknowledge of the manner of his death. But the difference between these almost casual references to his exceptional knowledge and observation, and the predictions and intuitions of Apollonius which are reported deliberately to create or enhance his reputation for supernatural skill and wisdom, is so obvious that it needs no emphasis. Whenever scholars speak of a 'hellenistic influence' on the accounts of Jesus' miracles, we should keep firmly in mind the striking absence from the gospel narratives of any explicit interest in this widely accepted mark of supernatural power.

A second option which seems to have offered some safety from the danger

---

[35] So in the traditions of Pythagoras' powers; cf. Iamblichus, *Vit. Pyth.* 8 and passim.
[36] *Vit. Ap.* 1.2; cf. above, n.19.
[37] Iambl. *Vit. Pyth.* 28.
[38] *Vit. Ap.* 1.19.

of being accused of sorcery was that of procuring a cure by means of prayer. A famous exponent of this style of activity was Hanina ben Dosa, who is reported to have actually given an account of the sensations by which he would know whether his prayer had been answered.[39] As we have already seen, a reputation for an exceptional degree of concentration in prayer must have run before the actual performance of a cure; and the divine (as opposed to demonic) origin of the miracle was authenticated by the fact that it evidently proceeded from that same activity of praying to the true God for which the sage had already acquired a reputation. Rather similar are the rain-making stories told of two of Hanina's near contemporaries, Honi and Nakdimon.[40] In their case it is not so much the inner concentration of the prayer which authenticates the miracle and removes from it the suspicion of sorcery as the familiarity with which the deity is addressed. This almost impudent style of arguing or bartering with God stands in a long tradition which goes back to Abraham entreating for Sodom and continues through many generations of rabbis. It was a style of address that no one would use to the devil; presumably, therefore, if Honi and Nakdimon were heard to use it when they procured rainfall for Jerusalem, they could not be accused of collaborating with demonic powers. But once again it is extremely striking that Jesus has no story of this kind told of him. All the conditions are there: Jesus both shows extraordinary powers of prolonged concentration and adopts an intimate (though not, in his case, bartering or bantering) style of address to God; and he instructs his followers in both the necessity and the power of prayer for performing miracles; but few of his mighty works are explicitly attributed to prayer. The style of the 'Charismatic' is not the one chosen by Jesus.

A third option which seems to have been available was that of performing a cure by normal medical means, but with an extra power and authority which might achieve success where the ordinary doctors had failed. It was not of course always easy to distinguish in practice between medical and magical or exorcistical techniques: the use of spittle, for example, is both a well-attested practice in primitive medicine, and also part of the exorcist's ritual when attacking an evil spirit.[41] Nevertheless both touching with the hand[42] and applying spittle[43] were normal medical procedures. That touching in particular was thought to be an effective treatment suggests that then as now there were people with a gift of healing in their hands. Most doctors might not achieve much in this way; but a person with a particular gift might occasionally effect a sensational cure. When Vespasian found he could cure a

[39] Cf. above, n.29
[40] Cf. above, n.8
[41] Cf. J. M. Hull, op.cit. 76–7.
[42] Solon fr. 13.61–2 (West); Seneca *Benef.* 6. 16.2
[43] Galen, *Nat. fac.* 3.7.

blind man and a cripple by these means, it was described as a piece of knowledge about himself miraculously imparted to him by the god Serapis, along with foreknowledge of his destiny to be Emperor. There is no suggestion in the very sober accounts we have of this episode[44] that magic was involved. The option of performing such cures by the exercise of a gift of healing was uncontroversial: it carried no sense of threat to the authorities or suspicion of collaboration with the devil. It could have been, therefore, an attractive option for Jesus, and indeed he is recorded as having adopted it on occasion: he made use of both touch and spittle,[45] and the healing of the woman with a haemorrhage has an explicitly 'medical' character: she had already received treatment by doctors, and after her cure Jesus tells her, 'Be cured of your wound'. The 'power' which Jesus felt to go out of him was a standard concept in healings of this kind,[46] and is seen by Luke to be the means by which Jesus carried out a number of cures (Lk. 6.18-19). Yet, though this offered a satisfactory model for describing a number of Jesus' miracles, it certainly was not his characteristic style of action. Healing or exorcism by a word (sometimes even when the sufferer was elsewhere) is recorded of him more often.

The proof (if proof were needed) that Jesus did not confine himself to any of these safer options is that five of his miracles, each reported by at least two of the synoptic gospels, were exorcisms, and that two summaries of his healing activity explicitly include the casting out of demons. That this was a more dangerous and ambiguous form of healing is clear from its very nature: if the cure depends on a kind of contest with demonic powers there is bound to be question about the weapons which the exorcist uses. We have a large amount of information about the techniques which exorcists had available to them, techniques which were mainly indistinguishable from magic.[47] The rituals and formulas they used show that they thought of themselves as fighting the demons on their own ground. The basic principle of exorcism was to enlist the help of a power greater than that of the demon which was causing the damage; but by so doing the exorcist would inevitably arouse suspicion that he had more knowledge and experience of the world of evil spirits than would be possible for anyone who did not himself dabble dangerously in the black arts. We know that Jesus was attacked on this very point: the accusation is made against him in the gospels, and is sustained in subsequent Jewish calumnies of him.[48] It is likely that his strongest

[44] Tacitus *Hist.* 4.81; Suetonius *Vesp.* 7; cf. A. D. Nock, *JRS* 47 (1957) 118 = *Essays* 2, 838, who relates these miracles to others which attended the birth or appointment of emperors. Cf. also D. Tiede, *The Charismatic Figure as Miracle-Worker* (1972) 90ff.

[45] Mk. 7.33; 8.23; Mt. 9.29; Jn. 9.6.

[46] Cf. Plut. *Q. conv.* 4.1.3 (663c) τὰς βασιλικὰς καὶ ἀλεξιφαρμάκους δυνάμεις: Plutarch is apparently referring to the healing 'power' in rulers' hands; cf. O. Weinreich, *Antike Heiligungswunder* 75.

[47] J. Hull, op. cit. 67ff.

[48] Cf. also Origen *C. Cels.* 1. 28.

defence was the success of his exorcisms. Though there were certainly other exorcists about, and an elaborate repertoire existed of skills for them to practise, we may guess that their treatment was not more than partially successful, and many improvements they produced were temporary. Their explanation of this relative failure will have been that in the game of playing off one spirit against another they had not been able to get a sufficiently powerful one on to their side, or that the expelled demon had found allies to return and take possession with – some such theory seems to lie behind Jesus' little parable about seven devils returning in the place of one.[49] But Jesus' cures were apparently dramatic and total; in which case (as Jesus had no difficulty in showing) the explanation of strife within the demonic world would not hold: if Satan were divided to this extent he would have no power at all. Jesus must have invoked a power of a different order altogether – nothing less than the Holy Spirit of God – to have produced such results. Indeed, the conduct of Jesus' exorcisms, as described in the gospels, is of a singularly 'pure' character. Certain details characteristic of known exorcism techniques can be found in the gospel accounts: the demon is directly addressed, and comes out of the sufferer in such a way that it is clear that something has happened. But, by contrast with the stories told by Lucian,[50] for example, there is a complete absence of technical language, mysterious rites and formulae or hocus-pocus of any kind. Even the story of the Gerasene swine, though it for once reveals the name of the demon and uses a sensational means of demonstrating its departure, has no trace of secrecy or esoteric techniques. Jesus evidently opted for a type of miraculous healing which was bound to be dangerously ambiguous; but, at least according to the records, he carried it out with the absolute minimum of those technical procedures which would most surely have aroused suspicion about his true credentials and motives.

According to the records: we can no longer dodge the question how far we can trust the reporting of the gospel writers. It could well be the case, for instance, that Jesus was in fact an exorcist who operated with all the paraphernalia and mysterious rigmarole of a common magician, and that it was the Christian tradition which censored the record and made out of it a Jesus who seemed totally removed from such dubious practitioners.[51] To which again the answer is that we cannot *prove* that this was not the case: apart from the gospels themselves we have virtually no information whatever about Jesus' exorcisms, and if anyone is to regard the gospels, in this respect as in others, as totally tendentious, there is no ground we can stand on in order to prove him wrong. On the other hand, it is fair to say that this is by no

[49] Mt. 12. 43–5; Lk. 11. 24–6; cf. also Acts 19.14ff.
[50] Lucian *Philops*. 31.
[51] This is not far from the view of J. M. Hull, op. cit. 116ff., who argues that Matthew represents 'the tradition purified of magic'. Cf. also E. Hoskyns and N. Davey, *The Riddle of the New Testament* (1947) 116–17.

means the most plausible interpretation of the evidence before us. The gospel miracle stories in general – and the healings are no exception – show an extraordinary restraint in the accumulation of any kind of detail. Emphasis is often laid, as might be expected, on the amazed reaction of the bystanders. But this emphasis is seldom reinforced by the addition of details that would heighten the miraculous impression. More than any other stories, miracle stories grow in the telling;[52] to regard the synoptic narratives as a deliberate stripping down of originally more sensational and elaborate accounts would be to go against all the normal canons of literary criticism.

In general, one can say that the miracle stories in the gospels are unlike anything else in ancient literature in that they avoid either of the tendencies which we find in any comparable accounts. They do not exaggerate the miracle or add sensational details, like the authors of early Christian hagiography; but nor do they show the kind of detachment, amounting at times to scepticism, which is found in Herodotus or Lucian and even to a certain extent in Philostratus. To a degree that is rare in the writings of antiquity, we can say, to use a modern phrase, that they tell the story straight.

This is not to say, of course, that they do not add their own interpretation of the events, or indeed reproduce an interpretation which was built into them right from the start. We have already observed that the miraculous, if it is to have any impact on the mind, needs some frame of reference. A miracle may demonstrate the power of God, the wisdom of a philosopher, the skill of a magician; but if it is not clear how it does any of these things it will remain a mere freak, something best forgotten or left out of account. Sometimes historical circumstances will be sufficient to provide a context. Josephus notes a whole series of apparently unnatural occurrences which took place shortly before the fall of Jerusalem.[53] In retrospect they could be understood as portents of the imminent disaster; at the time, they may well have been understood (such is the ambiguous nature of omens) as sources of encouragement by one side or the other.[54] But in any case historical events were moving to a climax: any abnormal event would be eagerly examined and reflected upon as a portent of the imminent but still unpredictable crisis; whereas, had it been a time of peace with no particular danger being apparent the same event – like the fall of the Tower of Siloam – would probably have presented no more than a tantalising question about the ultimate causes of things and

[52] Yet even of this there is strikingly little in the gospels. A 'tendency to heighten the element of miracle' (J. Jeremias, *New Testament Theology* 1 (1971) 86) is not really documented except by the fact (which may have a quite different explanation) that Matthew twice turns a single victim of blindness or possession into two victims. Moreover, even the apocryphal gospels (apart from the infancy narratives) do not add to the stock of miracle material; cf. Hennecke-Schneemelcher, *New Testament Apocrypha* 1 (E.tr. 1963) 435.

[53] *B.J.* 6.288-309.

[54] Cf. S. McCasland, *JBL* 52 (1932) 323-35, who shows that Josephus was adapting traditions which doubtless originated in apocalyptic circles to the omen-convention of Hellenistic historians.

have been quickly forgotten. But there is another factor which gives meaning to a miracle and which is more relevant to our purpose, that is, the motive or purpose of its author. We have seen that most of the miracles performed by Jesus consisted on the one hand of cures of the blind, the lame, the deaf and the dumb (cures which had virtually no precedent in his culture) and on the other hand of exorcisms (which laid him open to the charge of sorcery). We must ask, therefore, what was his motive and intention in choosing this singular range of options? Unless the gospels had allowed some answer to this question to be inferred from their narratives they would have failed to communicate anything by them. Indeed we can take the question one stage further back. Unless the original witnesses had been able to grasp what Jesus' purpose was, his miracles, though they might cause temporary amazement, would have made little sense to anyone. We have to ask the question, not just about the evangelists, but about Jesus himself.

It is perfectly possible, of course, that these cases just happened to be the particular ones which Jesus came across, and that his compassion moved him to deliver the victims from their sufferings. Indeed we cannot but believe that Jesus was supremely compassionate. But (to our surprise) we find that it is extremely rare for the gospels to mention the fact – so rare that it cannot have been this that they regarded as Jesus' characteristic motive for performing his cures. The gospels do of course describe Jesus as showing compassion. But on both the occasions on which this is referred to in Mark[55] and on three out of four in Matthew,[56] the object of his compassion is, not a particular sufferer, but the crowds in general, who are so sadly in need of shepherding, guidance and teaching. Only in the case of the two blind men in Matthew (20.34) and the son of the widow of Nain in Luke (7.13) is it said that Jesus acted out of pity; and only Matthew makes Jesus' compassion for the multitude a motive for the feeding miracle (15.32). That is to say: though the gospels allow for this motive on rare occasions, they clearly do not conceive it to be the primary one in the majority of miraculous incidents.

Another motive which it might seem plausible to attribute to Jesus is that of acquiring fame, popularity and authority through the performance of miraculous works. I have already quoted the observation of a social anthropologist that this might be the only way in which a messianic figure could establish his influence; and it seems reasonable to assume that one option which lay open to Jesus, in his own as in other cultures, was to gain attention for his teaching and his programme by a display of his exceptional power. Somewhat to our surprise, we find that the evidence tells strongly against that having been the case. In the first place, though analogies to this may be found in other societies, this is not so in the history of the Jewish people. Whatever may have been the original character of the miraculous deeds of

[55] 6.34; 8.2. $\sigma\pi\lambda\alpha\gamma\chi\nu\iota\sigma\theta\epsilon\acute{\iota}s$ in 1.41 I take to be an inferior reading.
[56] 9.36; 14.14; 15.32.

Moses, Elijah, Elisha and others, they are recounted in such a way in the Old Testament that it is always the glory of God, and not that of the wonder-worker, which is the consequence of their deeds. This biblical emphasis on the divine origin of the miracle, rather than on its human agent, must have affected attitudes in subsequent centuries. Certainly we can rely on the report given us in the gospels that the works performed by Jesus raised the question in peoples' minds whether he were Elijah or one of the prophets. That is to say, they sought to interpret him in the categories of wonder-working and prophetic activity already provided by the Old Testament; and those categories were marked by a tremendous emphasis on the author of their words and deeds being God himself. Moreover those latter-day prophetic figures who are often cited as affording some parallel to Jesus conform to this pattern: they arouse great expectations, not by a spectacular feat of their own, but by promising a sensational intervention by God on their behalf[57] – and it is significant that those other rebel leaders who are sometimes called messianic and who aspired to become king by organising revolt against the Romans[58] had no miraculous feats of any kind to their credit. When, therefore, we read in the gospels that after a notable cure or exorcism the crowds give glory to God, rather than to Jesus,[59] we are reading, not a cautious reinterpretation by the evangelist, but a response which was characteristic of the culture in which Jesus lived. This unwillingness to give credit to any individual for his exceptional powers is also, of course, a commonplace of later rabbinic thinking: any rabbi who performed a miracle in order to strengthen his own authority was regarded as highly suspect.[60] This doctrine, like that of the alleged cessation of prophecy, was probably a consequence of the need to maintain the authority of the established schools in the face of any threat from self-appointed (even if they claimed to be God-appointed) experts.[61] It may not be good evidence for the estimation in which ordinary people might hold a charismatic prophet: but it too must have relied for its strength on a general assumption that a miracle reveals the power and authority, not of any particular teacher, prophet or healer, but of God himself.

In the second place, the synoptic gospels themselves record a very striking reserve on the part of Jesus towards his own miracles. Certainly they evoked wonder and amazement from the crowds, as was inevitable; but it would be impossible to maintain that, according to these evangelists, they were performed for the sake of this reaction. Jesus nowhere appeals to the impression made by his own miracles as authentication for his personal authority and indeed he condemns the suggestion that signs and wonders are

[57] *B.J.* 2.259-61; *Ant.* 20. 167-70. Note Josephus' phrase, σημεῖα κατὰ τὴν τοῦ θεοῦ πρόνοιαν γινόμενα.
[58] Cf. Appendix II, p.175.
[59] The only clear exception is Mt. 14.33, on which see below, p.172.
[60] E.g. Eliezer b. Hyrkanus bB.M. 59b.
[61] See above, pp.58-9.

necessary in order to create faith.[62] It could of course be said that this reserve, along with the secrecy motif in Mark and the temptation narrative in Matthew and Luke, is the work of subsequent Christian reflection. The church, on this view, was anxious to deny that spectacular miracles had been the main achievement of the earthly Jesus (and to avoid thereby the awkward question why he had not therefore been universally acclaimed) and so introduced the notion that Jesus himself had played down their importance. But given that Christian apologetic was so soon to make use of all available miracles in arguing for Jesus' divine authorisation,[63] we are probably obliged to regard it as a well-founded fact about Jesus that he did not deliberately perform miracles to attract and to gain authority and influence for his message.

With that, we have exhausted the options which are exemplified by any other wonder-worker of antiquity, or indeed by any comparable type known to anthropologists. We have come to the remarkable conclusion that the miraculous activity of Jesus conforms to no known pattern. We are left no alternative but to interrogate the gospels themselves for their answer to the question why Jesus performed the miracles he did.

Our most precious evidence bearing on this question is the statement in Mark's gospel that on occasion Jesus' disciples themselves did not understand what he was doing (8. 17-21). As with his teaching in parables, so with the miracles, the meaning was not immediately apparent: the observer was not simply to be impressed or amazed, he was expected to reflect and perceive. Once again, we are confronted with a critical problem. The other gospels lay less stress on the difficulty of understanding and on the failure of the disciples to do so. We can explain this by assuming either that Matthew and Luke sought to tone down an authentic tradition which must have seemed discreditable to the disciples, or that Mark for reasons of his own was anxious to stress the obtuseness of the disciples and introduced this element into his account. Since neither of these alternatives can be proved against the other, the historical value of this statement in Mark has to be left open; yet it gains in significance, one way or the other, when it is placed alongside the fact that (with the exception perhaps of John) none of the gospel writers succeeds in presenting a uniform and consistent account of the motivation of Jesus' miracles. In Mark's gospel, for example, it is possible to suggest at least six different motives which the evangelist allows us to infer from the various miracle stories;[64] in Matthew, they are different again.[65] We can therefore

[62] In John they have a more positive function, but are still secondary to spoken and written testimony: 10.38. Cf. Harvey, *Jesus on Trial* (1976) 95.

[63] E.g. Arnobius 2.11. Cf. G. W. H. Lampe in *Miracles* (ed. C. F. D. Moule) 208ff.

[64] Cf. D. A. Koch, *Die Bedeutung der Wundererzählungen für die Christologie des Markus-Evangeliums* (1975), who suggests the following: (i) showing ἐξουσία; (ii) to illustrate 'Dämonenanrede und Schweigebefehl'; (iii) to illustrate impression made on the public, etc.; (iv) epiphanies; (v) to portray Jesus after Caesarea Philippi; (vi) interpretation imposed by context. To which one should surely add (vii) the motif of *faith*.

[65] See the study by B. Gerhardsson, *The Mighty Acts of Jesus according to Matthew* (1979).

take Mark's statement about the obtuseness of the disciples in the face of the miracles as historically correct to this extent, that the miracles of Jesus were not, or not all, so obviously intelligible that those who witnessed them *must* have known always what their meaning was.

This observation brings Jesus' miracles into relation with other aspects of his life and work. Even his most characteristic form of teaching – the parables – had a tantalising and mysterious character; and a number of his sayings seemed at first unintelligible without further elucidation (e.g. Mk. 7.17; 10. 10,26). That is to say, the difficulty of determining the meaning of the miracle stories is consistent with other well-attested features of the tradition about Jesus, and is only part of a wider question about his purpose and character as a whole. The first clue which the gospels offer us is the simple fact of the number of exorcisms which are reported among Jesus' miracles in the synoptic gospels (though they are absent altogether from the Fourth Gospel). These have neither the folkloric flavour of the stories in Tobit and Josephus, nor the concern for magical ritual found in the magical papyri, nor even the slightly humorous objectivity of rabbinic stories. They are told in earnest: that is to say, the reader is assumed to believe implicitly in the reality of the transaction, and to be impressed by the decisive effectiveness of Jesus' approach to what would have been recognised as a serious and normally almost incurable condition. But at the same time there is little attempt to engage the reader's curiosity still further by sensational details attached either to the condition or its cure. The symptoms given of possession are sufficient to show its seriousness, but not to make it exotic or unimaginable; the procedure of exorcism has a minimum of exorcist's apparatus.[66] The incidents are told as a straight contest between, on the one hand, a demonic power and, on the other, a person of supreme authority. That Jesus was in fact understood to be waging a contest of this kind is confirmed, not only by the temptation story at the beginning of the synoptic gospels, but by a number of sayings which use the same language and presuppose the same frame of reference. The saying about Beelzebub divided against himself; the parable of the strong man bound; the saying on seeing Satan fall from heaven; the sayings on the expected 'testing' of the disciples – all these provide a frame of reference for the exorcisms by representing Jesus as engaged, and victorious, in a contest with the devil.[67] Now it is true that this was not an indispensable way of speaking of the ministry of Jesus. It makes, at most, an occasional appearance in Paul,[68] and is absent altogether from the Fourth Gospel. But in those circles where the influence of demonic powers was

---

[66] *Ephphatha* can hardly be regarded as a typical exorcist's *vox barbarica*, being an evident reminiscence of the word Jesus used in his own language. It is true that *PGM* 7. 768ff. offers an interesting parallel to Mk. 1. 43. But it is a tenuous argument which asks us to see magical allusions in the verb ἐμβριμάομαι. Cf. J. Hull, op. cit. 84 and n.50.

[67] J. Jeremias, *New Testament Theology* 94–6.

[68] Col. 2.15; Eph. 1.21.

accepted and taken seriously, there was evidently no question but that Jesus had shown himself victorious over it. Of this victory, the exorcisms were related as signal demonstrations.

The second clue is also of a statistical kind. No less than eight of Jesus' healing miracles are cures of the deaf, the dumb, the blind and the lame.[69] Such miracles, though they occurred at pagan healing shrines,[70] were completely without precedent in Jesus' own culture.[71] Neither in the Old Testament nor in any subsequent Jewish writings do any such reports occur. In performing them, Jesus was breaking new ground, and seizing an option for which there was no precedent. When we ask why he did so – why, that is, the stories of his miraculous cures are so untypical of his culture – it is possible to give a purely pragmatic answer: it may just have happened that a number of people with complaints of this kind presented themselves to him, and that he naturally felt impelled to cure them. Or, somewhat more boldy, we may suggest that it was precisely because such cures were unknown that Jesus opted to perform them, in order to create a greater stir. But these explanations, quite apart from being unverifiable, are without any support in the gospels. On the other hand it can hardly be an accident that these four complaints are precisely those which Isaiah names as conditions which will be cured in a coming new age:

> Then the eyes of the blind shall be opened,
> and the ears of the deaf unstopped;
> then shall the lame man leap like a hart,
> and the tongue of the dumb sing for joy. (Is. 35. 5-6 RSV)

Matthew makes the connection explicit. In one of his summaries of Jesus' healing activity (15.30) he describes Jesus as curing the lame and the maimed, the blind and the dumb, and goes on

> . . . the multitude were amazed when they saw
> the dumb speaking,
> the maimed whole,
> the lame walking
> and the blind seeing. (15.31)

Such cures were not merely unprecedented; they were characteristic of the new age which, as we have seen, was expected one way or another by the majority of the contemporaries of Jesus. To use the jargon of New Testament scholarship, they were eschatological miracles.

[69] Dumb, Mt. 9. 32-4; deaf and dumb, Mk. 7. 32-5; blind, Mk. 8. 22-26, 10. 46-52, Mt. 9. 27-31, Jn. 9. 1-11; lame, Mk. 2. 1-12, Jn. 5. 1-9.

[70] The cure of limbs and of ears and eyes is attested by votive offerings at shrines of Asclepius at Corinth and Epidaurus (cf. M. Lang, *Cure and Cult in Ancient Corinth,* American School of Classical Studies at Athens: *Corinth Notes No. 1* (1977) 15ff.), of eye disease by Aristophanes, *Plut.* 683ff. On the possible existence of an Asclepeion in Jerusalem, see A. Duprez, *Jésus et les dieux guérisseurs* (1970) 63-97.

[71] The comment at Jn. 9.32, 'Never since the world began has it been heard that anyone opened the eyes of a man born blind', appears to be fully justified in the Jewish world.

However, we must beware of the temptation, so easily yielded to by students of the Bible, to assume that simply by relating some of Jesus' miracles to Old Testament prophecies of a golden age we have actually explained something. For one thing we must not imagine that we can do what the authors of the gospels were manifestly unable to do, that is, bring all the miracles of Jesus within one comprehensive frame of reference and force them all to yield the same significance. The material is far too varied and complex to tolerate such a simple explanation; and in any case we must at least allow for the possibility that Jesus on occasion made use of his exceptional powers simply in response to particular circumstances, without any intention of performing acts of deeper significance. Moreover we must not be taken in by the ease with which it is possible to formulate statements such as that Jesus, in his mighty works, 'anticipated the new age', or 'inaugurated a new period of history', given that, by the normal standards of historical reporting, history appears to have gone on as before without any notable change having been produced by the activity of Jesus. We shall do better to avoid such rhetoric, and to take our question one stage further back. We must ask why Isaiah should have used these terms in the first place to describe a state of affairs which lay in the remote and imagined future.

The answer to this question is not difficult to find. The prophets were not engaged in imagining a utopia, which is a literary exercise bearing no necessary relation to what may actually one day be realised on earth; nor were they indulging in childish wishful thinking or irresponsible day-dreaming. They were propounding a vision intended to inspire hope and action. As Ernst Bloch has so eloquently argued,[72] the only kind of promise of a new future which can genuinely nourish human hope is that which bears a close relationship to the actual limitations of human existence, and which lies only just beyond the threshold of what we believe to be possible. When the prophets spoke of a new dispensation which would be brought about by God, they started from the belief, which they shared with other cultures in antiquity, that the world has not always been as it is now. There was a primordial golden age, an original Garden of Eden, which was proof that a different order of things is possible and may one day be regained. The question to be asked was not so much, What will it be like, as, What are the constraints which prevent the present age from returning to that paradise? What limitations would have to be removed if mankind were once again to enjoy its original untainted heritage? One of the most obvious of these limitations was that imposed on Adam when he was expelled from Eden: only by the sweat of his brow could he and his descendants enjoy the fruits of an inhospitable earth. Surrounded as they were by desert, and living on land that was often arid and unproductive, it was natural for the prophets to imagine the overcoming of this limitation through a sudden abundance of water which would

[72] *Das Prinzip Hoffnung*, 165.

fill the dry river-beds and make the desert green. Visions of rich banquets for the poor and hungry belong also to this yearning, and doubtless provide at least part of the context in which Jesus' miraculous multiplication of loaves is to be understood. But there was another feature of everyday experience which seemed to place an absolute bar to the transformation of the world into the age of paradise. It was one thing if people lost limbs or faculties through war, or violence, or their own sin: these factors would presumably disappear of their own accord once the movement towards a better world had got under way. But what about those ailments which we call congenital, which appeared to be nobody's fault and yet were part of every human scene – deafness, blindness, deformity, paralysis? These surely could have no place in God's kingdom, yet mankind was powerless to do anything about them. They constituted an intractable barrier between the present age and the age to come. If a prophet were to inspire genuine hope of a new age in store for mankind, he must offer an assurance that this intolerable constraint on human dignity and freedom would, in God's good time, be removed.[73]

It is not therefore necessary to suppose that when Jesus cured the deaf, the dumb, the blind and the lame, people had consciously to bring these events into relation with a particular verse of Isaiah in order to understand their significance. It is rather that Jesus appeared to be demonstrating the possibility of overcoming those constraints and limitations – including even death – which were felt instinctively to stand as an intractable and inexplicable barrier in the way of mankind attaining to a better world. And the same is surely true of that other class of miracles we were considering a moment ago: the exorcisms. Here no reference is possible to the prophecies and visions of the Old Testament, for in Old Testament times people had not yet come to think of the world as dominated by demons and evil powers.[73a] But there is abundant evidence that in the time of Jesus one of the ways in which it was customary to express one's sense of constraint and impotence in the face of the irrational and apparently often malign accidents which attend every human enterprise was to postulate a world of demonic powers and evil spirits which was in constant conflict with the forces of good. Sometimes these were thought of as motivating the actions of rulers and so being responsible for political convulsions; sometimes they seemed manifest in individuals, causing that phenomenon of possession by an evil spirit which appears so frequently in the synoptic gospels. Not all the New Testament writers use this language: the author of John's gospel is a notable exception, and Paul shows a certain ambivalence towards describing the phenomena of evil in terms of demonic influences.[74] But for the most part the existence of the devil

[73] Jn. 9. 2–3 gains force when understood in this perspective. On the paradise-motif in Jesus' proclamation and activity, cf. B. F. Meyer, *The Aims of Jesus* (1979) 139–40.

[73a] The rare instances of an 'evil spirit' (Judg. 9.23; 1 Sam. 16.14ff.; 18.10) are not related to any general demonology.

[74] There is a number of texts (Romans 8.38, 1 Cor. 15.24, 2 Cor. 4.4, etc.) which justify the statement that, for Paul 'the world is in its unity and totality the domain of demonic powers' (J. Ridderboos, *Paul* (1977) 91). But at the same time Paul lays stress on the absolute responsibility of the individual for his moral choices.

and his agencies was taken for granted. His continued influence stood as another intractable barrier between mankind's present misery and its promised future of freedom and happiness. Both by his exorcisms, and by a number of sayings in which he proclaimed his superiority to these powers, Jesus seemed to demonstrate the possibility of final victory over this demonic constraint. Indeed we may say that such was the sense of enslavement to the spirit-world felt by so many of his contemporaries that Jesus could hardly have been acknowledged as their saviour had he not seemed to have struck a decisive blow against this redoubtable enemy.

By this route we reach a conclusion which is similar to that which we found to be true of Jesus' teaching. Even were he able to (and we have no historical grounds for thinking that he was), Jesus certainly did not sit light to the physical constraints which normally bear upon human life. His miracles were not random or freakish; but nor did they run in the channels of known techniques by which his contemporaries believed they could occasionally reverse the impact of the normal course of events. They seem not to have been performed in a spirit of competition with other charismatic figures, nor as a means of drawing attention to the power of the thaumaturge and investing him with unanswerable authority. They did not even have the prudential quality which would have protected their author from the suspicion of sorcery or the danger of a too enthusiastic reaction by the crowds. Instead, we find that an impressive number of them took the form of an attack on those limitations of the human condition which seemed most intractable, most inexplicable, and most stubbornly to prevent mankind from moving into that better world which is surely intended for us in the future purposes of God.

I have put all this in the past tense, as is appropriate to an attempt to reconstruct the historical constraints to which Jesus was exposed. But the same argument is capable of carrying significance for the present. I suggested in a previous chapter that Jesus' teaching has retained its power because of, and not in spite of, the fact that it contains an invitation to undertake what normally seems to lie on the far side of what is possible for human beings. It challenges us to do the impossible. The same is surely true of Jesus' mighty works. There have of course been times when this part of the record about Jesus has been passed over in embarrassed silence by apologists who were anxious not to offend the professed canons of a rationalistic age. But it is surely true here also that the story of Jesus has gained a response down the ages, and still does so today, not in spite of, but because of, the moments at which Jesus appears to have gone beyond the limits of the possible, or rather (if we may put it this way) to have pushed back to a significant degree the constraints of the impossible. It is perhaps once again certain Marxist thinkers who can help us most to see how this can be so. The Marxist has an extreme realism about the world as he finds it. He has no time for the comfortable liberal illusion that things will get better if only men will have the will to make them so. Bourgeois society, which stands obstinately in the way of any progress towards a condition in which human beings may have dignity and freedom, is not an entity which can be cajoled or levered out of the way. Only a violent convulsion will have any effect; and that will still leave human factors and constraints that are so hard to change that the most idealistic revolutionary may be tempted to despair. To have hope, we need to be assured that these obstacles are not immovable, that man can seriously undertake the impossible. Jesus' miracles offer such a challenge and such an assurance. To quote a Polish Marxist, for whom this aspect of Jesus' activity is a source of powerful attraction: 'a miracle is the radical answer to an urgent summons, an action which can be accomplished only if our whole personality – everything we are and possess – is brought into play; for this is the only way we can possibly make that crucial step which takes us beyond limits that have never been surpassed before.'[75]

[75] V. Gardavsky, *God Is Not Yet Dead* (E.tr. 1973) 47.

# 6
# Jesus the Christ:
# the Options in a Name

In exploring some of the constraints within which Jesus must have lived and worked, we have found more than once that he seems not to have been content with any one of the options normally open to a teacher, a miracle worker, or a religious leader, but to have combined these activities with the style and message of a prophet. I propose now to examine two particular episodes which are recorded in all the gospels, which have a strong claim to historical reliability and which are instructive illustrations of this prophetic side of Jesus' activity: the Entry into Jerusalem, and the so-called Cleansing of the Temple.

The suggestion that the former of these two episodes, the Entry into Jerusalem, may be confidently regarded as historical, requires a few words of justification. Indeed many critics would consider that the historical difficulties which it raises are such that it would be wiser to leave it out of account altogether in any reconstruction of Jesus' life. In the first place (they would argue) the story of the finding of a colt for Jesus to ride on is clearly regarded by the evangelists as evidence of Jesus' supernatural powers, and cannot therefore be regarded as sober reporting, but rather as a 'lengendary trait'.[1] In the second place, the absence from the gospel accounts of any of the political or practical consequences which would normally have followed such an ostentatious gesture arouses suspicion that the original kernel of the story was somewhat different: is it not more likely that Jesus was surrounded by a crowd of pilgrims going up to Jerusalem for the festival, and that a small demonstration of enthusiasm by his followers was subsequently magnified into the kind of major happening of which we read in the gospel accounts?[2] And in the third place, the whole incident is so blatantly written up to provide an exact fulfilment of Zechariah's prophecy (9.9) of a 'king coming humble and mounted on an ass' that we can hardly expect to be able to uncover a firm substratum of fact beneath it.[3]

[1] R. Bultmann, *HST* 261-2.

[2] Bultmann, ib. 281; M. Dibelius, *From Tradition to Gospel* (E.tr. 1971) 121-3.

[3] Cf. E. Haenchen, *Der Weg Jesu,* 377. Bultmann, loc, cit., calls the efforts to find history here 'absurd'.

These criticisms are not without weight; and I shall endeavour to do justice to them in what follows. But they fail to take account of one feature of the episode which, though seldom commented upon,[4] appears to me to be of decisive significance. Jerusalem, then as now, was a holy city. It is a deep religious instinct, shared by many peoples besides the Jews, that one approaches a place of pilgrimage on foot. When the Kaiser Wilhelm, in 1898, visited Jerusalem riding a splendid white horse, his action was entirely in character with himself, but it caused immeasurable dismay to the religious sensibilities of the inhabitants. By contrast, General Allenby, when taking possession of Jerusalem in 1917, prudently and appropriately dismounted when he came close to the city and made the final entry on foot.[5] The point is confirmed (if confirmation were necessary) by our earliest rabbinic sources, which explicitly exempted the infirm from the duty to make the pilgrimage on the grounds that they would be unable to accomplish it on foot.[6] To our astonishment, we observe that Jesus did the exact opposite. After making the long climb up from Jericho on foot, he apparently made special arrangements to secure a mount for the final stage from the Mount of Olives into Jerusalem. Far from being lost among the great crowd of pilgrims in such a way that the story could have grown out of a minor disturbance amidst a general pilgrimage, Jesus' action would have been extremely ostentatious, and would have attracted widespread and mystified, if not scandalised, comment. I find it impossible to believe that such an apparently gratuitous act of provocation to religious sensibilities could have been invented by the Christian tradition. For such an unprecedented act, we are surely justified in invoking the principle that 'odd is true': we may regard it as one of those pieces of information about Jesus which it would be unreasonable to call into question. Our task is to establish the meaning which such a gesture would have conveyed at the time.

There is a time-honoured answer to this question which seems at first sight to clear the matter up quite satisfactorily.[7] The entry into Jerusalem was an unambiguous acting out of the Zechariah prophecy of the humble king. This prophecy was certainly understood in rabbinic exegesis as an inspired description of one way in which the Messiah might come. By their acclamations the crowds showed that they read the message correctly; but their enthusiasm was so short-lived that no police or military action was necessary to repress the movement, and within a few days it had turned to such uncertainty that the same crowds were ready to support a demand for the execution of their erstwhile Messiah.

[4] The point is noted by I. H. Marshall, *The Gospel of Luke* (1978) 710, but no significance is attached to it.

[5] B. Vester, *Our Jerusalem* (1950) 278–9.

[6] M. Hag. 1.1. bHag. 6a.reports a discussion which presupposes that a pilgrimage must be accomplished on foot. The same implication is in M. Ber. 9.5, cf. J. Jeremias, *NTS* 23 (1977) 179.

[7] For a list of scholars who have taken this view, cf. V. Taylor, *The Gospel according to St. Mark,* 451.

Apart from the fact that a vital link in this chain of reasoning – the application of the Zechariah prophecy to the coming Messiah – is not attested in rabbinic tradition until the middle of the third century A.D.,[8] this explanation greatly oversimplifies the matter, in that it obscures one vital feature of the gospel narratives. Only two of these (Mt. 21.5; Jn. 12.15) make any explicit mention of the Zechariah passage at all, and of these one (that of the Fourth Gospel) states that it was only after the event that Jesus' disciples made the connection (12.16); at the time, the suggestion is that the Zechariah passage did not enter their heads. This may be something of an exaggeration: it is characteristic of John's gospel to allow the disciples to achieve their understanding of Jesus' true nature and intentions only at the very end of the story.[9] But the fact remains that two of the gospels – Mark, which appears to contain the earliest account, and Luke, which shifts the emphasis from the crowds to the disciples (19.37) – are content to tell the story with no explicit reference to the Zechariah prophecy. This is particularly striking, in that for once the episode carries no explanatory comment attributed to Jesus himself. That is to say, it was open to each evangelist to indicate the meaning of Jesus' action, but only two of them adopted this means of doing so. To form our own judgment, we must first try to rid our minds of this particular inter-pretation and study the episode as it is handed down to us in the gospel tradition as a whole.

The story falls into two parts, the first describing the means by which Jesus secured his mount, the second describing the actual procession. We must notice the surprising amount of space given in the synoptic accounts to the first part, which indeed constitutes two-thirds of the total story. John's gospel shows how it is possible to give the reader the necessary information in a single short clause ('Jesus, having found an ass . . .' 12.14). Evidently the synoptics saw a significance in this part of the story which justified them in entering into considerable detail. A possible explanation for their interest in it is that they saw it as a demonstration of Jesus' supernatural powers. Jesus could surely not have known by any normal means that there would be a foal awaiting him just when he needed it – let alone that it would be one (as Mark (11.2) and Luke (19.30) record) which had never been ridden before. There-fore the story is an exhibition of Jesus' supernatural foresight, and must have been told with this end in view. It also bears a formal similarity to the account of finding a room for the Passover: again, Jesus could not have known that there would be a man carrying a waterjar at just that moment who would provide his disciples with a room unless he had had supernatural means of knowledge. Yet it is fair to say that in neither of these stories is the slightest emphasis laid on this aspect of the matter. Elsewhere, if Jesus performs any feat that is out of the ordinary, the reaction of the witnesses is commented

[8] bSanh. 98a (R. Joshua b. Levi, *c.* 250 A.D.).
[9] 2.22; 6.6; 11.4; 13. 28-9; 16.12.

upon: they are amazed or frightened,[10] or they are brought to faith or discipleship.[11] But here there is no comment whatever. Indeed this silence has led many commentators[12] to take the opposite view: the episode is after all best understood as a natural piece of pre-arrangement. Jesus could easily have given orders in advance, particularly in a village where he already had friends. The synoptic gospels are simply telling us how his plans worked out in practice. So far as it goes, this explanation is perhaps more faithful to the spirit in which the story is told than is the supernatural one. But it leaves unexplained the point from which we started, namely the surprising length and detail of this part of the narrative.

We must therefore return to these details; and there are two features of them which suggest that the evangelists are concerned neither to emphasise the strangeness of the sequence of events as if it were supernatural, nor to accumulate trivial circumstances for the sake of historical accuracy, but rather to offer some clues to help the reader understand the episode as a whole. First, it has recently been shown[13] that Jesus' procedure was a perfectly normal example of the right of a king, a ruler (or his official representative), a general, or even a respected rabbi, to requisition transport in advance; the phrase, 'the master needs it', would be sufficient justification so long as the authority of the requisitioner was acknowledged.[14] But not only this: the manner in which Jesus' disciples took possession of the foal – even to the extent, according to Mark (11.3), of promising its immediate return (of which more in a moment) – shows Jesus to have exercised his right to requisition the animal only to the extent of overriding any possible inconvenience caused to its owner. From that moment on, Jesus in effect takes the foal on loan, and carefully observes the Jewish law of borrowing.[15] With these details, therefore, the evangelists allow the reader to infer two significant facts about Jesus: that he possessed the authority of a king or a leader to requisition transport, but that in his exercise of that right he behaved with impeccable righteousness according to the law. But this is not all. A further surprising circumstance is recorded by Mark and Luke (though omitted by Matthew): the foal was 'one on which no one had ever yet ridden' – surprising, not just because this would have been even harder to foresee or prearrange than the presence of the animal

---

[10] See the analysis in Bultmann, *HST* 225–6.

[11] The characteristic reaction to a 'sign' in the Fourth Gospel.

[12] E.g. V. Taylor, op. cit. 454.

[13] J. D. M. Derrett, 'The Palm Sunday Colt', *Nov. T.* 13 (1971) 241–53 = *Studies in the New Testament* (1978) 165–77.

[14] There is perhaps a touch of a more extensive and mysterious ('esoteric', Derrett op. cit. 247=171) authority if the phrase is translated '*its* master needs it' (NEB mg; T. Nicklin, *CR* 15 (1901) 203; Derrett, op. cit. 246=170 n.2): the requisitioner not only had authority to make this particular demand, but could in some sense be regarded as the master of all beasts of burden in Jerusalem. E. Stauffer, *Nov. T.* 2 (1956) 85 suggests that χρεία is here a technical term for a king's 'Adventslieferung'. For other possible senses cf. MM s.v. χρεία (2).

[15] Derrett, op. cit. 252–3 = 176–7.

in the first place, but because an unbroken donkey might have presented great difficulties as a mount down the steep road leading from Bethphage to the foot of the Mount of Olives. The detail must therefore have a symbolic value. The colt must be such as befitted a king, never ridden on by a mere commoner; or it must be fit for its sacred purpose, never having contracted ritual impurity from having been ridden by a man who might have been careless of such things.[16] Alternatively, it was the kind of ass on which the king of the Zechariah oracle would ride, which in the Septuagint is specifically described as a *pōlon neon*, a 'young' colt[17] – this would represent Mark's and Luke's single allusion to that passage. Either way, the point seems to be being made that the dignity and intentions of the rider required an unusual purity in his mount. Moreover, all three synoptic gospels include the statement that the foal was 'tied' (*dedemenos*). There is of course nothing odd in the circumstance itself: the foal would have needed to be tethered if it were to be available at all. The oddity is rather that the accounts should think it worth mentioning; and it is hard to believe that they did not have in mind a famous but obscure oracle[18] in Genesis (49.11) according to which Jacob prophesies to his son Judah eternal rule for his descendants until one should come[19] who would have the respect of the nations and would 'tie his foal' to a vine. Moreover, there is the unexpected promise of Jesus, recorded by Mark, that he would immediately restore the ass to its owner. As we have seen, this contributes to the carefully drawn portrait of Jesus as a righteous borrower. But may there not also be an allusion to the angry response of Moses when he was criticised by Dathan and Abiram: 'I have not taken from them so much as a single ass; I have done no wrong to any of them' (Nu. 16.15)? In short, the wealth of detail provided by the evangelists in this part of the story may be intended to alert the reader to a number of different models for understanding Jesus: he was a kind of king or authoritative leader; he was righteous; he was, like David, a descendant of Judah, heralding a new dispensation for the nations of the world; like Moses, he did no wrong. Whether or not our reading of all these symbolic meanings is correct, a point is gained of considerable importance. Here was an act of Jesus of which Jesus himself offered no explanation, but which was seen by the gospel writers to contain valuable pointers to his real purpose and identity.

All this, however, is introduction. The climax of the story is the actual entry into Jerusalem, with Jesus ostentatiously riding instead of proceeding

[16] Id. ib. 248-9 = 172-3; W. L. Knox, *Sources of the Synoptic Gospels* 1 (1953), 78 n.1.

[17] Cf. H.-W. Kuhn, 'Das Reittier Jesu . . .' *ZNW* 50 (1959) 82-91.

[18] J. Blenkinsopp, 'The Oracles of Judah and the Messianic Entry', *JBL* 80 (1961) 55-64, plausibly argues that this was the oracle referred to by Josephus, *B.J.* 6.312 and applied by him to Vespasian, and alluded to also by Tacitus *Hist.* 4.81; 5.13; cf. *Or. Sib.* 3. 49-51 etc.

[19] The mysterious phrase in the Hebrew text ('until Shiloh come') is taken to mean 'Solomon' by Klausner, *The Messianic Idea in Israel*, 29-30. It is Messianic in 4 Q Patr. Blessings. Cf. Kuhn, art. cit.

on foot.[20] Here again, there is no recorded commentary by Jesus explaining his action; such commentary as there is, is provided by the actions and words of the crowds. First, their actions: all three synoptics report that they spread their garments on the road, presumably[21] for Jesus' mount to walk on. Conceivably, this could have had a ritual significance, preventing any unclean matter on the ground from rendering unclean a person who was about to enter the temple;[22] but the readers of the gospels would more naturally have understood, and the evangelists must surely have intended, the gesture as the recognition by the crowd of Jesus as their leader or king.[23] This is evidently the interpretation intended by Luke, who adds no further details of the crowd's response to Jesus' action (indeed throughout his account it appears to be Jesus' own followers who make the demonstration, 19.37,39) and adds a word to make explicit the acclamation of Jesus as King.[24] Mark, however, introduces a further possibility by adding that other people cut straw or brushwood from the fields. The word he uses (*stibadas*) is rare, and occurs nowhere else in the Bible; in secular Greek it seems to mean 'mattresses', and the most natural implication of Mark's use of the word would seem to be the purely practical intention of making a steep and slippery path safer and more pleasant to ride on – the word hardly lends itself to any symbolic interpretation and perhaps the most likely explanation of its occurrence is that it contains a reminiscence of what actually happened. But Matthew and John appear to have allowed the hint to lead them in a different direction. In Matthew the straw has become branches cut from trees, and in John these have become palm branches. The change is significant. The kind of dry straw and leaves suitable for stuffing mattresses could have only a practical function; but green branches and palms were appropriate to a religious procession. At Tabernacles they were borne by pilgrims on their way into Jerusalem. Moreover – and we shall find that this is highly significant – the 'cleansing' of the temple by Simon Maccabaeus was accompanied by music and singing and the carrying of branches (1. Macc. 13.51), and the Festival of Dedication which was then instituted was deliberately modelled on Tabernacles (2 Macc. 10.6), and involved the carrying of 'garlands, fair branches and palms' (2 Macc. 10.7). This interpretation becomes more pointed still in the Fourth Gospel, where all mention of the spreading of garments is omitted, and the crowd is described as going out to

[20] The fact that the mount was an ass rather than a horse (as proved by Kuhn, art. cit.) does not itself diminish the dignity of the rider, cf. Jdg. 5.10; 10.4; Derrett, op. cit. 255=179.

[21] Luke makes the matter explicit by writing ὑπεστρώννυον for Mark's and Matthew's ἔστρωσαν.

[22] A possible inference from M. Zab. 4.7.

[23] Cf. 2 K. 9.13; Jos. *Ant.* 9.111. In Plutarch, *Cato Min.* 12, it is a gesture of respect from soldiers to their departing general.

[24] The words ὁ βασιλεύς are added by Luke after εὐλογημένος ὁ ἐρχόμενος.

meet Jesus[25] with palm-branches.

Thus the actions with which the crowd greets Jesus' ostentatious ride into Jerusalem are variously interpreted in the different gospels: Mark and Luke describe them as the reception of a leader or a king, John as a religious procession; Matthew combines the two. But further interpretation is offered by the reports given of the acclamation that was shouted or chanted by the crowd. Here it is important to be clear about what kind of reporting this is. As F. C. Burkitt pointed out long ago,[26] if a crowd utters a shout that is intelligible to the hearer it will consist of not more than a word or two: *Hosanna* is exactly the kind of cry we should expect, but not the longer rigmarole which follows it in the gospel accounts. Alternatively, a crowd will sing in unison a familiar hymn or religious song. There are in fact clear traces of such singing in the narratives. But again, we must beware of assuming that the evangelists would have been content to transcribe the text of the song without any comment or modification. Rather, they are likely to have used the material offered by the original singing to show how the whole scene was to be interpreted. This incidentally explains why none of the gospel accounts contains the exact text of any known psalm or prayer. But it also helps us to see how we may best approach the narratives. First we must ask what the crowd is likely to have been shouting or singing; then we can judge what interpretation the evangelist chose to lay on these shouts or songs.

With the exception of Luke (who likes to avoid all barbarous-sounding expressions[27]) all the evangelists report that the crowd shouted *Hosanna*. In the Old Testament, the word occurs only once, in Ps. 118.25. But this psalm was one of those used at the major festivals of Passover and Tabernacles[28] and also presumably at that of the Dedication.[29] Moreover, the phrase *Hosanna* (in Hebrew *hoshia-nna*, meaning literally 'save now') was part of the ritual chant with which the branches were carried round the altar at the festival,[30] and in due course became a familiar way of referring, not only to the festival prayers,[31] but to the branches themselves.[32] It was, that is to say, a familiar liturgical chant,[33] and one that would naturally come to the lips of a crowd that was waving branches in a procession. To this extent, therefore, the gospel accounts offer a realistic description of the actual shouting of the

---

[25] C. H. Dodd does well to draw attention to this detail, which effectively makes the Johannine story *quite different* from the synoptic: *Historical Tradition in the Fourth Gospel* (1963) 155-6. The point is also noticed by W. L. Knox, op. cit. 78.

[26] *JTS* 17 (1916) 144.

[27] Cf. H. J. Cadbury, *The Making of Luke-Acts* (1958) 125.

[28] References in Str.-B. 1. 845-9.

[29] For which indeed it may have been composed; cf. Burkitt, art. cit. 141.

[30] M. Sukkah 4.5

[31] Lev. R. 37.2 on 27.2.

[32] bSukkah 37b; Tg 2 Esther 3.8.

[33] E. Lohse, *TWNT* 9 682: 'Liturgische Formel'.

crowd.[34] But they do not leave it at that. They all agree in continuing the quotation from Psalm 118 (following now the Greek text, doubtless more familiar to their readers), 'Blessed is he that comes in the name of the Lord'. As we have seen, there is no difficulty in accepting this as a literal account of what the crowd is alleged to have done. It was just as possible for them to chant a familiar psalm-verse as to shout out Hosanna all together. The chant need have meant no more than it normally did when sung at the festivals: it was a way of welcoming a pilgrim as he drew near to the temple. It would have been entirely natural for the crowd to have sung these words when they found themselves greeting Jesus with their branches; there is no need to assume any esoteric significance in them.[35]

But, once again, the evangelists are not content to leave the matter there. What was the significance of this solemn riding into Jerusalem, this liturgical greeting of a pilgrim? Mark adds the words, 'Blessed is the coming kingdom of our father David'. We can safely recognise this as the evangelist's own interpretation: the sentence comes from no known scriptural or liturgical text, and is far too long to decribe any spontaneous shouting of the crowd. Moreover it contains an odd phrase: 'our father David' is not attested in Jewish literature,[36] and is perhaps more likely to be a Christian invention;[37] and 'the coming kingdom of David' has also no exact parallel in Jewish writings.[38] But this is not to say that Mark or his source made it up out of his head. The word 'blessed' would start immediate echoes in the mind of any Jew. It was the opening and recurring motif of the daily prayer enjoined upon every Jew and known as the Tefillah or Eighteen Benedictions.[39] The fourteenth of these is likely to have contained the following clause:

> Be gracious . . . to the kingdom of the house of David,
> thy righteous Messiah.[40]

This petition is often regarded as early evidence of Messianic expectation in Palestine,[41] and indeed the somewhat similar words in Mark are the grounds

---

[34] The addition by Mark and Matthew of ὡσαννὰ ἐν τοῖς ὑψίστοις is no less realistic. Once Hosanna is understood as a liturgical response, there is no difficulty about singing it 'to' (with the dative) God or his emissary. But Jews would not have sung ὡσαννὰ τῷ θεῷ; they would have used a periphrasis, which is what ἐν τοῖς ὑψίστοις represents (cf. Ps. Sol. 18.10; G. Bertram, *TWNT* 8. 617 n.44). Luke replaces ὡσαννὰ with a midrash along the lines of the angel-hymn in 2.14.

[35] The so-called 'messianic' interpretation of the psalm is not attested in the Tannaitic period. E. Lohmeyer, *Das Evangelium des Markus* (1937) 231 rightly leaves the question open whether the words would have been felt more appropriate to a prophet or a 'messianic king'.

[36] But this may be an accident: the phrase would not have been impossible (the Rabbinic evidence cancels itself out: Str.-B. 1. 918; 2. 26).

[37] Though it occurs in Christian literature only at Acts 4.25, an ungrammatical verse where it may well be an early interpolation, cf. *Beginnings of Christianity* 4 ad loc., Lohmeyer, op. cit. 231 n.4 rightly refuses to invoke this verse as evidence for either Jewish or Christian usage.

[38] V. Taylor, op. cit. 457

[39] Cf. G. F. Moore, *Judaism* 1. 291ff.

[40] For a convenient text and discussion, cf. G. Vermes, *Jesus the Jew* 132.

[41] E.g. G. Vermes, loc. cit.

on which many commentators describe the crowd's acclamation of Jesus as 'Messianic'.[42] But it is important to be precise: the word Messiah in the Benediction appears to be an honorific title of the historical David rather than of a figure in the future; and the whole prayer is one for the restoration of Israel as a 'Davidic Kingdom' rather than for the appearance of a Messiah-figure.[43] There can be little doubt that it was some form of this prayer which inspired Mark's text. It is possible that the crowd actually chanted this prayer, and that Mark is offering a Greek paraphrase of it; if so, they will have been expressing their habitual longing for a new era in their history, no doubt with an expectation of its fulfilment sharpened by Jesus' striking assertion of authority. Perhaps it is more likely that Mark (or his Christian source) followed the train of thought suggested by the word 'blessed', and incorporated an idea about the coming kingdom which was suggested by one of the familiar 'blessings'. At any rate the drift of his interpretation is clear enough: the acclamation of the crowds was no ordinary religious chanting. It expressed the recognition that this moment was a significant one for the restoration of the kind of kingdom for which the Jews prayed every day.

The adjustments made by the other evangelists need not detain us long. Matthew regularly likes to abbreviate Mark; and here he found that sufficient commentary on the crowd's chanting would be provided if he simply noted that Hosanna was sung, not just in honour of God, but also of 'the son of David', whom the Christian reader would identify as Jesus, but who, in the context of the crowd's understanding, could be any Davidic figure who seemed to raise expectations of a coming new era.[44] Luke and John both replace the reference to David and his Kingdom by identifying the blessed one who comes in the name of the Lord as 'king'. We cannot think that they intended by this to describe the procession as an actual claim to the throne by Jesus. The complete absence of any consequences rules this out; and in any case it would hardly have been the crowd's first reaction to Jesus' strange decision to ride into Jerusalem and to the religious significance of the palms. Rather, they have simply shifted the emphasis from the kingdom, such as all Jews prayed for, to the king who would (under God) bring it into being. John's gospel has much to say about the nature of this kingship;[45] but a preliminary interpretation of it is offered (as also in Matthew) by the explicit quotation of the Zechariah oracle of 'the king who comes seated upon an ass'.

[42] E.g. F. Hahn, *The Titles of Jesus in Christology* (E.tr. 1969) 255; E. Lohse, *TWNT* 9. 683 and numerous commentaries.

[43] This is acknowledged by E. Lohse, *TWNT* 8. 485. The Babylonian Recension, 'Make the Branch of David soon spring forth' etc., is more explicitly 'messianic', but this has no verbal connection with Mk. 11.10.

[44] If Matthew's phrase ὡσαννὰ τῷ υἱῷ Δαυίδ is to be regarded as historically plausible at all, it must be kept general and indefinite: the use of a liturgical phrase normally addressed to God in honour of a specific individual would surely have been felt to be blasphemous. But it is surely more probable that this is a Christian commentary on the crowd's shouting of *Hosanna*.

[45] Cf. especially 18.36ff.

These adjustments, though not important in themselves, are evidence for a process of interpretation by the evangelists which gives further support to the approach I have adopted. The kernel of historical fact within the fairly elaborate layers of interpretation which we have analysed is Jesus' startling and ostentatious reversal of the normal constraint which would have obliged him to enter Jerusalem on foot. There may well have been some who were shocked or bewildered by such a gesture; but there is no reason to doubt that the majority of those who witnessed it responded by acknowledging Jesus' authority to proceed in this way and by greeting him with chants and actions appropriate to a religious occasion. We have also noticed a point that will take on some significance in the sequel, namely that the closest historical precedent to the spontaneous waving of branches is provided by the celebrations which accompanied the purification and rededication of the temple under Simon Maccabaeus. In order to complete our understanding of this episode, we must follow up our study into its immediate sequel, the so-called 'cleansing of the temple'.

In contrast to the story of the Entry, this one seldom arouses any suspicion of having owed its origin to a misunderstanding or a legend. Jesus' brusque attack on the traders in the temple is unprecedented, and it is difficult to think how it could have entered the gospel tradition had not something of the kind occurred. This is easy to say; but when we go on to ask what it was exactly that happened, we find ourselves in great difficulties. According to Mark Jesus began to expel from the temple precincts all who were engaged in buying and selling, he overturned the tables of the bankers and the seats of those who sold doves for temple offerings, and prevented people from using the temple as a thoroughfare. Now there are, as is well known, good grounds for thinking that none of these activities ought to have been taking place.[46] The whole temple area, though of great extent, and furnished with colonnades which would naturally attract commercial and social activities,[47] was nevertheless a holy precinct.[48] A number of trades connected with the temple cult would naturally have been carried on as close to it as possible, and the clear implication of the gospel accounts (which is supported by a small amount of independent evidence[49]) is that they had actually penetrated into the precincts. But even if they had no clear right to be there, the task of ejecting them could hardly have been seriously undertaken by Jesus. In the first place,

[46] See the circumstantial discussion by J. D. M. Derrett, 'The Zeal of thy House', *Downside Review* 95 (1977) 79-94, esp. 81-4. For the relevance of M. Ber. 9.5, cf. J. Jeremias, *NTS* 23 (1977) 179-80.

[47] Philo, *Spec. leg.* 1. 68-70.

[48] The regulations applying to synagogues, M. Meg. 3.3, would apply equally to the temple.

[49] The presence of 'money changers' to provide the Tyrian coinage required for the payment of temple dues, at least in the period before Passover (M. Shek. 1.3), is not disputed. That trading in animals took place in the temple, apart from occasional abuses, seems not to be proven even by the argument of J. Jeremias, *Jerusalem in the Times of Jesus* (E.tr. 1969) 49.

the so-called 'Court of the Gentiles' was a huge open space, and the various businesses would have been too numerous and scattered for one man to have been able to launch a serious attack on them. Secondly, the traders themselves would certainly not have failed to invoke the protection of the temple police; thirdly, the pilgrims themselves would hardly have welcomed and supported an action which would have deprived them of necessary facilities;[50] fourthly, the attack, which would have involved violence, seems out of character with all that we know about Jesus; and fifthly, it seems inconceivable that the Roman garrison, which was situated overlooking the temple area, would not have intervened to quell the disturbance.[51] We seem to be confronted by a paradox: it is unlikely that the story could have been fabricated; but the more we think about it the more improbable it appears.

The difficulty is a real one. We cannot therefore dismiss out of hand the solution proposed by a small but influential group of scholars, namely that we hear in the gospels only a muffled echo of an attempt by Jesus to gain control over the temple area by force. In the words of S. G. F. Brandon,[52] 'it is improbable that his action in the Temple was unsupported; indeed, far on the contrary, it is likely that it was achieved by the aid of an excited crowd of his supporters and was attended by violence and pillage'. Once again, we cannot refute this view by appealing to the evidence of the gospels to show that there is no trace of mob violence in the narrative, that the lack of reprisals or of police or military action tells against a demonstration on this scale, or that the character and policy of Jesus as described in the entire New Testament is incompatible with any such revolutionary gesture. For we shall be told that this is of course exactly the impression which the gospels intended to give, whereas the facts were quite otherwise, and it is only the very improbability of their story[53] which allows us to reconstruct the real course of events which they were so anxious to conceal. But what we can do is suggest an alternative solution to the admittedly substantial difficulties inherent in the gospel narratives, and allow the reader to judge for himself which interpretation does more justice to the evidence that we have. I would suggest that we follow the clue provided by one of the options which we know Jesus to have followed, namely that of the prophetic style of action and utterance. It was characteristic of the Old Testament prophets that they might be directly commissioned by God to perform some striking and challenging gesture in order to arouse attention to the message they proclaimed.[54] But the gesture is symbolic: when Jeremiah was ordered to place a yoke on his neck (Jer. 27) he was not effecting the submission of his nation to the king of Babylon, but by

[50] E. Haenchen, *Der Weg Jesu* 384 well describes these practical factors.

[51] Cf. Acts 21.31; S. G. F. Brandon, *Jesus and the Zealots* (1967) 334.

[52] Op. cit. 333.

[53] 'Our sources have purposely presented the matter in an idealistic manner . . . The Gospel account is . . . unsatisfactory', Brandon, op. cit. 338.

[54] 1 Kings 11.29ff.; 22.11; Is. 20.1ff.; Hosea 1.2, etc.

means of the startling gesture giving a symbolic demonstration of the policy which would have been in accord with the divine will. The prophet does not physically change things by his actions; but his actions may represent the change which God wills to bring about and which the prophet is charged to proclaim. Seen in this light, some of the practical difficulties involved in Jesus' action in the temple disappear. One option open to a prophet who was moved to comment on an institution such as the banking and commercial facilities of the temple would have been simply to denounce it, and our task would be very much easier now if Jesus had chosen this course, since he would presumably have given explicit reasons for doing so. But to be effective this would have had to be addressed to those who bore ultimate responsibility for the institution, that is, not the traders, but the priestly officials, and these were doubtless not available. It need not therefore greatly surprise us that he chose another established option, that of the prophetic gesture. To make his point, he had only to disrupt the normal routine of the bankers and merchants sufficiently to attract attention and to make clear the nature and object of his attack.[55] The practical consequences need not have been serious. Loss may have been sustained by a few tradesmen; but if (as we have seen) there was doubt about the legality of their trade, they would not have found it easy to argue their case against Jesus. But in any case to make his point Jesus need have attacked only one or two stalls: the action need not have been on a scale sufficient either to attract the notice of the police or the military, or to affect Jesus' reputation as one who stood fundamentally for persuasion rather than force, The only serious question which need have been raised by his action is that which is in fact discussed a few verses later (Mk. 11.28): the authority by which Jesus performed these actions. It is significant that Jesus replied by a comparison with John the Baptist, whom the crowds regarded as 'really a prophet'. The authority required for a prophetic gesture was that he who performed it should be a real, not a false, prophet.

If then, Jesus was performing a prophetic gesture, what did it mean? Here again, we find ourselves in difficulties if we think of Jesus as making a serious attack on the temple arrangements. For one thing, what he could accomplish single-handed or even with a few supporters would have made little impression on a complex and well-established commercial system; and for another, the action seems to have been directed at the wrong people: it was surely not the tradesmen themselves, but the authorities who sanctioned their trade, who were responsible for anything that was amiss. But as soon as we read the episode as a gesture illustrating the proclamation of a prophet, these difficulties again disappear. What is being expressed in symbolic action is the divine judgment on a particular use which was being made of the temple; and

---

[55] A certain amount of violence was necessary to give visible effect to a claim: and Jesus was establishing his claim to prophetic authority. Cf. J. D. M. Derrett, *Law in the New Testament* (1970) 298–9, with literature there cited.

therefore our question must be, What was the object and content of this judgment? In the normal way we would expect the prophet himself to answer the question for us by providing his own commentary on the action.[56] And in fact all four gospels provide such a commentary; but apart from the suspicious fact that the Fourth Gospel provides one quite different from that of the synoptics, there must be real doubt whether any of these commentaries goes back to Jesus, given that no words of his own are recorded, but only quotations from the Old Testament, which, as we shall see, neither bear the meaning they had in their original contexts nor serve to give a satisfactory explanation of Jesus' intentions.

But we should not dismiss these fragments of commentary without studying them in detail. Mark offers two quotations. The first is from Isaiah 56.7, which in the Septuagint runs, 'for my house shall be called a house of prayer for all nations'. Standing in the so-called 'Court of the Gentiles',[57] in sight of a prominent notice in red letters forbidding Gentiles entry into the inner courts,[58] the quotation would have been appropriate enough on the lips of a prophet who wished to plead for the destiny of the temple as a centre of universal worship.[59] But this was certainly not the original meaning of the text in Isaiah – indeed it could hardly be extracted from the Hebrew version which Jesus would have used.[60] Moreover, however appropriate it might have been as a comment on the topography of the temple area, it has no relevance whatever to the action against tradesmen and bankers (who had no responsibility for the exclusion of Gentiles); indeed Matthew and Luke, who omit the words 'for all nations' from the quotation, may have correctly sensed that they had no bearing on the meaning of Jesus' action. For all these reasons it seems extremely unlikely that this quotation represents Jesus' own commentary on his gesture. Much the same goes for the phrase drawn from Jeremiah 7.11 ' a robbers' cave'. In the circumstances of the time, when the use made of the temple by brigands (*lēstai*, as in Jeremiah and the gospels) was soon to become outrageous,[61] the quotation would have had a general appropriateness; but again it bears a sense somewhat different from the text in Jeremiah (where it is a comment on the inhabitants of Jerusalem in general); and since there is no hint in the narrative that the tradesmen were behaving like 'robbers' – indeed the word (suggesting violence) is totally inappropriate to them[62] – the quotation is just as irrelevant to the action as the previous one.

[56] As in Jeremiah 27 and regularly in the Old Testament.

[57] This is a modern term, and must not be used to support the view that Jesus was attacking the Jewish exclusivism of the temple.

[58] Jos. *B.J.* 5. 194: the famous inscription is in Istanbul.

[59] So, e.g., Lohmeyer, *Markus* ad. loc.; R. Lightfoot, *The Gospel Message of St. Mark* (1950) 67-8.

[60] 'I will make them (sc. the nations) joyful in my house of prayer'.

[61] Jos. *B.J.* 5. 402.

[62] Cf. M. Hengel, *Die Zeloten* (1976) 25-47, 389 n.1: the word always means a violent raider, never a swindler.

In short, both quotations, though they are intelligible as attempts by the evangelists to provide a scriptural explanation of the episode, can hardly be regarded as authentic reports of Jesus' own commentary.

The situation is little better in John's gospel. The scene is described in more detail: Jesus uses a whip of cords, and his action is more energetic, and perhaps on a larger scale,[63] than in the synoptics. His one word of commentary contains an allusion[64] to Zechariah 14.21, 'On that day there will be no more a trader in the house of the Lord' – a prophecy of a coming age when the worship of the temple will be purified, and it is certainly true that Jesus' actions, as described in John's gospel much more than in the synoptics (where there is less emphasis on traders, more on banking), are an appropriate gesture to give force to these words. But even here, to make them fit the action, the evangelist has to specify that they were spoken especially to those who sold doves. He seems to have sensed that they were somewhat inapposite to the episode as a whole. He then adds that the disciples were reminded of another text altogether, 'Zeal for thy house devours me' (Psalm 69.9), which is appropriate enough as a general description of Jesus as a righteous and pious sufferer,[65] but is certainly not an elucidation of the action which has just been narrated.

We seem, then, to be forced to the conclusion that the scriptural quotations or allusions introduced by the evangelists are more likely to represent an attempt by the Christian tradition to relate Jesus' action to biblical prototypes than a recollection of any commentary by Jesus on his prophetic gesture.[66] It is not of course difficult to suggest other texts which might have come to the mind of either Jesus himself or the witnesses of the episode, and commentators have not been slow to do so.[67] In particular, a number of prophecies can be adduced along the lines of Zech. 14.21, which is alluded to in the Johannine account, to suggest that Jesus' action might have been recognised as 'Messianic', or at least as a sign of the inauguration of a new age.[68] But the inconvenient fact remains that none of the first narrators of the scene thought these passages necessary or useful to elucidate it; or (to put the matter the other way round) the gesture of Jesus did not seem to them to be one which lent itself to elucidation by scriptural texts other than the ones which (somewhat artificially in our modern judgment) they proposed themselves. In short, the probability is that this action of Jesus, like his ostentatious riding into the city, was not immediately understood by the spectators and the first

[63] πάντας ἐξέβαλεν is a literal impossibility (see above); it must either be hyperbole, or else πάντας is used distributively, 'every kind of'. Cf. C. H. Dodd, *Historical Tradition in the Fourth Gospel* 157 n.3.

[64] Cf. C. H. Dodd, op. cit. 159.

[65] Id. ib.

[66] So Haenchen, *Der Weg Jesu* 386.

[67] Derrett, art. cit., offers a rich selection: Is. 59. 14–20; Hosea 6. 5–6; Mal. 3. 1–3; Neh. 13. 4–13.

[68] Especially Mal. 3. 1–3.

narrators (and so should not be understood by us) as the deliberate acting out of an Old Testament prophecy, but as a new and creative prophetic gesture with which Jesus (as with so much of his teaching) challenged his contemporaries to draw their own conclusions.

It is of course possible that the gesture was more easily intelligible at the time than it was to later generations, and would therefore have needed no commentary. It has been suggested,[69] for example, that an actual dispute was in progress between parties within the priestly administration, one wishing all temple commerce to take place on the Mount of Olives, the other encouraging it in or near the temple precincts. Jesus' action would then have been understood as a clear demonstration in favour of the Mount of Olives party. Alternatively, we may assume that the trading and banking within the precincts was an abuse which was both recognised and generally connived in, and Jesus' gesture would have been understood as a proper judgment on the complaisancy of the desecrators.[70] But we are on surer ground if we follow the one clue which is offered us by the gospels as to the question which Jesus' action actually provoked: 'By what authority do you do this?'[71] (Mk. 11.28). As we have seen, Jesus' reply took the form of a comparison with the activity of John the Baptist, whose authority was that of a prophet. The question, therefore, addressed to Jesus was whether he had the necessary prophetic authority to carry out this symbolic action. In the precincts of the temple, this question had a very pointed application. We have already noticed that Jesus' entry into Jerusalem had only one historical precedent, namely the approach of Simon Maccabaeus to cleanse the temple of pagan objects in 141 B.C. But this ceremony had included the proviso that certain matters in the temple could be regulated only by 'a prophet who was to come'[72] – and the tradition long remained alive in Judaism[73] that only a prophet has authority to control and rectify temple procedures. It follows that a person who assumed the right, even by a symbolic gesture, to pass judgment on any temple institution was thereby claiming the authority of a prophet. Whatever else Jesus' action may have signified, it was a clear demonstration of prophetic authority. And so (we are told) it was understood.

I have argued that these two episodes – which may plausibly be regarded as having originally formed a single sequence – are securely based in history and

[69] V. Eppstein, 'The Gospel Account of the Cleansing of the Temple', *ZNW* 55 (1964) 42–58. The suggestion is ingenious, but offers no explanation of the place of money-changers in the story.

[70] Perhaps in the spirit of Jesus' frequent citation of Hos. 6.6, Hos. 6.5 being also appropriate. Cf. Derrett, art. cit. 91.

[71] Commentators are mostly agreed that ταῦτα here refers at least primarily to the action in the temple, though it may include also the Entry. In John (2.18) it refers explicitly to the expulsion of traders. Only in Luke (20. 1-2), with perhaps a hint in Matthew (διδάσκοντι 21.23) is the question generalised so as to include Jesus' teaching.

[72] 1. Macc. 4.46; cf. 14.41-2; R. Meyer, *TWNT* 6. 816–17.

[73] Derrett, art. cit. 87 and n.35.

are examples of Jesus deliberately and ostentatiously seizing the option of a prophetic style of action. We have already seen that there is a saying of Jesus which offers good evidence that he thought of himself as a prophet (Mk. 6.4), and that there are aspects of his teaching which are best understood in the context of a prophetic view of the importance of the hour. Moreover the gospels record a large number of occasions on which Jesus was recognised and acknowledged as a prophet.[74] There can be no doubt, therefore, that Jesus did in fact act and speak as a prophet. And yet it is equally clear that his followers never felt this to be an adequate description of him. There is no occasion in the New Testament on which he is so referred to after the resurrection; 'prophet' never became a standard description of the risen Jesus. That is to say, however much Jesus may have invested his teaching with a prophetic tone, and fashioned his actions in a prophetic style, it can never have seemed to his followers that this was the primary option he followed or that a description of him as 'prophet' would adequately convey the essence of his work and nature. To the question, what description did they in fact find adequate, there can be only one possible answer. They called him 'Messiah', 'Christ'. We have to ask, What led them to use this title of Jesus, and what options would have been open to one to whom it was felt to be appropriate?

It might appear at first sight that the episodes which we have just been studying offer a clue to the transition from prophet to Christ. Jesus' entry into Jerusalem was a clear fulfilment of the prophecy in Zechariah about a humble king riding on an ass (9.9), a prophecy which was taken to refer to a coming Messiah; and the attempt to reform the institutions of the temple could best be understood in terms of another text in Zechariah (14.21) which also referred to a messianic age. Do not these two episodes therefore show Jesus reaching beyond the option of prophet towards that of Messiah? This view, which is endorsed by a large number of scholars,[75] is nevertheless exposed to formidable difficulties. As we have already seen, it is sheer supposition that Zech. 9.9 was understood as an oracle about a future Messiah in the time of Jesus: our earliest piece of evidence for this interpretation dates from two centuries later. Moreover, two of the evangelists could tell the story with barely a hint of an allusion to this passage: it cannot therefore have seemed to them to be the key that was necessary to understand it. As for the cleansing of the temple, it is true that some kind of reform and renewal of temple worship was described by Zechariah and others as events heralding a new age; but there is no hint in those writings that the agent of this reform was necessarily to be regarded as the Messiah, and we found that the authority required by Jesus to perform such an action seems to have been that, not of Messiah, but of a prophet. In short, the links between these actions and the claims of a

---

[74] Mk. 6.15; 8.28; Mt. 21.11; 21.46; Lk. 24.19, etc.
[75] E.g. J. Jeremias, *Jesus als Weltvollender* (1930) 35–44; W. Kümmel, *Promise and Fulfilment* (E.tr. 1957) 118 and n.53.

Messiah are exceedingly tenuous and those scholars who refuse to see any 'messianic' implications in these episodes[76] cannot be easily refuted.

In addition to these difficulties, there is the important point made in an earlier chapter that it is far from certain that the option to represent oneself as 'the Messiah' actually existed. The title was apparently not a common one, nor would it necessarily have carried much meaning unless qualified and explained; and the expectations of the Jews, though they certainly included in many quarters a lively longing for a new and (in certain respects) supernatural age, did not necessarily specify an individual who would help to bring it into being, and even if they did envisage such a person their interest in him was secondary: the primary object of hope was the new age itself. Our question ought therefore to be, not whether and when Jesus adopted the option of acting as Messiah, but rather when and why his followers began to refer to him by this name. To this question modern scholarship may be said to have established an impressive and cogent answer: it was after, and as a result of, the resurrection that Jesus' followers recognised him to be the Messiah, the Christ. Of the two occasions in the synoptic gospels on which the title was accepted by Jesus, one (the answer to the High Priest) is manifestly unhistorical,[77] the other (Peter's confession) bears clearly the marks of subsequent Christian reflection.[78] Therefore the older view that Jesus saw himself in these terms rests on an uncritical view of the texts; the title must have been given to Jesus only after his followers had come to the conviction that he was indeed the uniquely authorised and victorious agent of God's purposes which this title described – that is, after his resurrection and exaltation.[79]

There is of course one major difficulty in this view, of which its advocates are fully aware. The person who, in Jewish texts of this period, is expected to be instrumental in bringing about a new age and who is sometimes described as 'Messiah' is a figure in whom are invested mainly nationalistic, if not actually military, hopes. He would be a leader, victorious over his enemies, and by no means averse to the use of force.[80] How then did it come to seem appropriate to describe Jesus by a title with these connotations? The answer generally suggested is that there were certain elements in the conception of Messiah – the uniqueness of the role, its responsibility for fashioning a new and purified people of God, its power as a focus of Old Testament expectations – which made it the only possible one for describing a person such as

---

[76] E.g. F. Hahn, *The Titles of Jesus in Christology* (E.tr. 1969) 156-7.

[77] See above pp.32f.

[78] Bultmann, *HST* 257-9 describes the whole story as a legend, and has been followed by a large number of German scholars. Others (e.g. F. Hahn, *The Titles of Jesus in Christology* 223-6) regard it as a composite *pericope*, containing early elements. But few regard the attribution of the title χριστός to Jesus as authentic, and most would concur with the judgment of e.g., W. Grundmann, *TWNT* 9. 530, that the gospels provide no evidence for any 'messianic consciousness' in Jesus.

[79] F. Hahn, op. cit. 164 goes further: the title became established only a generation later.

[80] E.g. Ps. Sol. 18 passim.

Jesus had been and now continued to be after the resurrection; but that at the same time a radical reinterpretation was necessary (perhaps assisted by certain hints given by Jesus himself),[81] such that Jesus could be understood not only to have been and to be the Messiah but also to have given this concept an entirely new orientation. Jesus was indeed identified as Messiah after the resurrection; but this identification involved a drastic revision of previous messianic ideas.

In favour of this reconstruction must be reckoned the fact that it appears, at least in broad outline, to be identical with that proposed by the author of Acts. In Peter's first speech we are told that God has made Jesus 'both Lord and Christ', and the context leaves us in no doubt that the means by which this has been done is the resurrection (2.36).[82] But it is not without significance that there is no other instance in the New Testament where it could be said that Jesus' messiahship was understood as being conferred by the resurrection. We must come back to this text at the end of this chapter; but meanwhile we must take note of three very serious difficulties to which the whole reconstruction is exposed.

(i) We may ask, first, whether the difficulty already mentioned of the difference between the popular expectation of a victorious Davidic Messiah and the actual life and achievement of Jesus has been fully confronted. E. Schillebeeckx has recently drawn attention to the sheer improbability of the Christians, immediately after the resurrection, having been able, not merely to claim that the crucified Jesus was the Messiah (if 'Messiah' meant a victorious Davidic leader) but to have coined, and persuaded others of, an entirely new meaning for that term. He writes: 'Without already existing models it was out of the question for a triumphalist, Jewish messiah concept to be reshaped within a few years by the Christians into a suffering Messiah.'[83] We may put the point another way by saying that so long as there is a basic similarity between the concept and the person who is said to embody that concept, it makes sense to talk of re-interpretation; a number of details or aspects may be modified, so long as the essence of the concept remains recognisable. But is not the figure of the suffering and crucified Jesus too far from the concept of the Davidic Messiah for any re-interpretation to have saved the day? Is there not a basic incompatibility here which calls the whole theory into question? Attempts have been made to overcome this difficulty by arguing that the idea of a suffering Messiah already existed in Judaism in the time of Jesus, so that, in effect, the 're-interpretation' had already (at least in part) taken effect;[84] but the evidence for this is, at best, exceedingly

---

[81] A view vigorously defended by C. F. D. Moule, *The Origin of Christology* (1977) 31-5.

[82] Cf. H. J. Cadbury, *The Making of Luke-Acts*² (1958) 278.

[83] *Jesus* (E.tr. 1979) 514.

[84] J. Jeremias in W. Zimmerli-J. Jeremias, *The Servant of God* (E.tr. 1957) 57ff. (=*TWNT* 5.685ff.).

thin.[85] Alternatively it may be suggested[86] that given that the story of Jesus fulfilled both texts from the Old Testament which were held to foretell a Messiah and texts which described a righteous sufferer, the Christians will at once have discerned the scriptural 'necessity' of such a suffering Messiah and have set about persuading others of it; but this presupposes a process of biblical exploration which must surely have taken some time, and can hardly have been completed soon enough for the church to make its initial proclamation that Jesus is Christ. None of these arguments lessens the sense of a certain improbability involved in Jesus' followers having of their own initiative chosen this title as their prime designation of Jesus.

(ii) A second difficulty is that it is by no means obvious why, if the disciples had not recognised Jesus as Messiah during his lifetime, they would have been led to think of him as such by the resurrection. It is not difficult to see a logical connection between the resurrection and other possible titles. It meant, at the very least, that Jesus was vindicated by God, and therefore 'just' (a designation which occurs three times in Acts).[87] It implied that he was exalted, and so had fulfilled the destiny of the Son of Man.[88] It was an intelligible demonstration that he was truly a Son of God.[89] But it is not so easy to see why it would have been thought to indicate messiahship; for if no one expected the Messiah to die, how could they have expected him to be raised from the dead? The best answer that can be given to this is that since, after the resurrection, the followers of Jesus felt themselves to be living in the new, Messianic age, they must suddenly have grasped that Jesus had been, and (through the resurrection) was still, the 'Messiah' who had brought all this about.[90] But in reality this answer only shifts the question further back. We have seen that the primary expectation of the Jews was for a new age: the identity of the messiah was a secondary matter. By calling this age a messianic age, we beg the question. We may grant that the Christians may have been aware of the inauguration of a new age after Easter, and have associated this with Jesus' resurrection. But we are no nearer to the answer why they should have thought of this age as (in our terms)[91] messianic, and therefore have identified Jesus as 'Messiah'.

(iii) A further difficulty is caused by a curious feature of the usage of

[85] Cf. B. Lindars, *New Testament Apologetic* (1961) 75 n.1; O. Cullman, *Christology of the New Testament* (E.tr. 1959) 122: 'it is difficult to connect suffering with the Jewish Messianic expectation.'

[86] Cf. Lindars, op. cit. 75ff., who seeks to uncover the various stages of this exploration.

[87] 3.14; 7.52; 22.14. In these passages it is often regarded as a relic of 'primitive' Christology.

[88] The connection appears to be made explicitly by Luke in his version of Jesus' reply to the High Priest (Lk. 22.69), which is picked up in Stephen's vision (Acts 7.56).

[89] Wisdom 5.5,15. A connection of this kind seems to lie behind the apparently early formulation in Romans 1.4

[90] Cf. e.g., O. Cullmann, *Christology of the New Testament* 134–6.

[91] 'Messianic' is of course a modern term. Later rabbinic writers spoke of 'the days of the Messiah', etc.; but there is no equivalent of any kind in the New Testament period.

St. Paul. Here (somewhat to our surprise, in view of the prevailing consensus) Jesus is never named as 'Jesus the Christ'. He is Jesus, or Christ, or the Christ, or Jesus Christ, and there is no occasion on which 'the Christ' stands for a predicate that could be applied to Jesus. On the other hand, later Christian literature (including Ephesians and the *textus receptus* of 1 Cor. 3. 11) displays a re-emergence of the predicative expression, 'the Christ'.[92] The usual explanation of this phenomenon is that Jesus was first (after the resurrection) identified as 'the Christ' of Jewish expectation, and that this was soon such a commonplace on the lips of Christians that the title became a name: 'Jesus the Christ' became 'Jesus Christ', or even simply 'Christ'. This process was apparently complete even by the time Paul wrote his first letter; but subsequently (so it is suggested) Christians began reflecting on the meaning of the name, and remembering – indeed actually reminding each other – that it originated in the claim that Jesus was *the* Christ.[93] On the usual assumption that Jesus was called Christ, or the Christ, only after the resurrection, this is perhaps the only possible explanation.[94] But if it were the case that Jesus was known by this additional name during his lifetime, then the facts fall into place with a great deal less shuffling. Paul will have known this name, and used it without further discussion. A subsequent generation – that during which the gospels were written – will have begun to reflect on the meaning and implications of the name, and from time to time to use it with an intentional emphasis on the dignity which it ascribed to Jesus. Such an explanation[95] cannot of course stand if the usual hypothesis is maintained that Jesus was called 'the Christ' only after the resurrection; but it would come into its own, and indeed would offer a supporting argument, if it could be shown that the whole hypothesis is false and that Jesus was known as Christ even in his lifetime.

In an earlier chapter[96] I advanced linguistic and historical arguments for the view that this was in fact the case, that is, that the phrase, 'Jesus called Christ' represents one of the ways he was known in his lifetime, and is not by any means best explained as a title acquired only after the resurrection. Our review of the difficulties involved in the usual reconstruction offers further support to the argument. The reason why this suggestion has not commended

[92] The facts are set out and commented on by W. Grundmann, *TWNT* 9. 532-4; N. Dahl, 'The Messiahship of Jesus in Paul', *Studia Paulina* (ed. Sevenster and Van Unnik 1953) = N. Dahl, *The Crucified Messiah* (1974) 37ff. Cf. W. Kramer, *Christ, Lord, Son of God* (E.tr. 1966) 203-14.

[93] Cf. 1 Cor. 3.11 T.R.; 1 Clem. 42.1; Ign. *Eph.* 18.2, etc.

[94] Possibly supported by the fact that Paul never uses 'Lord' and 'Christ' side by side – naturally, if both were originally *titles*; Kramer, op. cit. 214.

[95] Which would also illuminate the usage in Acts, where Χριστός is certainly used as a proper name, but where there is also a surprising number of occurrences of it as a predicative title, and where the title is also explicated with the verb χρίω (4.27; 10.38). This usage is more easily explained if Luke was commenting upon the meaning and implication of an already accepted name of Jesus than if it represents 'a primitive stratum of christology' (cf. S. S. Smalley, 'The Christology of Acts Again', in *Christ and Spirit in the New Testament* (ed. B. Lindars and S. Smalley, 1973) 79-93 at 86-7; H. J. Cadbury, in *BC* 5.358 makes a similar suggestion: 'a successful attempt at archaism').

[96] Chapter 4, pp.80-2.

itself in the past is that it was assumed that 'being called Christ' necessarily involved laying claim to messianic status; and it is precisely this claim which scholars quite rightly call into question as a plausible one for Jesus to have made in his lifetime. But if, as we have argued, there was no generally recognised 'messianic title' which could have been appropriated by any individual, then the way becomes open once again to allow for the possibility that Jesus had 'Christ' for one of his names (indeed his distinguishing name) during his lifetime. and that it was the implications of this name as one of messianic authority which were explored and exploited after the resurrection. But this suggestion, however much it relieves the strains inherent in the alternative explanation, still requires, before it can be accepted, an answer to one decisive question: if 'the Christ' was not a title implying a messianic claim, then what did it mean, and how did it become attached to Jesus?

We have already noticed that, of all the New Testament writers, it is Luke who shows the greatest sensitivity to the comparative strangeness of the word 'Christ' and who most faithfully reflects the linguistic usage of the period. It is therefore reasonable to begin with the explanation which he offers of the name as applied to Jesus. In commenting on the verses quoted from Psalm 2 by the enthusiastic Christian community in Jerusalem, which end with the words, 'against the Lord and against his anointed', Luke describes Jesus as the holy servant (or son) whom God has 'anointed' (Acts 4.27). In Peter's speech before Cornelius the same phrase is used, but with a further precision: Jesus is one whom God 'has anointed with holy spirit and power' (Acts 10.38). This leaves no doubt of the reference. There is just one passage in the Old Testament in which anyone is said to be anointed with the Holy Spirit, and this is Isaiah 61.1: 'The Spirit of the Lord is upon me, because he has anointed me'. To clinch the matter, Luke places early in his gospel an anecdote according to which Jesus explicitly refers this prophecy to himself. All this, of course, might be no more than a deliberate piece of antiquarian research by Luke: confronted by the title 'Christ' he might have made his own research into the scriptures to account for it, and written up the story accordingly.[97] But in fact this reference to Isaiah has so many points of contact with the gospel tradition as a whole that it is exceedingly unlikely to be the invention of any one evangelist or even (as we shall see) of the early church as opposed to Jesus or his disciples. Indeed it introduces us to a complex of ideas which pervade the whole gospel record and are bound up with the style of preaching and action adopted by Jesus.

This is a point which can be established only by a detailed and somewhat technical argument, which is presented below.[97a] For the present we may summarise it by saying that there is a number of what may be called thumbnail sketches of Jesus in the gospels and Acts, all of which make use of

[97] Cf. P. Stuhlmacher, *Das Paulinische Evangelium* 1 (1968) 228: 'wir betrachten also Lk. 4. 16–30 als novellistische Entwicklung.'

[97a] In the *Note* on pp.152–3.

a complex of Isaiah passages which were already interpreted in the light of each other in pre-Christian times. Two of these descriptions take the form of an extended quotation: Matthew (12. 18–21) quotes from Isaiah 42. 1–4, Luke (4. 18–19) quotes Isaiah 61. 1–2. These are doubtless to be attributed to the evangelists themselves. But the presence of allusions to the same complex in the baptism and transfiguration narratives, and also in a saying of Jesus describing his own activity (Mt. 11.4–6; Lk. 7.22) which we have already seen[98] to have a strong claim to authenticity, suggests that we have here a very early model for summarising the work of Jesus, one which may indeed go back to Jesus himself.

These texts centre round a figure who is a servant and a son, a herald, and an anointed one. Moreover, as a herald he has a specific message to pronounce: he proclaims that God is king, he has good news for the poor and he comforts those who mourn. Now there can be no doubt that the heart of Jesus' message concerned the Kingdom of God, and that he laid great emphasis on preaching to the poor[99] and the outcast;[100] moreover his healing ministry was concentrated upon those manifestations of the new age – the cure of the blind, the deaf, the dumb and the lame – which are mentioned in related Isaiah-passages. That is to say, if one wished to offer a classic and concise description of the character of Jesus' work and message, it was to these passages that one would naturally turn. But who was the person to whom all this belonged? He might be the Son or the Servant; he might be the Messenger or the Prophet; but by far the most striking designation is offered by Isaiah 61.1 and echoed in Is. 42.1: the one whom God *anointed*. It is perhaps tempting to ask what episode in particular in Jesus' life would have been regarded as an 'anointing'; and it is perfectly reasonable to answer that (in view of the allusion to Is. 42.1 in the synoptic accounts) his anointing was his baptism. But we must remember that 'anoint' had come to be used metaphorically even before the completion of the Old Testament: it meant 'appoint', 'instal in office'.[101] We must imagine then that when asked what distinguished this Jesus from any other man of the same name, someone who had seen something of him might reply that he was 'from Nazareth', 'a prophet', 'a teacher'. But followers of Jesus, who had observed both the range and the primary emphasis of his teaching and healing, would have instinctively summed it all up in a few

---

[98] Cf. above, p.83 and n.57.

[99] The first beatitude in Luke's version (6.20) is the clearest expression of this, and the theme is prominent throughout the third gospel. Matthew's addition, ἐν πνεύματι, does not correct this, but modifies it in the direction of relating the saying to the *anawim* of the Old Testament, who are not merely poor (though they are this) but pious besides; cf. J. Jeremias, *New Testament Theology* 1. 112–13. The theme is not prominent in Mark, but is implicit in the saying (which was, for its time, too revolutionary to have been invented) 'how hard it is for those who have possessions to enter the Kingdom of God' (10.23), and its parabolic explanation (10.25, which is also surely too characteristically exaggerated to have been invented).

[100] ἁμαρτωλοί cf. Jeremias, op. cit. 109ff.

[101] Cf. G. Vermes, *Jesus the Jew* (1973) 158–9.

sentences from Isaiah, and have described him by means of the striking phrase contained in those texts: Jesus was the one 'anointed' or 'appointed' to preach the kingdom, to bring good news to the poor, to cure the blind, the deaf and the lame. He was – Christ.

We are now in a position to give a more comprehensive answer to the question from which we started, that of the option or options chosen by Jesus out of those which would have been available to him within the constraints imposed by his own time and culture. The name given to both the story and the message of Jesus in the earliest gospel, and indeed throughout Paul's letters, is *euangelion*, 'good news' – a phrase which is best explained as deriving from the proclamation of Isaiah's messenger in Is. 61.1 and 52.7. The content of his preaching concerned above all the Kingdom of God, and it was addressed particularly to the poor and the distressed. His works of healing were directed towards overcoming those obstacles which seemed to stand most stubbornly in the way of the inauguration of a new age – blindness, deafness, lameness and possession by demons. All these ideas (with the exception of the last, which involves a way of understanding illness that was strange to the Old Testament) occur in what we have seen to be a small complex of Isaiah prophecies which were already in people's minds as a sequence of related texts.[102] The agent of all this has various names in Isaiah: he is the Servant, the Messenger, and (most characteristically of all) 'one anointed with the spirit', that is, Messiah, or Christ. If this name (as I have suggested) came to be attached to Jesus in his lifetime, and became the name by which he was most commonly distinguished from all other men called Jesus, it would have been a powerful indicator of the fundamental orientation of his life and work. The unprecedented options he chose were those which were charted by a small group of Isaianic prophecies: to herald a new age by overcoming the physical obstacles to it, by announcing good news to the poor, and by proclaiming the kingship of God.

But we must beware, once again, of yielding to any sense of achievement if we have merely indicated the congruence of certain aspects of the record about Jesus with certain prophecies in the Old Testament. Unless we can show that these ideas not only occur in scripture but were themselves of fundamental importance to Jesus' contemporaries we shall have achieved nothing more than a somewhat antiquarian exercise of detecting the 'fulfilment' of certain Old Testament texts in the New. An option for his style and activity would not have commended itself to Jesus merely because it happened to be laid out for him in the Old Testament. What we have to show is that this scriptural description of a prophetic and authoritative messenger-figure in fact responded to the deepest longings of the Jewish people in the time of Jesus, and so represented a kind of constraint within which Jesus could work and which would help to make his life and death intelligible both

---

[102] These related eschatological ideas created a complex of citations somewhat different from the modern isolation of so-called 'Servant songs' identified by the word *'ebed*, παῖς.

to his followers and to the world beyond. For this purpose we need to spread our net a little wider and ask, not merely what these texts might have meant in Isaiah, but what importance was subsequently attached to them and what kind of resonance they would have had in people's minds in Jesus' own time.

A part of this question has already been answered. There was undoubtedly among the Jews, as among many people at various times in the ancient world, a vigorous longing for a new age in which those conditions of human life which seem most intractably to exclude us from the promised paradise would be fundamentally changed or removed. This longing was classically expressed by Isaiah, whose words had naturally helped in turn to shape people's expectations and to set the parameters within which any serious harbinger of new possibilities of existence would be constrained to work. But we have still to mention one essential element in this vision. Besides the intractable facts of illness, drought and hunger there was also present in people's minds a factor of which we are as conscious today as they were then, that is, the obstinate way in which, for all our striving, it appears to be a fact of life that the rich get richer and the poor get poorer, and all our efforts to overcome the basic inequity of society seem of little avail. In relative terms Jewish society had a good record in this respect. The law contained many humanitarian provisions for the relief of poverty,[103] and charitable giving to the poor was practised[104] and commended[105] to an extent unknown in pagan culture.[106] Yet the economic facts remained obdurate and apparently immutable. Jesus would have received general assent to the observation that the poor you have always with you.[107] Therefore an essential element of any real advance towards the reign of God and a new age would have to be some radical change in economic circumstances. Good news to the poor was prominent in the prophetic vision; it was also necessarily prominent in the option chosen by Jesus, who (according to Luke and Matthew) placed it at the very forefront of his proclamation. And the one who proclaimed this was described in Isaiah 61 as a person who was 'anointed' (or appointed) to do so. That is to say, it would have been natural to call him 'Christ'.

A second recurring feature of this general longing for a new age was expressed in terms of the Reign of God. That God is King had of course been an absolutely basic article of faith for the Jews as for other near eastern peoples from very early times;[108] but it was a claim which was seldom made simply as

---

[103] Lev. 19. 9–10, etc.

[104] Str.-B. 4. 536ff. ('Die altjüdische Privatwohltätigkeit').

[105] Prov. 3. 27–8; Sir. 4.3; Tobit. 4.7; Ps. Phok. 22–3, etc.

[106] Cf. H. Bolkestein, *Wohltätigkeit und Armenpflege* (1939) 129; J. Bergmann, 'Die Stoische Philosophie und die Jüdische Frömmigkeit' in *Judaica* (F. Cohen) 1912.

[107] Mk. 14.7. The parabolic saying in Mk. 4.25 ('To him that hath shall be given, etc.') seems to presuppose a recognition of the facts of economic life.

[108] Cf. G. von Rad, *TWNT* 1. 567, who argues that it emerged only after the establishment of the monarchy in Israel. W. Eichrodt, *Theology of the Old Testament* 1 (E.tr. 1961) 194–8, regards this early reserve towards the divine title *melek* as a notable feature of Israelite religion.

a timeless truth: God *is* king, but the present state of affairs is hardly to be thought of as the perfect and final manifestation of his kingship; there must surely be a time in the future when his reign will be established and acknowledged in a way that is not yet the case.[109] The development of this theme is explicit in Deutero-Isaiah,[110] and was perhaps a natural consequence of the exile, with its recognition that the people of Israel could no longer have any pretensions to be a kind of paradigm and representative of God's kingdom on earth. It received further definition in Daniel, where reflection on the transient nature of a succession of earthly kingdoms sharpened the sense of contrast with the eternal kingdom of God which only a radical change in the ordinary course of history could bring about.[111] In subsequent Jewish literature – that is, between the Maccabean period and the fall of Jerusalem in 70 A.D. – the theme receives frequent emphasis;[112] and its hold on the popular mind can be confidently inferred from its occurrence in the Kaddish prayer:[113]

> May he establish his kingdom
> in your lifetime and in your days . . .

This theme was naturally one which could be expressed in a variety of modulations. The kingship of God might be demonstrated by means of his sovereignty over Israel in particular[114] or else as a universal sovereignty over all nations.[115] It might be exercised directly by God himself, or through an earthly king who would bring about the necessary changes on earth,[116] and who would perhaps be 'anointed' or appointed to reign.[117] That is to say, in so far as the option chosen by Jesus was one which involved the proclamation of this theme, it left him wide latitude for interpretation, which indeed he appears to have used to the full: his concept and understanding of the kingdom is nothing less than a radical and unprecedented[118] reinterpretation of the whole notion of God's influence upon the ways of men. Yet however original Jesus' presentation of this theme may have been, it could hardly have avoided raising the question whether it was one in which he himself would be the king. That the question was raised is historically certain: it provided the basis of the charge on which Jesus was crucified by Pilate, and the statement in John's gospel that, after the feeding of the five thousand, the crowds sought 'to make him king' (6.15) may well preserve a historical

---

[109] von Rad, loc. cit.
[110] Is. 52.7. Eichrodt, op. cit. 198, who overstates the case: there is only one instance.
[111] Dan. 2.38–44; 4.17,25,32.
[112] Ps. Sol. 17.3f.; Ass. Mos. 10.1; Or. Sib. 3.47,176; 1 QM 6.6
[113] For the text, cf. J. Jeremias, *New Testament Theology* 1 (E.tr. 1971) 198 and literature there cited.
[114] Is. 41.24; 43.15; 44.6
[115] Is. 52.10; Dan. passim; Mal. 1.14, etc.
[116] The two are found side by side in Ps. Sol. 17.3,23.
[117] As in Ps. Sol. 17.36; 18.6,8; 1 QS 9.11, etc.
[118] J. Jeremias, op. cit. 32–5, well draws attention to the unprecedented use of language in Jesus' teaching about the kingdom; though of course this might be due to accident; cf. above, pp.86–7.

memory which has been suppressed in the other gospels.[119] How far Jesus' conduct and teaching actually gave rise to such a movement is a question which our evidence does not permit us to answer with any certainty. The explicit repudiation of any earthly dominion in the temptation narratives in Matthew and Luke, and the almost laboured interpretation of Jesus' kingship as one 'not of this world' in John's gospel, may well be deliberate creations by the evangelists or the traditions they used to minimise the political implications of the Christian movement. But we can perhaps say with some confidence that the whole of Jesus' teaching as it is presented in the gospels conforms consistently to the pattern we would expect of teaching about the new age. What is important is the character of that new age itself, the nature of God's ultimate kingship. The identity and role of any human agent is a secondary matter. We have seen that the manner of Jesus' entry into Jerusalem could not but have given a regal impression, and this is acknowledged in the narratives of Luke (19.38) and John (12.13). But even if there were other acts and sayings of Jesus which had a similar implication, but which have been eliminated from the gospel tradition, it would still be the case that the primary emphasis in his teaching was the kingdom itself, and not the status of his own person. The correct interpretation of his name, then as now, will have been that he was one anointed or appointed to make a proclamation. That he was anointed to be king, though it might be true in a certain sense, could never have seemed to be the most important thing about him. The words which Luke ascribes to the disciples just before the ascension – 'Lord, are you now about to restore the kingdom to Israel?' (Acts 1.6) – represent, of course, a misunderstanding of Jesus' teaching about the kingdom, but preserve (as we have seen to be often the case in Luke)[120] an authentic use of idiom: the question which occurs to them is not whether Jesus is going to establish himself as king, but whether it is now time for the 'kingdom' to be established.

But there is also a third element in the expectations expressed in our Isaiah passages which, though lying a little further below the surface, is perhaps ultimately of greater religious importance. The Jewish religion has always seemed to contain a fundamental paradox. On the one hand it claims to possess the most comprehensive revelation of God which has ever been available to men: the Torah (in G. F. Moore's phrase) is nothing less than 'a revelation of religion'.[121] In it may be found in every detail the way of life which God enjoins upon men, along with a total understanding of the universe as God's sovereign creation. At the same time, God remains a mystery. His ways are inscrutable,[122] his action in human history baffling and at times

[119] Cf. C. H. Dodd, *Historical Tradition in the Fourth Gospel* 213-17.
[120] Cf. above, pp.80,140.
[121] G. F. Moore, *Judaism* 1.248.
[122] Is. 40.12; Job 38ff., etc.

apparently discouraging.[123] Even the scriptures, which promise to contain
the sum of possible knowledge about him, turn out to be obscure, puzzling
and apparently (at times) self-contradictory.[124] Expert knowledge and an
inspired tradition are required to interpret them.[125] A symptom of this
paradox is the identification, made well before the close of the Old Testament
canon and taken for granted in rabbinic Judaism,[126] of Law with Wisdom.
Law is written in a book, and in principle is accessible to all. But Wisdom has
to be searched for and pursued, it is given only to the wise and the pious,
indeed (according to a myth which appears in 1 Enoch 42 and may well have
been known long before)[127] it was a gift of God to men which found so little
acceptance that it returned in resignation to the place whence it had come.
Small wonder, then, that any vision of a new age included some relief to the
strain of this paradox. The time would come when God would be known
with a clarity that was withheld in the present age; the veil would be
removed, the mystery resolved.[128] Evidence for the vitality of this
expectation may be seen most clearly in the literary form of apocalyptic
writing. The pseudonymous seer is one who has had revealed to him some
part of the secret purpose of God,[129] which at present is hidden from all but
the privileged seer and his circle, but will soon be made plain to all. But the
desire to penetrate behind the inevitable obscurities of God's self-revelation[130]
continued for centuries to be manifested in the long tradition of Jewish
mysticism on the one hand, and on the other in the expectation that the new
age will make possible a new and immediate knowledge of God.

Once again this new revelation may be thought of as simply being made
available to all: God will make himself known. But though the revelation
remains primary, the person of an ultimate revealer is naturally the object of
hope and speculation. The first revelation, of the Torah, was given through
Moses, who had the unique privilege of seeing God face to face. All the
scriptures (so ran the dogma in first-century Judaism)[131] were written by
prophets; and the oracle in Deuteronomy 18.15 that God would raise up

---

[123] Ps. 74 etc.

[124] See M. Hengel, *Judaism and Hellenism* 2. 113 n.438.

[125] Prov. 8.22-3; Sir. 24.23. Cf. Moore, op. cit. 1. 263ff.

[126] Moore, op. cit. 265; M. Hengel, *Judaism and Hellenism* (E.tr. 1974) 1. 169ff.

[127] Cf. U. Wilckens, *TWNT* 7. 508-10.

[128] E.g. Test. Lev. 2.10 ἐγγὺς κυρίου στήσῃ . . . καὶ μυστήρια αὐτοῦ ἐξαγγελεῖς. The idea is present
in the Old Testament, especially Hos. 6.2-3 LXX, Jer. 38.34 LXX. In Rabbinic Judaism it occurs
in the form of 'God's Name' being revealed in the Age to Come, R. Pinchas ben Jair, Str.-B.
1.311; cf. C. H. Dodd, *The Fourth Gospel* 163-4. Is. 54.13 and Jer. 31.33-4 are also relevant: see
the suggestive discussion in J. D. M. Derrett, *Biblica* 62 (1981) 372-86.

[129] Note the emergence of the Aramaic word *raz* in this context. Cf. A. E. Harvey, *JTS* 31
(1980) 326-7. G. Scholem, *The Messianic Idea in Judaism* (E.tr. 1971) 17 conveys the sense of
paradox when he writes that the transition from the public proclamation of the prophets to the
esoteric mysteries of Apocalyptic is 'the enigma of Jewish history'.

[130] 1 Cor. 13.12.

[131] Jos. *C. Ap.* 1.41; bB.B. 14b–15a.

another prophet 'like Moses' was naturally regarded as a prophecy of a new and definitive revelation such as all the intermediate prophets were not able to give.[132] The sense of this expectation is well conveyed in the opening verses of Hebrews. God had indeed spoken of old through the prophets, who had in various ways sought to interpret God's law. But in the last days had come one who had given a definitive interpretation: the Son. Such was precisely the expectation evinced in numerous expressions of the Jewish hope: someone would come who would at last explain what God was really like, what God really demanded of men.

It is therefore not surprising that the appearance of such a person should have figured prominently in prophecies of a new age, and indeed should have provided one of the connecting links between the texts of the Isaiah complex which we have been studying. In Isaiah 42 the 'servant' has the task of establishing judgment (*mispat*) and providing revelation (*torah*) for which distant peoples are eagerly waiting: these terms are generally recognised to bear in this passage a meaning beyond that of the judicial or interpretative activity of an ordinary priest, king or prophet.[133] Moreover, it is also said of this servant-revealer that he will be 'a light to all peoples' (Is. 42.6), a conception with a long career before it in messianic speculation. But of interest to us now is the way in which this function becomes prominent also in wisdom literature. Wisdom is herself a revealer of God's nature and purposes, and the wise man therefore is one who both acquires knowledge of God and also is able to offer those who will receive it authoritative teaching on these matters. By the time of Christ, therefore, the expectation that an individual revealer would be a factor in the coming new age[134] was expressed with a considerable richness of content. This individual would be like Moses, who saw God face to face and was the mediator of the fundamental historic revelation; he would be a prophet, with the authority at the very least to arbitrate in matters affecting the temple, but also anointed to proclaim and even bring about the conditions of the new age; and he would be the wise man *par excellence*, possessing and imparting final and authoritative knowledge about God. It is surely significant that Jesus seems deliberately to have opted for all these roles. It was his very combination of them which, as we have seen, made it appropriate to assign to him the further name of 'Christ'.

But as soon as this function of ultimate revealer is attributed to an actual human being who appears on the stage of history, awkward questions arise. How are we to know that he speaks the truth? What is his authority, what is the source of his knowledge? How shall we know that we are right to attend to him? We have already met this issue in the form of the dogma that there

---

[132] The Samaritan belief expressed in Jn. 4.25 is presumably based on Dt. 18.15. For the belief in a new Moses expressed in CD 6.3ff. and 1 QS 9.11, cf. N. Wieder, *JJS* 4 (1953) 158–75, who suggests that the rabbis suppressed this tradition in reaction to Christianity.

[133] C. R. North, *The Suffering Servant in Deutero-Isaiah* (1955) 140–1.

[134] 1 Enoch 51.3; cf. K. Berger, *NTS* 20, 1973, 28ff.

could be no new prophet in Israel. Exactly the same goes for the claim of anyone who purported to be a teacher or a revealer. So far as the establishment was concerned, wisdom – that is, the greatest degree of knowledge about God available to men – was identified with the Law, the Torah;[135] and the understanding and interpretation of this law was vested in a tradition to which only those who were properly trained and authorised had access. Anyone claiming to speak of the mysteries of God independently of this tradition represented a threat that must be energetically opposed. But there was also a deeper and more strictly religious reason to expect opposition, if not persecution, for anyone who sought to proclaim the nature and demands of God in all their immediacy. It was recognised to be inherent in human nature that the bearer of God's revelation – however much it might be 'good news' to some and 'light' to others – was likely to present a challenge too demanding and unwelcome to be acceptable to the run of mankind. The classic model of the innocent sufferer, mocked, abused, and persecuted for his piety was familiar from the Old Testament;[136] the fate of groups within Judaism – particularly Pharisaism in its formative period – whose convictions forced them to oppose the general trends of the society around them is vividly expressed in inter-testamental writings.[137] But most significant for our purpose is the dramatic account in the Wisdom of Solomon of the righteous man who claims to have knowledge of God and who is mocked and hounded by the ungodly to the point of death, but finally vindicated by God.[138] The echo of this in Matthew's passion narrative (27.43) – and indeed in one of the earliest Christian writings we possess[139] – shows that this paradigm of suffering and death inflicted on one who was wise and righteous, though it is fully developed only in a writing which is characteristic of a deeply hellenised Judaism, must nevertheless have been familiar in Palestine.[140]

This realisation that the role of mediating a revelation of God to men was likely to involve suffering and rejection could be expressed in various ways. The recipient of God's self-disclosure might be a prophet; and it was becoming an accepted feature of the popular biography of the great prophets that they risked or suffered martyrdom in reward for their proclamation of God's word[141] – a presupposition which seems also to have been taken for granted by Jesus (Mt. 23.37; Lk. 11.47). Or he might be described simply as a servant or son of God – one entrusted with a specific task, whose role was

---

[135] Cf. above n.126.

[136] Is. 53; Ps. 22, etc.

[137] Ps. Sol; 1 QH, etc.

[138] L. Ruppert, *Der Leidende Gerechte* (1972) 70–105 identifies an original 'diptych' in Wisd. 2.12–20; 5.1–7 which is an elaboration of Is. 53, perhaps originally written in Hebrew and inspired by a situation of oppression such as that of Pharisees under the Hasmoneans.

[139] Phil. 2. 8–9; cf. 2 Macc. 9.12 which is itself related to Wisdom 2–5.

[140] This is accounted for by Ruppert's theory.

[141] Cf. H. Fischel, 'Martyr and Prophet', *JQR* 37 (1946) 265–80, especially 279; H. J. Schoeps, *Aus frühchristlicher Zeit* (1950) passim.

defined by the servant-texts in Deutero-Isaiah, and who there endures humi-liation and suffering, apparently for no reason other than that he has been faithful to the commission given to him by God. Or he might be the typical righteous man, persecuted and despised by those not disposed to hear his wisdom, and whose rejection could be given mythological expression in the story of wisdom herself finding no welcome on earth. Scholars have devoted much effort to trying to establish precise connections between these various representations. In particular, they have asked whether 'the Messiah' was ever identified with 'the servant',[142] or whether 'the prophet' of the future was ever thought of as 'the Messiah'.[143] But the approach which I have been proposing suggests that these questions are wrongly phrased. We have found a classic paradigm of hopes for the future in a complex of passages from Isaiah which were already read in the light of each other in the time of Jesus. We have seen that these passages allow for an individual who through his proclamation and preaching would make possible in the coming new age an understanding of the nature and purposes of God which in the present age must remain veiled and mysterious. Further reflection on these texts might develop one or other of the descriptions offered of such an individual; but we need not be greatly concerned if the writings which embody this reflection do not explicitly bring these descriptions together: they stood in combination in the basic complex of texts from which all this reflection arose. What is important for our purpose is that the one really distinctive designation, which serves to embrace them all, is 'the one who has been anointed' (or appointed), that is: the Christ. When this name came to be attached to Jesus, it conveyed the recognition that he promised to fulfil, not just certain scriptural prophecies, but the deep longings and expectations of which those prophecies were a classical expression.

If we are right that this was an option that presented itself to Jesus, and was the option which in fact he chose, then a number of problematical aspects in the story of Jesus immediately fall into place. We can now understand, not only how the first Christians were able to accept and preach the fact that one called 'Christ' had been crucified, but how Luke was able to go so far as to say that 'it was necessary' that the Christ should suffer. For the name Christ, as we have seen, was given to Jesus in virtue of the fact that he responded to the expectation that someone would come with a prophetic message, an evan-gelistic proclamation, and a revelation of wisdom, which were felt to be necessary constituents of a new age. But it was sensed also that this was a role which, men being what they are, must involve rejection. Prophets are murdered, the servant with his proclamation is despised and insulted, wisdom finds no welcome and the wise and righteous man is persecuted. If

---

[142] E.g. J. Jeremias, *TWNT* 5.680ff.
[143] E.g. K. Berger, 'Zum religionsgeschichtlichen Hintergrund . . .' *NTS* 17 (1971) 394ff.

'the anointed one' had been an expression capable only of suggesting a royal and nationalistic figure, this would not be expected; but the anointed prophet-messenger of good news and wisdom would be bound to incur this fate. In the second place, we can see why the question raised again and again by the teaching and activity of Jesus was the question of his authority – or perhaps we should say more accurately, his authorisation. Given that the new age which he proclaimed was not such (as many would have expected it to be) as to carry all before it, but was rather a seed growing secretly, a mystery to be received only by those ready to do so, then the claims inherent in this proclamation could not but have caused a crisis. If Jesus was indeed of God, authorised and commissioned to speak and act as he did, then he must be obeyed and followed. If not, he must be eliminated. No middle position was possible. Christians, in effect, are those who have acknowledged this divine authorisation, and have sought ever since to clarify the implications of the precise relationship of Jesus with God (this will be the subject of my last chapter). But the majority of Jesus' contemporaries took the opposite view, and having done so had no option other than to press for the due penalty of the law[144] to be exacted from one who had made such a blasphemous claim.

But the third matter which now falls more easily into place is that of the Resurrection. In considering the background of this article of Christian faith, scholars have tended to be influenced by the relative unanimity of later rabbinic sources and to regard the resurrection of the body as a cardinal Jewish doctrine of which the origin can be found in writings from the Book of Daniel onwards.[145] This presupposition has led them to make little of the fact that Jewish writings of the Hellenistic and early Roman periods show remarkable diversity in their accounts of life after death, and if we did not possess such clear evidence of subsequent Jewish doctrine on the matter it would surely not have occurred to us to conclude that there was a single, or even a dominant, belief among Jews in the time of Christ.[146] Few scholars, for example, have faced the fact that Josephus, when describing the beliefs of the Pharisees, uses language which unmistakably suggests a doctrine of trans-migration of souls;[147] that Daniel's account of the righteous 'shining like

144 Dt. 18. 18–20. See below pp.170f.

145 E.g. G. F. Moore, *Judaism* 2.295.

146 Cf. H. Cavallin, *Life after Death* (1974) 213: 'Concepts and symbols from widely different anthropologies are used in order to express the hope of personal survival of death.' Cf. also 200. It is also notably difficult to find any reference to resurrection in the Dead Sea Scrolls (cf. J. Carmignac, 'Les dangers de l'eschatologie', *NTS* 17 (1971) 376 n.1) or in pre-70 rabbinic traditions; cf. J. Neusner. *Rabbinic Traditions* 3.304–6; 318–19; *Kairos* 14 (1972) 57–70.

147 μεταβαίνειν in *B.J.* 2. 163 is technical Pythagorean language; cf. Diog. L. 8.5; ἐκ περιτροπῆς in *C.Ap.* 2.218 and *B.J.* 3.374 also seems unambiguous. H. St. J. Thackeray, *Selections from Josephus* (1919) 159 faced the issue, but has been shouted down by those determined to see in Josephus orthodox rabbinic doctrine at most 're-interpreted' so as to be intelligible to Greek readers. Cf. E. Schürer, *History* 2 (1979) 543 n.103; G. Mayer in *Josephus-Studien* (ed. O. Betz, 1974) 264–5. Even H. Cavallin, op. cit. 141–7, though he observes that Josephus' language has a Platonic colour, does not adequately represent his apparent Pythagoreanism.

stars' is echoed in Wisdom 3.7, where it is the *souls* of the righteous which live for ever; or that the language used by the martyred brothers in 2 Macc. 7 includes not only resurrection but eternal life and even an expectation of physical resuscitation.[148] It is not, in other words, the concept of resurrection which provides the connecting thread between these fragmentary references to life after death, but rather a theme which is much older in biblical thinking but begins to take on this particular form in the inter-testamental period: the vindication of the righteous man, whose faithfulness has brought him even to a martyr's death, but whom God not only rewards but vindicates by giving him a place in heaven such that his erst-while enemies are confounded.[149] All that we have said earlier about those options chosen by Jesus which led him to be called 'Christ' implies a similar vindication as the only possible dénouement. His proclamation of good news of the kingdom, his teaching and activity as a prophet, even his miracles, raised in a sharp and urgent form the question of his authority. Law-abiding Jews of his time had no alternative. If they did not accept as authentic Jesus' claim to divine authorisation, they were bound by law to secure his death, and this death would itself seem to be proof of the spuriousness of the claims. But those who took the opposite view, and saw Jesus as authorised by God to bear the name of Christ and to act and speak as he had, inevitably expressed their belief in terms of divine vindication. Jesus had necessarily been rewarded with life after his death, and had been exalted by God to unique dignity. Precisely what event or events brought them to this conviction, and why they chose 'resurrection' as their invariable way of expressing this moment of divine vindication, are questions to which we may not be able to recover more than probable answers.[150] We ought to take seriously the statement that the disciples were on one occasion puzzled to know 'what resurrection from the dead might mean' (Mk. 9.10). But whatever their experience might have been, it enabled them to affirm the correctness and appropriateness of the name 'Christ', which Jesus had borne in his lifetime.[151] To return to a text which we left on one side at an earlier stage in the argument, but which our conclusion makes fully intelligible, 'God has made him both Lord and Christ' (Acts 2.36). How much more this enabled them (and enables us) to say about him – how far the authorisation given to him by God was unique and implied a relationship with God such that Jesus has properly been regarded by Christians as (in some sense) divine – must be the subject of the final chapter.

[148]ἀναβιώσκεσθαι (cf. 2 Macc. 7.9 ἀναβίωσις) occurs in Plato, *Phaedo* 71e, where it means 'come to life again', sc. in a new body.

[149]Cf. G. Nickelsburg, *Resurrection, Immortality and Eternal Life in inter-testamental Judaism* (1972), especially 81-2.

[150]It may possibly be a sufficient explanation that ἀναστῆναι and ἐγείρεσθαι are the terms used in the cardinal Old Testament texts: Is. 26.14,19 (LXX); Dan. 12.2Θ; cf. Ps. Sol. 3.13; cf. G. Kegel, *Auferstehung Jesu, Auferstehung der Toten*, who relates this terminology also to the second of the Eighteen Benedictions.

[151]A similar conclusion is reached by K. Berger, *Die Auferstehung des Propheten und die Erhöhung des Menschensohns* (1976) 146.

## Note: A pre-Christian interpretation of Isaiah 61

(i) In Isaiah 61.1 the one who has been 'anointed with spirit' has a specific task: 'to bring good news to the humble, to bind up the broken-hearted, to proclaim liberty to captives'. In Luke the verse is quoted according to the Septuagint, which adds the clause, '(to proclaim) sight to the blind'. Clearly this version could not have been available to Jesus or to his immediate followers; but this addition in the Septuagint text is evidence from early (indeed pre-Christian) times that this passage of Isaiah was read in conjunction with Isaiah 42, which begins with a 'servant' on whom God has 'bestowed his spirit', and goes on to give him the task of 'opening eyes that are blind' (42.7).

(ii) But there are further ramifications of the allusion to Isaiah. The anointed one of Is. 61.1 is to 'bring good news' to the poor. The Hebrew root is the same as that of the 'herald' (*mebasser*) of Is. 52.7, whose feet are lovely upon the mountains and who 'brings good news' to the effect that 'God is king'. The herald is an important figure in Deutero-Isaiah; his news is good: he brings peace and announces God's kingdom.[152]

(iii) That these connections were made in pre-Christian times, and in Palestine, is proved by certain texts from Qumran. In 1QH 18[153] we have the progression, 'thou didst shed thy holy spirit upon thy servant . . . to be a herald (*mebasser*) of thy goodness . . . to the poor'. In the Melchizedek fragment (11 Q Melch)[154] a commentary on the 'herald' of Is. 52.7 is offered by reference to 'the one anointed by spirit', of Is. 61.1. These two passages between them display the fusion of all three Isaiah texts: the servant on whom the spirit is bestowed of Isaiah 42, the herald who brings good news of Isaiah 57 and the one anointed with the spirit who brings good news to the poor of Isaiah 61. This confirms that the apparent association of Isaiah 42 and Isaiah 61 in the Septuagint was a widespread and accepted piece of exegesis.

(iv) Later rabbinic tradition occasionally applied Isaiah 61.1 to the messiah who was to come: the text referred to 'the anointed one' *par excellence*.[155] But the Targum is perhaps more significant for our purpose, since it accepts the most obvious literal meaning of the text, namely, that the prophet is speaking of himself.[156] This at least provides early evidence that it was not felt strange that a prophet would be 'anointed' or (to put it the other way round) that 'an anointed one' might be a prophet. Moreover the connection is confirmed by Sirach 48.8, where Elijah is said to have 'anointed' prophets, and by CD 6.1 and 1 QM 11.7 where the prophets are 'anointed ones'.

(v) We have seen that Luke makes explicit the references to Isaiah 61 both in Acts and in the synagogue scene at the beginning of the gospel, and that he also relates the name 'Christ' to Isaiah 42.[157] But these are by no means the only instances of allusions to this complex of Isaiah passages. In Mt. 12. 18–21 there is an extended quotation of Isaiah 42. 1–4, offering a general commentary on the style of Jesus' works of healing; in

[152]Cf. G. Friedrich, *TWNT* 2. 706–7, who, however, somewhat overstates his case that in Dt.-Is. *mebasser* is 'ein geprägter religiöser Terminus'. Its only occurrence is in 52.7, and 61.1 provides at most an echo of it. Cf. also P. Stuhlmacher, *Das Paulinische Evangelium* 1 (1968) 116–22.

[153]In 1 QH 18.14 there is doubt whether MBSR should be pointed *mibbasar* or *mebasser*. G. Vermes, *DSSE* 200 prefers the latter, as does P. Stuhlmacher, op. cit. This uncertainty does not affect the argument: it was the root, not its inflection, which carried the associations.

[154]For the text, cf. M. de Jonge, A. Van der Woude, *NTS* 12 (1966) 301–26. Cf. also J. T. Milik *JJS* 23 (1972) 96–109; English text in Vermes, *DSSE* 265–8. The 'Messiah of the spirit' is surely a way of referring to the one 'anointed with the Holy Spirit' of Isaiah 61.1. It is immaterial whether the original reference was to the Teacher of Righteousness, as Milik suggests.

[155]Str.-B. 2. 134,156: the earliest instance is fourth century (R. Acha).

[156]Tg. 'The Spirit of prophecy is upon me'.

[157]Acts 4.27.

the baptism and transfiguration stories in the synoptics there is an unmistakable allusion to the beginning of the same passage; and the Q-saying in Mt. 11.4–6, Lk. 7.22 contains a clear reference to Isaiah 61 ('the poor have the good news preached to them') alongside a description of Jesus' activity based on the list of the signs of the new age (the blind seeing, the deaf hearing, the lame walking, the dumb speaking) in Isaiah 35. 5–6.

# 7

# Son of God:
# the Constraint of Monotheism

I must now introduce one further instance of those historical constraints which, I have argued, give definition and content to the bare general statements which constitute the main part of our reliable information about Jesus. This is the constraint of that instinctive and passionate monotheism which lay at the heart of all Jewish religion and (at least in the eyes of pagans) constituted a great part of its identity. 'The Lord our God is one God': so begins the prayer (the *Shema*) which every Jew said, and still says, daily; 'Thou shalt have no other gods besides me': so began the Decalogue which, in the time of Jesus,[1] was recited every day in public worship. The belief that there is only one God, and that he is Lord of all, was fundamental to the one religion in antiquity which offered determined and uncompromising opposition to the tolerant polytheism of the pagan world. It was within a culture indelibly marked by this monotheism that Jesus lived and died and was proclaimed. It was within this constraint that he had to convey his conviction of divine authorisation and that his followers had to find means of expressing his unique status and significance.

It is important not to oversimplify: as with all credal statements, the precise meaning of what is being asserted is difficult to define. Even the meaning of the Shema itself has always been a subject of debate.[2] The force of the constraint of monotheism can be grasped only when it is clear what it is that is being denied; and in the case of the Jews this was by no means always the same at different times and places.[3] Early in their history their proclamation of the one true god, though it excluded the worship of any other god among themselves, by no means excluded the existence of the gods of other nations; it merely asserted the complete superiority of Yahwe over all other deities. Later on, the oneness of God became exclusive: officially no other gods could

[1] M. Tamid 5.1. On the cessation of this practice recorded in yBer. 1. 3c, cf. G. Vermes, *Post-biblical Jewish Studies* (1975) 169-71.

[2] W. Eichrodt, *Theology of the Old Testament* 1 (E.tr. 1961) 226-7; L. Jacobs in *Enc. Jud.* 14 (1971) col. 1373.

[3] Cf. G. F. Moore, *Judaism* 1. 359-64.

exist;[4] yet an uneasy feeling that the gods of paganism possessed some kind of malign existence lingered on well into the New Testament period,[5] and the use of the word 'god' for them was not necessarily a term of abuse or mockery. Within the Jewish community, the power of the monotheistic confession is seen perhaps most clearly in the criminal code: the most grievous offences were those which in any way diminished the unique majesty and honour of God.[6] Blasphemy stood conspicuously at the head of the list of capital sins.[7] Moreover any intellectual or religious opinion which seemed to postulate a second celestial being independent of the one god was firmly anathematised.[8] But it was of course when Jews looked outside their own culture that their monotheism received its sharpest definition. From the prophetic denunciation of idol-worship to the strident polemics of Hellenistic Judaism against any manifestation of paganism, faith in the exclusive oneness of God is felt to be totally incompatible with the recognition of any other divine being.

This constraint, at the very least, precluded an option which would have seemed to any pagan the most natural way of describing Jesus, that is, as a god. The Greek pantheon was essentially an open one: there was no difficulty in adding further members. The one formal qualification that was necessary was that there should exist a cult in honour of the new god. This might spring up spontaneously, as in the case of founders of cities who received divine honours from the grateful inhabitants; or it might be instituted by the decree of the prestigious ruler who, from the time of Alexander onwards, thought fit to claim divinity for himself or for his deceased predecessor.[9] Such deification of distinguished rulers placed no strain on Greek or Roman religion.[10] The king or emperor could be thought of either as one of the traditional gods visiting the earth in human form, or else as a new deity now added to the pantheon. The only resistance felt by the Greek-speaking world was against the extravagant courtesies and obeisance which became due to such a 'god' in his lifetime, and which seemed too redolent of the manners of oriental courts (from which they were derived) to be readily accepted by the spiritual descendants of Peisistratus or the Scipios;[11] but even this resistance was soon overcome. In the case of Alexander, contemporary Greek observers

[4] Eichrodt, op. cit. 221; G. Bornkamm, *BZNW* 21, 87-8.
[5] 1 Cor. 8.5.
[6] G. F. Moore, *Judaism* 1.466.
[7] Siphre Dt. 21.22 (Fr. 114b). Cf. J. D. M. Derrett, *Law in the New Testament* 453-5.
[8] Moore, *Judaism* 1. 364ff.; A. F. Segal, *Two Powers in Heaven* (1977).
[9] On this topic, see L. R. Taylor, *The Divinity of the Roman Emperors* (1931) ch.1.
[10] Even among intellectuals, to whom 'emperor worship seemed little more than an extravagant compliment to a man whose virtue and understanding had some share in the divine', G. Bowersock, *Fondation Hardt – Entretiens* 19 (1972) 190.
[11] Arrian *Anab.* 4.12: two stories describing Callisthenes' unwillingness to pay Alexander the honour of *proskynesis*. Such honours were regularly declined by Roman emperors, Suet. *Aug.* 52. For other examples, cf. M. Charlesworth, *PBSR* 15 (1939) 1-10.

had no theological difficulties: they merely registered their scorn of his foolish presumption.[12]

Clearly this kind of promotion to divine honours would have been totally abhorrent in any Jewish milieu[13] and also totally inappropriate to any person save a ruler distinguished by signal victories or exceptionally wide dominions. But there was another, less formal, kind of deification which comes closer to our concern. If a man was found to have gifts and powers that were out of the ordinary, and seemed supernatural, the Greeks saw no reason not to describe him as a 'god', or as 'divine', even if there was no cult in his honour.[14] In remote antiquity, Pythagoras had been acknowledged as a god in virtue of what we would now call his psychic powers,[15] and Empedocles had proclaimed himself one.[16] The great philosophers of the past were repeatedly called 'divine'.[17] The later Pythagorean writer Philostratus similarly attributed divinity to his hero Apollonius of Tyana on the grounds of apparently supernatural powers of perception.[18] Here it is not so much a matter of seeking to secure a place in the pantheon for a particular philosopher as of using the words 'god' and 'divine' to express the exceptional nature of the person so described, and to account for the feats of which he appeared to be capable and the impression which he made on others. As in the case of rulers, such language posed no threat to the religious sensibilities of a pagan: the notion that someone who appeared to be a man might turn out after all to be a god was as old as Homer, and we read of Paul and Barnabas stumbling into just such a situation in Asia Minor.[19] The consequence of such an identification might again be the institution of a cult; but it need not be, and it is clear that in the case of someone who was more of a philospher than a freakish miracle-worker the question was semantic rather than ontological. Calling him 'a god' was a way of describing his exceptional powers and character: it did not imply that divine honours should be paid to him.

It is this more analogical use of the language of divinity which has caused

---

[12] Hyperides 6.21; Aelian, *Var. Hist.* 2.19.

[13] The first recorded Jewish reaction to the Hellenistic ruler cult is associated with Antiochus IV's assumption of the titles Epiphanes and Theos: Dan 3.1ff. etc. Cf. M. Hengel, *Judaism and Hellenism* 1. 285. But in the time of Hadrian we find a Jewish woman in Palestine prepared to swear by the τύχη κυρίου Καίσαρος: *IEJ* 12 (1962) 260.

[14] Cf. A. D. Nock, *JHS* 48 (1928) 31f. = *Essays* 1. 145f.: 'θεός does not necessarily imply more than a being possessed of greater power than humanity has and immune from death . . . It is not easy to draw a definite line between comparison and identification'. Cf. C. H. Dodd, *The Fourth Gospel* (1955) 251: 'In popular Hellenistic usage . . . υἱὸς θεοῦ represents a certain confusion of divinity and humanity.'

[15] Iambl. *V.P.* 28.143.

[16] Fr. 115, 118, 119 Diels.

[17] Cf. A. D. Nock, art. cit. 32 = 145 and n.51.

[18] *Vit. Ap.* 1.2.

[19] Acts 14.11; cf. A. D. Nock, *JRS* 47 (1957) 119 = *Essays* 2. 840: 'the constant comparison and equation of rulers, as of lesser personages, with specific deities . . . was well worn currency.'

the question to be raised whether the uncompromising monotheism of Palestinian Judaism may not have been significantly modified when Jews (writing in Greek) sought to commend to pagan readers the exceptional virtues and powers of the great personalities of the Old Testament. Moses, Solomon, Isaiah and others are occasionally described by Josephus[20] as having 'divine' characteristics and by Philo[21] as possessing a certain divinity, and the question is much discussed whether these Hellenistic Jewish writers have departed significantly from the rigid distinction between God and man which is implied throughout the Old Testament, and have compromised their ancestral monotheism in their attempt to emphasise the god-given characteristics and qualities of the heroes of biblical history.[22] To which it may be replied that what we find in these authors is not so much a religious as a linguistic phenomenon. In the idiom of the readers for whom they were writing, to call Moses (in some sense) divine was to insist on the altogether exceptional nature of his gifts and to imply that these gifts were from God. But it was not for one moment to suggest that Moses should be (or ever had been) acclaimed or worshipped as a god,[23] or that his existence qualified in any way the unique divinity of the Creator of the world.[24] The constraint of monotheism exercised its hold on these writers as firmly as it did on those of the Bible itself.

It is therefore no cause for surprise that the New Testament writers appear to have submitted to this constraint, and to have avoided using the word 'god' or 'divine' of Jesus. Jesus himself is recorded as having endorsed the standard Jewish confession of monotheism[25] (Mark 12.29) and accepted the prohibition which this implied of any moral comparison between himself and God (Mark 10.18); moreover in the Fourth Gospel he is made to deny vigorously the accusation that he set himself up as a being equal to and independent of God.[26] The New Testament writers similarly are insistent about the absolute oneness of God, and show no tendency to describe Jesus in terms of divinity: the few apparent exceptions are either grammatically and textually uncertain[27] or have an explanation which, as we shall see, brings them within the constraint of Jewish monotheism.[28] It was not until the new

[20] *Ant.* 3. 180; 8. 34, 187; 10. 35.

[21] *Vita Mos.* 1. 158.

[22] For a recent study, cf. C. H. Holladay, *'Theios Aner' in Hellenistic Judaism* (1977) and the judicious discussion of it by W. Telford, *JTS* 30 (1979) 246-52.

[23] The nearest thing to this is the reaction to him of Egyptian priests, ἰσοθέου τιμῆς καταξιωθῆναι, Artapanus ap. Euseb. *Praep. ev.* 9.27.6.

[24] As expressed e.g. *De op. mund.* 170, cf. Justin *Dial.* 55 (Trypho).

[25] Justin cites Jesus as a teacher of traditional Jewish monotheism, 1 *Apol.* 13.

[26] Most explicitly at Jn. 10.33: Jesus' reply makes the semantic point that there is precedent in his own culture for using the word θεός for beings who are other than the one God; but the main burden of his reply, as throughout the gospel, is that, far from being a second or rival god, he is totally dependent on and united with the Father.

[27] The point is important but controversial, and is given detailed discussion in Appendix III.

[28] See below, pp.166,172

religion had spread well beyond the confines of its parent Judaism that it became possible to break the constraint and describe Jesus as divine;[29] and it is significant that Jewish Christian churches continued to exist for at least a century which refused to take this step.[30] But given that this option was closed, only one alternative remained. If no divine attributes were possible, only human categories could be used. Jesus' unique authority must somehow be expressed by a model or paradigm drawn from human experience and human relationships. We have seen already that one designation that was chosen (and was apparently inspired by the character of Jesus' activity) was that of the person anointed to proclaim good news to the poor and bring sight to the blind: the Christ. Another, which has become of critical importance in subsequent Christian doctrine, was Son of God.

That this was felt to be a highly significant title is shown by the remarkable fact that in all four gospels it is given to Jesus only by supernatural beings or voices or by men speaking on supernatural authority.[31] The only exception (apart from one instance in Matthew's gospel to which we must return later) is the significant one of the cry of recognition by the centurion at the cross. We shall suggest in a moment the reason for this restraint in the use of the title; for the present it is enough to note that it was evidently not felt to be a description which could be used indifferently alongside others, but that it had a particular connotation such that it could be applied to Jesus only on the highest authority. Precisely what this connotation was is a question on which a certain amount of light is thrown by the observation that the title is known to have been applied by Jesus' contemporaries to angels, to the Jewish race as a whole, and (a recent development) to men of particular piety and innocence.[32] But to gain more precision in the matter, it is necessary to ask how the relationship between a son and his father was normally understood, and what kind of relationship with God would therefore have been implied by the title. To do this, we have first to rid our minds of that somewhat sentimental ideal of intimacy and partnership between father and son for which there is no evidence before the Enlightenment[33] and which became widely accepted only under the influence of the Romantic Movement. We must set on one side also that interest in the physical and metaphysical implications of the relationship which lay at the heart of the christological debates of the early patristic

---

[29] The first unambiguous instances are in Ignatius of Antioch, writing *c*. 110 A.D.

[30] Justin, *Dial*. 48.

[31] Cf. A. E. Harvey, *Jesus on Trial* (1976) 41-5.

[32] For a convenient summary of the evidence, see M. Hengel, *Son of God* (E.tr. 1976) 41ff.

[33] Cf. L. Stone, *The Family, Sex and Marriage in England, 1500-1800* (1977) 239-44: the old patriarchal model of the family was first assailed in the period 1690-1750 under the influence of new philosophical and religious insights.

period[34] and which owed more to Greek philosophical speculation than to the social *mores* of the Jews. I suggest that there were in fact three aspects in particular which seemed important, if not defining, characteristics of the relationship of a son to his father.

(i) The first of these aspects is one which only the permissive social conventions of today prevent us from taking for granted as the ancients did. What the son owes to his father is above all – obedience. In the Book of Proverbs a father says to his son: 'Let your heart hold fast my words: keep my commandments and live' (4.4). And this was no empty exhortation. A clause still stood in the Law to the effect that a son's stubborn disobedience was punishable by death.[35] A son's duty to his father was to obey him implicitly throughout his active life and to support him materially in his old age.[36] The fifth Commandment was felt to be properly at the head of the list of those which governed the relationships between human beings: honouring one's parents came next to, and was indeed an aspect of, honouring God.[37] Throughout the ancient world, an appropriate comparison to the relationship of son to father was felt to be that of subject to king, or even slave to master;[38] and when men were called sons of God in the Bible or in later Jewish literature, it was this quality of obedience which was primarily suggested by the metaphor.[39] To say, therefore, that Jesus was 'son of God' was to say, first and foremost, that he showed perfect obedience to the divine will. Moreover, just as a human father would seek to perfect this obedience in his son by imposing discipline and chastisement ('A father who loves his son will whip him often', Sirach 30.1) so God in his role as father could be expected to discipline his children.[40] Indeed the father–son relationship offered a clue to understanding Jesus' sufferings. As the author of Hebrews expressed it, 'he learnt obedience from what he suffered, and was perfected' (5.8–9).

---

[34] The earliest formulation known to me of an identity of *nature* between father and son is in Origen, *De princ.* 1.2.6: 'Ita etiam scriptum est: "Et genuit Adam Seth secundum imaginem suam et secundum speciem suam". Quae imago etiam naturae ac substantiae patris et filii continet unitatem' – a unity conceived on a Platonic understanding of θεότης; and even here the precise formulation may be due to the later hand of Rufinus. Later on, identity of nature is taken for granted. Cf. Cornelius à Lapide *in Rom.* 8.15: 'sic enim apud homines pater dicitur, qui naturam suam filio communicat.'

[35] Deut. 21. 18–21; M. Sanh. 7.4; 8.1–4. In Roman law a father had absolute power of life and death over his children until the second century A.D.; cf. J. Carcopino, *Daily Life in Ancient Rome* (E.tr. 1941) 76ff.

[36] Cf. J. D. M. Derrett, *Jesus' Audience* (1973) 35.

[37] Cf. Philo, *De spec. leg.* 2. 224ff.

[38] Ar. *Eth. Nic.* 1160b: ἡ μὲν γὰρ πατρὸς πρὸς υἱεῖς κοινωνία βασιλείας ἔχει σχῆμα. Cf. *Pol.* 1259a fin . . . τέκνον δὲ βασιλικῶς. Aristotle, as a true Greek, finds the oriental family 'tyrannical', and rejects the master–slave model; but Philo has no such reservations: *De spec. leg.* 2. 227, children are ὑπήκοοί τε καὶ δοῦλοι; ib. 234 ὡς ἄρχουσι πειθαρχοῦντες . . . ὡς δεσπότας εὐλαβούμενοι.

[39] Jeremiah 3. 19–20; Mal. 1.6; for rabbinic instances, cf. J. Jeremias, *The Prayers of Jesus* (1967) 18–19.

[40] Prov. 3. 11–12.

(ii) There is a second aspect of the relationship of son to father which is equally strange to our own culture, in which learning and knowledge is sought from teachers and experts rather than from parental experience. But in antiquity (and by no means only among the Jews) the basic instruction and apprenticeship offered by a father to his son served as a model both for general education and for the transmission of esoteric knowledge.[41] 'Hear, O sons, a father's instruction, and be attentive, that you may gain insight' (Proverbs 4.1). The teacher was a father to his pupils, the student was a son to his instructor.[42] Whatever might happen in practice – and education of course became diversified and specialised even in antiquity – the ideal remained constant of the father passing down his wisdom, knowledge and experience to his son. What has been called 'a hidden parable' in John's gospel[43] makes full use of this basic model: 'the son does nothing on his own unless he sees his father doing it . . . the father shows him everything that he does.' The model may have originated in the father's workshop, where the son learns the ancestral trade as an apprentice. But it was felt to extend to every aspect of the transmission of knowledge from teacher to learner.

We have seen that one of the most powerful yearnings of the Jewish people was for one who would come to give the decisive and ultimate revelation of God's nature and will. We can now see why, once the conviction had gained ground that Jesus was indeed this ultimate revealer, it was appropriate to call him, not only 'Christ', but 'Son of God'. It was he who had learnt, to a unique degree, the truth about God; in this respect, therefore, he was uniquely qualified to be called 'Son of God'. As the prologue to the Fourth Gospel expresses it: 'The only-begotten son,[44] being in the bosom of the father – he has revealed him.' Or as Hebrews puts it: 'God has spoken in these last days by his son.' Indeed the full force of this aspect of the son–father relationship is exploited in a saying which has come increasingly to be regarded as an authentic reminiscence of Jesus' manner of speech about himself,[45] the second part of which would have been held to be axiomatically true of any teacher of esoteric wisdom:

> Everything has been committed to me by my father,
> And no one knows the son but the father,
> And no one knows the father but the son
> And he to whom the son is willing to reveal him.
>
> (Mt. 11.26–7; Lk. 10.22)

[41] See the long list of instances adduced by A. J. Festugière, *La Révélation d'Hermès Trismégiste* (1950) 1. 332–54. For further references, cf. F. Boll, *Aus der Offenbarung Johannis* (1914, repr. 1967) 139 n.1.

[42] S. Dt. 34 on 6.7, bSanh 99b; M. B.M. 2.11; cf. E. Lohse, *TWNT* 8. 358. In the Hermetic literature, the teacher of esoteric wisdom is called 'father' again and again, e.g. *C.H.* 13.1–3. Cf. also 3 Enoch 48C. 7, 45. 1–2 MS.E.

[43] 5. 19–20; cf. C. H. Dodd, *More New Testament Studies* (1968) 30–40; P. Gächter, *Neutestamentliche Aufsätze* (ed. J. Blinzler et al. 1963) 65–8.

[44] See below, Appendix III, p.177.

[45] Cf. J. Jeremias, op. cit. 48ff.; *New Testament Theology* 1 (1971) 56–61. J. Dunn, *Christology in the Making* (1980) 200.

(iii) But there is still a third aspect of the relationship of son to father which is of significance for our purpose but which may easily escape our notice because it too is far removed from the conventions of our time. This is the aspect of *agency*. The Jews have always been a great commercial people and the importance of securing reliable agents for the successful expansion of business was well understood. As soon as you start getting on as a trader, you will need to extend your interests beyond your own little shop or office. You need to know and employ people who can carry on your business in your absence and who can be trusted to carry through transactions to your advantage. Indeed it could be said that success in business depended more than anything else on the ability to choose and make use of reliable agents.[46] In these circumstances there was just one person whom a businessman would wish if possible to have as his agent in preference to any other – and that was his son. Not only, as we have seen, should he be able to rely on his son's absolute obedience, but in the long run the interests of the son, who was also the heir, would coincide with the father's. A classic instance of this agent-son is in the Book of Tobit: Tobias is sent on a long journey to recover an old debt for his father and is duly accredited as his father's authorised agent.[47] A more sinister example is Jesus' parable of the wicked vine-dressers, where the son is instantly recognised as the agent[48] having full authority as well as (being the heir)[49] a personal interest, and is accordingly murdered.

Further precision may be gained from the Jewish law of agency as it prevailed at the time.[50] Agency was an effective means of conducting business only if the acts of the agent could be assumed to be approved by his principal, and therefore to bind the principal in respect of legal liability. To express this relationship, the maxim was coined that 'A man's agent is like himself';[51] that is to say, for the purpose of the transaction for which the agent was authorised, it was as if the principal himself were present, and the agent must receive the respect which would be due to the principal – a good biblical instance is Abigail's prostration before the messenger-agents of David who came to seek her consent to marriage (1 Sam. 25.41).[52] It is of course important not to extend this principle beyond its specific application. An

[46] Cf. J. D. M. Derrett, *Jesus' Audience* (1973) 76.

[47] Tobit 5.2 א. The significance of this use of σημεῖον for understanding Johannine usage is discussed in my *Jesus on Trial* 95 and n.34.

[48] Though the matter involves some technicalities, cf. Derrett, *Law in the New Testament* 302-3 and 303 n.1.

[49] This follows from Mark's phrase, ἕνα υἱὸν ἀγαπητόν: an only son was necessarily both heir and agent.

[50] Cf. Derrett, op. cit. 52 n.4 for the literature, and add Z. W. Falk, *Introduction to Jewish Law of the Second Commonwealth* 2 (1978) 191-4; J.-A. Bühner, *Der Gesandte und sein Weg* (1977) 196-8.

[51] M. Ber. 5.5.

[52] Marriage and divorce were the classic instances of the use of agency: Derrett, op. cit. 53; Falk, op. cit. 192-3.

agent was not his master's representative under *any* circumstances: he carried his principal's authority and prestige only for the conduct of the transaction for which he had been appointed as agent.[53] Nevertheless, so long as his master was absent and he was seen to be managing his master's affairs, there would be a presumption that he was acting as an authorised agent, and he would receive the appropriate respect. Indeed the same principle finds expression in the notion of an envoy 'representing' the sovereign. If you knelt before him, you were kneeling, not to him, but to the absent king. If you insulted him, the insult was taken personally by his sovereign and you were at war (2 Sam. 10.1ff.). The king was present in the ambassador just as, for certain purposes, the principal was present in his agent: 'a man's agent is like himself'.[54]

That this procedure of agency was sufficiently familiar to be used as a figure of speech is proved, not only by the saying in John's gospel, 'the agent (*apostolos*) is not greater than him who sent him',[55] but by the rabbinic application of the term to Moses, Elijah, Elisha and Ezekiel who acted as 'agents' in performing wonders that were normally the prerogative of God alone.[56] The figure is not used directly of Jesus, nor could it be argued that in calling a person a 'son' one was necessarily thinking of him as an 'agent'. On the other hand, there were circumstances under which the recognition that a man was a certain person's son might well carry the implication that he was also that person's agent. As we have seen, the best agent a man could have was his son. If the son were observed going about his father's business; if he were known to be an only son (*monogenēs*) and 'beloved' (i.e. not dispossessed) and therefore with a personal interest in the inheritance; and (still more) if the son claimed to have been 'sent' by his father for the purpose – there would be a strong presumption that the son was acting as his father's agent, and it would be wise to treat him accordingly. Now it happens that a number of sayings attributed to Jesus and well-attested in different strands of the gospel tradition[57] show Jesus to have spoken of himself as one who was 'sent'; and in each case the context permits no doubt about what was meant: Jesus was sent by God. If then the one who claimed to be sent by God was acknowledged to be the Son of God, the title cannot but have carried the implication that he was also God's representative, God's 'agent'.

A study of the Fourth Gospel reveals that an understanding of Jesus as the authorised agent and representative of God is one of the controlling themes of

[53] Well stated in K. H. Rengstorf's classic article on ἀπόστολος *TWNT* 1. 414: 'Beauftragung mit ganz bestimmten Aufgaben'; cf. Bühner, op. cit. 210.

[54] Philo well expresses the principle when he writes (*De dec.* 119) ὁ δ' ὑπηρέτην ἀτιμάζων συνατιμάζει καὶ τὸν ἄρχοντα.

[55] The comparison is evidently taken from everyday life, and ἀπόστολος must represent *shaliach*, not (Christian) 'apostle'. Cf. Harvey, *Jesus on Trial* 115-16.

[56] Rengstorf, art. cit. 419.

[57] Mk. 9.37 par.; Mt. 10.40; Lk. 9.48; Jn. 13.20; Mt. 15.24; Lk. 4.18,43; Jn. 12.49 etc. It is significant that Paul twice refers to God having 'sent' his son, Romans 8.3; Gal. 4.4.

the whole narrative.[58] But we can now see that it is implicit also in the synoptics' use of the title, Son of God; indeed, it is the explanation of the surprising phenomenon we observed earlier, namely that Jesus is acknowledged as Son of God only by supernatural beings or on supernatural authority. For if one who is Son of God is so called not merely because he is obedient and just, but because he is known to be sent by his Father and is therefore God's representative, agent and authorised revealer of the truth, then to give this name to a living person in respect of his work, his mission and his teaching is to say something very serious indeed. It amounts to the recognition that how you respond to him – what you say to him, whether you attend to him, obey him and consistently acknowledge him – is equivalent to how you respond to God himself. It is, in effect, your judgment and your salvation: and there is more than one saying attributed to Jesus in the synoptic gospels, quite apart from whole discourses on the theme in the Fourth Gospel, which have precisely this implication.[59] Small wonder therefore that so grave and portentous a designation of Jesus was one which, it was instinctively felt, no one would normally have dared to give him in his lifetime unless supernaturally prompted to do so.[60]

'He claims to have knowledge of God, and calls himself son of God . . . he boasts that God is his father' (Wisdom 2.13,16). In view of the evident allusion to this passage in Matthew's Passion narrative[61] there can be no doubt that some version at least of it, which we know only as part of a writing characteristic of Hellenistic Judaism, must have been familiar to the very first Christians.[62] In this context the phrase 'Son of God' probably meant no more than a righteous and innocent man who had perhaps achieved an unusual degree of piety,[63] and there is no convincing evidence that it had come to have any further meaning by the time of Christ.[64] It certainly was not a 'title' waiting to be assigned to an individual who would be recognised as worthy

[58] Harvey, *Jesus on Trial,* esp. ch.5.

[59] Mk. 8.38 par.; Lk. 9.26; Mt. 10.33 par.; Lk. 12.9.

[60] Two passages in Lk. suggest this evangelist's sensitivity to the point: (i) 2.49. The translation (A.V.) 'about my father's business' is not only correct (despite papyrus evidence supporting the R.V. rendering; cf. C. F. D. Moule, *Idiom Book of New Testament Greek* (1953) 75) but entirely appropriate to the agent-son taking up his work of authoritative exposition (ἀποκρίσεις 2.47). (ii) 20.16 μὴ γένοιτο is not just an expression of 'horror' (cf. I. H. Marshall, *The Gospel of Luke* (1978) 731) but is apotropaic, a repudiation of a sacrilegious thought (the rhetorical use, denying a false conclusion from a premise, as in Epictetus and Paul, is quite inappropriate here). Jesus' hearers are appalled at the consequences of maltreating one whom they discern to stand allegorically for God's agent and representative, and repudiate the thought that such a thing could happen.

[61] Mt. 27.43: an application to Jesus of Ps. 22.19 which shows striking similarities to Wisdom 2.12–20 (which itself alludes to the same verse of Ps. 22). Cf. D. P. Senior, *The Passion Narrative according to St. Matthew, A Redactional Study* (Bibl. Ephem. Th. Louv. 39, 1975) 288–90.

[62] See above, p.148.

[63] Cf. G. Vermes, *Jesus the Jew* (1973) 194–200; M. Hengel, *Son of God* (E.tr. 1976) 41ff.

[64] Even Kl. Berger, who relies on the evidence of late Jewish writings such as 3 Enoch and the problematical *Joseph and Asenath,* has to admit that the further meaning 'divinely authorised messenger' is by no means established: *NTS* 17 (1971) 424.

of it. In this repect we are justified in adopting an approach to it similar to that which we followed in the case of 'Christ'. Instead of assuming that its meaning can be discovered from its occurrences as a title in Hellenistic or even pagan writings, we must ask what were the connotations of the phrase itself which would have made it seem an appropriate designation for a person such as we believe Jesus to have been.[65] I have argued that in certain contexts the word 'son' itself connoted obedience to a father's will, an inherited knowledge of his skills and experience, and the authorisation to act as a fully empowered agent. These contexts are all present in the narratives concerning Jesus, and are taken for granted in sayings which may reasonably be regarded as authentic. To call Jesus Son of God was therefore to accept the claim implied in his words and actions that he was totally obedient to the divine will, that he could give authoritative teaching about God, and that he was empowered to act as God's authorised representative and agent. To this extent, the phrase 'Son of God' as applied to Jesus acquired new precision and a new range of meaning; but there was nothing new in the conceptions it made use of. Indeed the notion of a teacher and leader fully authorised by God, disobedience towards whom would be tantamount to repudiation of God himself, was well understood in the Old Testament.

The crucial text is Deuteronomy 18. 18-20:

> I will raise up for them a prophet like you from among their brethren; and I will put my words in his mouth, and he shall speak to them all that I command him. And whoever will not give heed to my words which he shall speak in my name, I myself will require it of him. But the prophet who presumes to speak a word in my name which I have not commanded him to speak, or who speaks in the name of other gods, that same prophet shall die.

This is related[66] to a text in Exodus (23.20-1) where the subject is some kind of supernatural being, but where the consequences of disobedience are equally serious:

> Behold I send an angel before you, to guard you on the way and to bring you to the place which I have prepared. Give heed to him and hearken to his voice, do not rebel against him, for he will not pardon your transgression; for my name is in him.

Whatever may have been the original purpose and meaning of these passages,[67] they represent a fundamental conviction about the nature of

---

[65] I find myself in agreement here with B. Gerhardsson, who writes (*The Mighty Acts of Jesus* (1979) 88), '"The Son of God" is not treated as a ready-made title for a specific figure for which people are simply waiting and with which Jesus is simply identified. It is used as an interpretative designation . . .'.

[66] 'Bears a generally deuteronomistic stamp', M. Noth, *Exodus* (E.tr. 1962) 192.

[67] The fact that Ex. 23.20 was combined with Mal. 3.1 in pre-Christian Jewish exegesis (J. Jeremias *TWNT* 2.938 n.66; R. H. Gundry, *The Use of the Old Testament in Matthew's Gospel* (1967) 11-12) shows that the notion of mission and agency was felt to be primary. Rabbinic exegesis passes over the prophetic sense of these passages (Str.-B. 2.626 on Acts 3.22), perhaps in reaction to the Christian exploitation of it.

God's self-manifestation which is the religious equivalent of the legal concept of agency. Divine authorisation had of course been given to the great teachers of Israel – Moses and the prophets – to disobey whom was to disobey God himself. Yet such disobedience was inevitable, as inevitable as sin itself. The Bible therefore stops short of regarding these figures as the actual *representatives* of God on earth, for in that case disobedience would have amounted to a blasphemous repudiation of God's authority and would surely have been followed by death. The only instances of such a life-and-death encounter with a representative of God are expressed in the form of an 'angel' of God (*mal'ak yhwh*), where it is as if God himself is present (e.g. Gen. 16.13; Gen. 31.11-13).[68] The passages just quoted from Deuteronomy and Exodus are significant as evidence of the expectation (held at least as early as the Deuteronomist) that such a divinely authorised figure – a true representative of God – would appear at some time in the future, and this expectation was accompanied by the practical, or legal, considerations that any alleged appearance of such a figure would need to be authenticated before it could be acknowledged, but that once acknowledged the figure would demand total obedience, being nothing less than the agent and representative of God himself. This expectation was certainly still held in the time of Jesus,[69] and it is highly significant that the same two passages are alluded to in the narratives of Jesus' transfiguration:[70] the designation of him as Son of God clearly implied that he was God's authorised agent and representative.

If the question is now asked, when and how was Jesus actually acknowledged as Son of God, we can see that it could hardly have been in his lifetime. To have said of a person who appeared (as we have seen) to speak and act with absolute authority that he was 'Son of God' was to say much more than that he was innocent or pious: it was to acknowledge him to be God's actual representative on earth, to whom the same homage and obedience would be due as if one were suddenly in the presence of God himself. It is a sign of the historical faithfulness of the gospels that they give so few instances of Jesus' followers ever having reached this point: there is only the prostration of the disciples and their address to Jesus as Son of God after the walking on the water in Matthew's account (14.33), and this probably reflects the language of the church;[71] as does Peter's confession in the same gospel (16.16), which in any case is said to be based on a supernatural source of knowledge ('Flesh and blood have not revealed this to you'). Otherwise the only people to use the

[68] Cf. W. Eichrodt, *Theology of the Old Testament* 2 (E.tr. 1967) 23-4.

[69] Cf. above, n.67.

[70] The connection is assured by the phrase ἀκούετε αὐτοῦ (Mk. 9.7 and pars.) corresponding to εἰσάκουε αὐτοῦ Ex. 23.21, ὅς ἐὰν μὴ ἀκούσῃ . . . ὅσα ἐὰν λαλήσῃ ὁ προφήτης ἐκεῖνος Dt. 18. 19,22.

[71] The episode appears anomalous at this stage in the narrative (it anticipates Peter's confession in 16.16), and doubtless reflects church language; cf. H. J. Held in Bornkamm, Barth and Held, *Tradition and Interpretation in Matthew* (E.tr. 1963) 266; E. Schweizer, *Good News according to Matthew* (E.tr. 1976) 323; but, as my argument suggests, it is not necessarily 'Hellenistic' as claimed by e.g. F. Hahn, *The Titles of Jesus* (E.tr. 1969) 299.

title of Jesus in his lifetime are those who doubt or deny Jesus' authority (Mk. 14.61; Mt. 27.40-3): they have been led by appearances to disbelieve Jesus' claims, and therefore conclude they can safely reject the suggestion that he is (in any sense at all) 'Son of God'. The alternative – to accept the designation – would have involved total obedience and submission to him. This his enemies could never contemplate; and it is surely highly probable historically that none of the disciples, during his lifetime, reached the point of being able to say it, even though they understood and eventually recorded those indications of his obedience and authority which would have made the description appropriate. As we have seen, it was only heavenly voices, or the demons who recognised[72] and were made powerless by Jesus' divine authorisation, and who acknowledged him as Son of God in their moment of defeat, who could safely be reported as having used the phrase.

But all this was changed after Jesus' death. When the centurion at the cross pronounced Jesus to have been Son of God, this could have been taken to mean no more (on the lips of an outsider) than the statement that Jesus, like the just sufferer of Wisdom 2, was innocent despite the guilt implied by his execution. But to those who were aware of his constant obedience to the divine will, his apparent intimacy in prayer with his heavenly father, and his claim to authority in word and deed, the description implied nothing less than that Jesus was to be obeyed and revered as God's agent and representative: it was as if God himself were present in him. If during his lifetime they had hardly been able to risk this identification, the resurrection seemed to make it both plausible and possible. Accordingly, two 'resurrection appearances' are recorded in which the presence of Jesus is acknowledged to amount to the presence of God himself (the disciples 'prostrated themselves' Mt. 28.17, and Thomas addressed him as 'My Lord and my God', Jn. 20.28). In retrospect, there was no risk attached: it became a profession of faith that Jesus had indeed been Son of God – that is, God's authorised representative and agent on earth.

It is therefore not surprising that what may well be the earliest recorded instance of the Christian confession of Jesus as 'Son of God' (Romans 1. 3-4) should have associated the designation with the resurrection. Whatever else may have been meant by the statement that Jesus had 'been raised from the dead', this at least was intended: that he whose righteousness and whose exceptional claims to authority had been made problematic by his handing over to execution had been utterly vindicated by God. However much Jesus may have conducted himself in a way appropriate to one who could be described (in the various senses suggested above) as 'Son of God', the fact of the crucifixion had caused the question to remain open: it could either be a sign (as his enemies would maintain) that Jesus' claim to authority was

---

[72] That they were in a position to do so accords with contemporary demonology; cf. G. Vermes, *Jesus the Jew* 206-10.

spurious; or else (as Christians came to interpret it as early as the hymn preserved in Philippians 2) it could be seen as the ultimate act of obedience of the son who was to receive the name that is above every name. It was only by the resurrection that God (even for Christians) settled the matter by designating Jesus finally and definitely[73] as his Son (Romans 1.4; Acts 13.33). This did not mean that Jesus *became* Son of God only after the resurrection; but (as we have seen) there were good reasons for doubting whether anyone who encountered him in his lifetime would have taken the risk of acknowledging him as such. Only the demons must be supposed to have recognised Jesus' full authority, for this was the reason for their defeat. Otherwise it could only be supernatural attestations that would have articulated Jesus' divine authority: the voice of God at the Baptism and the Transfiguration,[74] and (according to subsequent reflection) the explanation (attributed to an angel) of the mysterious circumstances of his birth, which made him in some sense 'Son of God' from the moment of his conception.[75]

This review of the evidence confirms what we should in any case have expected: that the immediate followers of Jesus were strictly bound by the constraint of that monotheism which, as Jews, they instinctively professed, and in their attempts to declare who Jesus was they stopped well short of describing him as 'divine'. But at the same time the importance they assigned to the title 'Son of God' suggests that when it was accorded to such a person as Jesus was remembered to have been it was felt to imply the truth of those claims to divine authority which were characteristic of his whole style of action and utterance: Jesus had indeed shown that absolute obedience to God, had spoken of God with that intimate authority, and had acted with the unique authorisation which belonged to God's representative and agent on earth, which would be characteristic of one who was (in the senses usually ascribed to 'sonship' in antiquity) in very truth 'Son of God'; and the reversal of the world's judgment upon him, which was implied by the event his followers called 'the Resurrection', enabled them to describe Jesus with absolute confidence as 'the Son', a title which would certainly have been

[73] I accept the argument that ὁρισθείς in Romans 1.4 cannot mean *merely* 'declared', but a ὅρος is the definitive and acknowledged marker of a territorial situation which may have existed previously by consent.

[74] This proposal would make it unnecessary to assume that the application of Ps. 2.7 to Jesus at his baptism and transfiguration represents a *later* stage of christological development, as argued by, e.g. E. Schillebeeckx, *Jesus* 550ff.

[75] It has often been argued (e.g. H. A. Wolfson, *The Philosophy of the Church Fathers* (1956) 169–76, 292–3) that the virgin-birth story reflects a quite un-Jewish interest in God as the 'begetter' of the Son, Jesus Christ, and is therefore a 'Hellenistic' accretion. But Psalm 2.7 ('Thou art my son: this day have I begotten thee') was always understood metaphorically in Judaism (A. George, 'Jésus fils de Dieu dans St. Luc', *RB* 72 (1965) 185–209 at p.191), and even when brought to bear on the manner of Jesus' birth did not cause reflection on any form of physical or sexual divine parentage: 'the Holy Spirit is the agency of God's power, not a male partner in marriage' (R. Brown, *The Birth of the Messiah* (1977) 137). The gospel narratives in no way anticipate the later patristic interest in Jesus' precise relationship with God.

correct in his lifetime, and was presumably acknowledged by supernatural beings, but was too momentous to be openly acknowledged even by those of his followers who had found their way to faith in him.

Can we now take the argument one stage further back, and use this constraint (as we have used others) to increase our knowledge of Jesus himself? We may surely start from the assumption that he, as much as his followers, was subject to it: there is no evidence whatever that he spoke or acted as if he believed himself to be 'a god', or 'divine'. Even the attacks on his memory which are preserved in the Talmud make no reference to any such pretension, and the accusations levelled against him by 'the Jews' in the Fourth Gospel are not based on any explicit claims to divinity, but on inferences drawn from certain acts and sayings – inferences which are countered by showing that, far from usurping God's authority and power, Jesus was fully authorised to act as God's accredited agent. At the same time there is (as we have seen) an impressive body of evidence that Jesus combined and transcended the options normally available to a religious teacher and leader in his own culture. He assumed an authority to declare the will of God for men, and to act in accordance with that will, such as had not been claimed by any previous figure in the religious history of the Jews. 'By what authority?' was the question raised again and again by his teaching, his healing acts and his prophetic stance;[76] and he seems deliberately to have made the question more insistent by speaking of the present moment as one of crisis and ultimate decision. My argument so far would suggest that to describe himself, directly or by implication, as 'the Son of God' would have been a way – perhaps the only available way – of claiming such unprecedented divine authorisation, at the same time as preserving intact that respect for the indivisible oneness of God which was the instinctive possession of any religious Jew. Is there any evidence that this was in fact the option chosen by Jesus? I suggest that there are two factors which point clearly in this direction:

(i) There is a remarkably consistent body of evidence in the gospels that Jesus addressed God as his father with a singular and possibly unprecedented intimacy. I say 'possibly' because it is important not to overstate the case. It is true that the use of *abba* as a form of address to God, which was undoubtedly characteristic of Jesus and was subsequently adopted by his followers, has no precedent in any Jewish literature known to us, and may well represent a radical innovation;[77] but it must also be remembered that the so-called 'charismatic' teachers of the time – those whom the Jewish tradition called

---

[76] Only once explicitly (Mk. 11.28 pars.), but it is implied by the recognition of the crowds of his ἐξουσία (Mk. 1.22, Mt. 9.8, Lk. 4.32, etc.) and by the alternative explanations offered by those who could not accept his authority, that he was out of his mind (Mk. 3.21) or an agent of the devil (3.22).

[77] The argument has been stated many times by J. Jeremias, e.g. *The Prayers of Jesus* (E.tr. 1967) 9-67. For a careful evaluation, cf. J. Dunn, *Jesus and the Spirit* (1975) 22-4.

'men of deed'[78] – adopted a style of almost bantering intimacy with God which is not so very different. Moreover one of them – Honi – was remembered as referring to himself as a 'son of the house',[79] which was evidently understood to convey an authority that stemmed from at least an unusual degree of intimacy with the divine will.[80] The closeness to God which is suggested by many of Jesus' prayers and sayings is therefore not necessarily to be seen as a radically new assault on that sense of distance from God which was characteristic of the religious thinking of his people. In the same way, to stress (as Jesus did) the fatherhood of God in general in the context of prayer and worship was not to say anything which would not have been readily grasped and accepted by his contemporaries, whether Jews or pagans; and to address God as one's father in a more personal way was recognised, at least in some circles, as a privilege which might possibly be claimed by an exceptionally wise and god–fearing man. But Jesus' *abba*-father language, even if not completely unparalleled, seems to have struck his contemporaries as going beyond such familiar examples: it was felt to be his characteristic mode of prayer, well documented in the synoptic gospels, greatly elaborated in the Fourth Gospel, and boldly adopted (doubtless on the authority of Jesus' teaching) by his followers. Moreover there are three sayings recorded in the synoptic gospels which confirm Jesus' claim to a particular degree of 'sonship'. One I have already discussed: 'No one knows the father but the son' (Mt. 11. 27). The second is complementary to it: 'That hour no one knows, not even the son, but only the father' (Mk. 13.32). In view of the manifest concern, first of one of the evangelists,[81] and then of a number of copyists,[82] to eliminate this apparent restriction of Jesus' supreme authority, the saying must be accepted as authentic. Indeed on our agency model it is not difficult to understand. The son is the authorised agent of his father's interests. But just as in business the principal will keep certain matters in his own hands, so the divine father can be expected to restrict the sphere even of his son's agency in certain respects: Jesus might be 'the son', but still not be entrusted with knowledge of the Hour. The third passage is the parable of the Wicked Vinedresser. It has often been doubted whether the original hearers of this parable would have identified the son, sent by the father to claim the harvest, with Jesus.[83] The saviour whom the Jews expected (it is argued) was thought of as Messiah, not Son of God, and therefore the story

[78] See above, pp.104,107.

[79] 'I am as a son of the house before thee', M. Taan. 3.8

[80] S. Safrai, 'The Teaching of Pietists in Mishnaic Literature' *JJS* 16 (1965) 15–33 at p.19 denies that it meant more than 'domestic slave'; G. Vermes, *Jesus the Jew* 210 and n.86 argues that it was understood to mean 'son of God'.

[81] Luke (21.33–4) omits the verse altogether, though he implies it at Acts. 1.7.

[82] From a corrector of Sinaiticus onwards in Matthew (24.36), from a tenth–century uncial onwards in Mark.

[83] E.g. K. Klostermann, *Das Markus-Evangelium* (1936) Mk. 12.6; W. Kümmel, *Promise and Fulfilment* (E.tr. 1957) 83.

(if it goes back to Jesus at all) must have made its point, not as an indication of Jesus' authority and mission, but as a general illustration of the dangers of unfaithful guardianship. But apart from the fact that an allegorical interpretation was built into the parable right from the beginning with the allusion to Isaiah's allegory of the vineyard, so that its hearers could expect to find at least God and themselves depicted in it, the connotations which (I have been arguing) belonged to the idea of 'son' itself would have made it clear that the story turned on the arrival of the one who was at last the father's fully authorised agent. And since the question of authority and authorisation had been raised again and again by Jesus' activity, the connection would hardly have been difficult to make. Now it is notable that in none of these three sayings does Jesus explicitly say that he *is* the son. But it seems to be one of the most securely established characteristics of Jesus' manner of speech that often he left it to his hearers to make the decisive connection; indeed his fondness for the self-designation 'Son of Man' may be explained, at least in part, as a means by which Jesus could speak of himself without forcing his hearers to acknowledge him as the possessor of ultimate authority – the Son of Man always *could* be understood (if one wished to evade the issue) as someone else.[84] That Jesus referred to himself as Son of God in a similarly oblique way would be of a piece with his chosen style.

(ii) When I observed at the beginning of this enquiry that Jesus' conduct seems to have raised the question of legality without being indisputably illegal, I reserved discussion of the one charge which is explicitly laid against Jesus in both the synoptics and John's gospel, that of blasphemy. Our ability to understand the significance of this charge has been much impaired by the rabbinic definition of it (i.e. the offence of pronouncing the divine Name[85]) according to which Jesus would apparently have been innocent of the offence. But there is evidence to suggest that the charge would have been more widely interpreted by a court in the time of Jesus,[86] and it remains the one on which he is most likely to have been arraigned (even if, as I have argued, the court could not agree on his guilt). The offence consisted, fundamentally, of diminishing God's honour by usurping some privilege or prerogative due to him alone.[87] Note was taken of the fact that the death penalty was incurred by dishonouring one's father and mother just as by blaspheming God; and analogies were drawn between the two offences, such that blasphemy could be understood along the same lines as filial disrespect: you must not deprive

[84] Cf. M. Casey, *Son of Man* (1979) for a recent statement of the view that the original Aramaic phrase could be used to make a general statement which the listener might (but need not necessarily) see exemplified by the speaker.

[85] M. Sanh. 7.5

[86] Cf. Harvey, *Jesus on Trial* 77-81. My argument has little to add to the points made long ago by G. Dalman, *Der Gottesname Adonaj* (1889) 43-9.

[87] Cf. J. D. M. Derrett, *Law in the New Testament* 454; H. Beyer, *TWNT* 1.621, 'Antastung der Majestät Gottes'.

God of his rights and dues any more than your parents. In each case the penalty is death.[88] This understanding of blasphemy is neatly exemplified by the cure of the paralytic: Jesus is said to be 'blaspheming' on the grounds that he is usurping God's prerogative of pronouncing the forgiveness of sins (Mk. 2.7). Similarly in John's gospel: by claiming the right to work (as only God can) on the sabbath day, Jesus is making himself 'equal to God' – which is a capital offence (5.18).[89] Such a charge would normally be countered by denying that the utterance or action in question had taken place, or, if it had, that its intention or effect were blasphemous. But there was a further possible line of defence. The alleged blasphemer might have been authorised by God to act or speak as his agent. Far from being an infringement of God's prerogative, the deed might have been carried out or the word spoken on God's behalf: it was as if God himself were present. In this sense, as we have seen,[90] certain Old Testament figures were rescued from the imputation of having usurped God's prerogatives by being recognised as God's 'agents'. It follows from our earlier discussion that one way of describing such a divine agent was as 'Son of God'. The son would be presumed to be acting with his father's authorisation; therefore his conduct could not be blasphemous. If Jesus claimed to be Son of God, and if this claim were true, then words or actions which would normally have seemed blasphemous would not be so, for they would have been authorised by God. Equally, if the claim were false, the defence would fall. To put the matter another way: to call oneself 'Son of God' was not in itself blasphemous or punishable at law (though it might be unjustified and reprehensible). But if one did so as a defence against the charge of blasphemy, it would be understood as a claim to be speaking or acting with the authorisation of God. If the defence were found to be false, it would be as blasphemous as the original offence. This explains why the designation 'Son of God' appears in connection with blasphemy in the synoptic accounts of the hearing before the Sanhedrin. It explains also the statement attributed to the Jewish leaders in John's gospel (which otherwise would have no foundation in the Jewish legal system): 'We have a law, and by that law he ought to die, because he said I am the Son of God' (19.7). That Jesus claimed (even if only implicitly) to be Son of God is a probable inference from one of the most securely attested facts about him: that he was charged with the offence of blasphemy.

The sharper delineation of Jesus' relationship to God which we have obtained by this study is the result of the tension between two factors: on the one hand there was the constraint of monotheism, which I have argued was implicitly submitted to by Jesus and by his immediate followers, and which

[88] Philo, *De dec*. 107, 111, 119-20. For a possible juridical connection between the two offences, cf. Z. W. Falk, *Introduction* . . . 2. 156-7.

[89] Cf. 2 Macc. 9.12: Antiochus (called βλάσφημος in 9.28) remorsefully declares that a just man should not θνητὸν ὄντα ἰσόθεα (v.l. ὑπερήφανα) φρονεῖν.

[90] Cf. above, n.56.

excluded any style of action on his part, or any form of acclamation on theirs, which would have imputed to him a claim to divinity; on the other was the necessity felt by Jesus to assume a unique and god-given authority for his words and deeds, and the concern of his followers to find means of expressing his superiority to any other person who had claimed to speak and act with the authority of God. It was this tension which caused Jesus to challenge his contemporaries again and again with the question of his own authority, and which led his followers (once they had come to the point of acknowledging this authority) to advance for him the claims which were implied in the designation 'Son of God'. Jesus, it was believed, had shown total obedience to the divine will, he had given his teaching with the authority which only a son can have when instructed by a father, and he had acted as nothing less than God's representative and agent on earth. Therefore he was, in all these senses, 'God's son'; and since, when the son is known to be acting as the father's authorised agent, it is as if the father is actually present in the son, it followed that it was appropriate to pay to the son the respect and honour which are due to God himself. This was as far, indeed, as the constraint of monotheism would allow them to go. But perhaps it was as far (in their culture at least) as anyone needed to go.[91] When Thomas called Jesus 'My Lord and my God', we do not have to suppose that he, or the evangelist, was flouting the constraint of his instinctive monotheism; rather he is portrayed as acknowledging Jesus to be the fully accredited divine agent, to speak to whom was as if to speak to God himself.[92] In much the same way, when Matthew tells the story of Jesus walking on the water, he ends by reporting that the disciples prostrated themselves before him (14.33). We need not think that Matthew is here ignoring the normal constraint of monotheism and for once allowing his narrative to be influenced by Hellenistic stories of gods appearing on earth thinly disguised as human beings. It is rather that at this moment (as it seemed to this evangelist) the disciples momentarily recognised Jesus as the fully authorised son and agent of God, and registered the momentous consequences of this recognition by prostrating themselves as if in the presence of God himself.

This understanding of the implications of sonship, and of the over-whelming authority possessed by Jesus if he was indeed (in all the senses described) 'Son of God', enabled the first followers of Jesus to use the title as a way of stating his unique relationship with God, and his total authority over

---

[91] Though there were other ways of seeking to express Jesus' unique authority within this constraint: hence the attempt in the early Jewish-Christian church to formulate christology in terms of a superior 'angel', i.e. one invested with power to act on God's behalf (like the *mal'ak yhwh*): this is the σεμνότατος ἄγγελος of Hermas *Vis.*, 5.2 (other instances collected by J. Barbel, *Christos Angelos* (1941) 47-50); or in terms of God's 'name' (cf. J. Daniélou, *Théologie du Judéo-Christianisme* (1958) 199ff.). Trypho the Jew is a typical witness to the difficulties for Christology caused by the Jewish constraint of monotheism, Justin, *Dial.* 48-9.

[92] There is good Old Testament precedent for this in the *mal'ak yhwh*, Gen. 16.13; 31.11, etc. Cf. W. Eichrodt, *Theology of the Old Testament* 2.24.

us which flows from that relationship. Jesus, in his teaching, his prophetic actions, and in the obedience which led to his death, was acting as God's agent and representative on earth. It was as if, when he spoke and acted, God himself was present. In Luke's phrase, 'God was with him'; in Paul's, 'God was in Christ'. That this was so had been demonstrated by the resurrection, after which Jesus had necessarily been given the highest place, under God, which could be awarded to any living being. Christians could now confidently join in the worship and praise due to one who had been given (again under God) a name which is above every name, and through whom the Holy Spirit was now active among those who acknowledged his lordship. It was as far as one could possibly go (these Christians felt) in ascribing unique dignity to Jesus consistently with respecting the constraint of monotheism. In later times the church, no longer perhaps perceiving the power and decisiveness of the agent–son–representative model, and having among its members men used to a more philosophical analysis, felt it necessary to go considerably further in the direction of a metaphysical identity between Jesus and his heavenly father: released from the constraint of Jewish monotheism, gentile Christians began to think of Jesus as also, in some sense, God. In the last few years it has come to be questioned whether the resultant construction of Jesus as 'God incarnate' is either credible or intelligible today. I have argued that the earliest Christians were constrained to stop considerably short of this; but that by acknowledging Jesus to be Son of God in all the senses which that phrase suggested to them they were able to say all they needed about his unique authority and power. Indeed the fact that they felt able to do this is itself a piece of hard historical evidence which throws light not only on the nature of the conviction they had reached at and after the resurrection, but also on the nature of the challenge presented by Jesus in his lifetime, a challenge which is capable of being presented with as much force today as it ever has been in the past.

# Appendix I

## The Interpretation of Acts 13:27-8
### (see p.21)

The passage in Acts runs (13.27-8): οἱ γὰρ κατοικοῦντες ἐν Ἰερουσαλὴμ καὶ οἱ ἄρχοντες αὐτῶν τοῦτον ἀγνοήσαντες καὶ τὰς φωνὰς τῶν προφητῶν τὰς κατὰ πᾶν σάββατον ἀναγινωσκομένας κρίναντες ἐπλήρωσαν, καὶ μηδεμίαν αἰτίαν θανάτου εὑρόντες ᾐτήσαντο Πιλᾶτον ἀναιρεθῆναι αὐτόν. This passage appears to contain an oxymoron. κρίναντες should mean 'having condemned (him)', but the very next clause states that 'they found no cause of death in him'. To make sense of the passage, it is necessary to reduce the tension between the clauses by taking one of them in a different sense.

The great majority of commentators choose to take κρίναντες at its face value, and pay no attention to the remarkable omission of the 'judgment' at Lk. 22.71 (though Blinzler sees the difficulty, and suggests that Luke was anxious to spare his gentile readers the confusion they would have felt if they had been told that Jesus was twice convicted in two different courts, *Prozess*[4] (1969) 172, 428 n.10). They then have to explain the phrase 'having found no cause of death in him', and seek to do so by suggesting that it represents the point of view of the speaker (Peter) or of the author of Acts – they found nothing that was *really* a cause of death in him. So, e.g., D. R. Catchpole, *Trial* (1971) 184-5; Blinzler, *Prozess*[4] 435; U. Wilckens, *Missionsreden* 134-5. D. Flusser, *Jesus* 141 n.209 goes so far as to say, 'Lk. selbst hat offenbar gemeint, die Juden hatten Jesus zum Tod verurteilt'!

The strain placed by this approach on the plain meaning of the words is only too evident. The alternative is to take this phrase at its face value, and see whether κρίναντες can easily be taken in a different sense (so P. Winter, *On the Trial* 28, 48). This is not nearly so difficult. A glance at the dictionary shows that κρίνω can mean simply 'take a decision'; indeed there is an excellent parallel in Acts itself, when Festus says 'I decided to send him', ἔκρινα πέμπειν (25.25). We do no violence to the word if we take it in this sense in 13.27 ('they fulfilled the scriptures by their decision') and we remove the apparent contradiction.

That this is the correct solution is confirmed by a number of other arguments:

(i) Apart from the account of the trial in Mk. and Mt., and three passages related to it (Mk. 10.33; Mt. 20.18; Mt. 27.3), the treatment of Jesus by the Jews is nowhere in the New Testament referred to as a 'judgment' or a condemnation, always as a 'handing over'.

(ii) Luke omits those words in Mark which might be taken as a verdict (Lk. 22.71; Mk. 14.64).

(iii) Luke omits the word κατακρινοῦσιν from the third passion prediction (Lk. 18.32; Mk. 10.33).

(iv) In Acts 5.39 Gamaliel is made to allow for the possibility that the Christian movement is of God. He could not plausibly have done so if (in Luke's view) he had known that the Sanhedrin had condemned Jesus.

(v) Jesus' burial in a private tomb, which is stressed by Luke (Acts 13.29), would have been impossible, according to the Mishnah (Sanh. 6.5), if Jesus had been condemned to death by a Jewish court.

(vi) The malefactor's statement (Lk. 23.41) οὐδὲν ἄτοπον ἔπραξεν would lose its plausibility if Luke intended us to understand that Jesus had just been convicted in a Jewish court.

The cumulative force of these arguments seems to me to make it impossible to take κρίναντες in 13.27 in the sense of 'condemn', in which case Luke's view must be represented by the plain meaning of the statement that the Jews 'found no cause of death in him'.

# *Appendix II*
## Alleged Messianic Pretenders
### (see p.85)

(a) Judas son of Ezechias, Simon and Athronges (Jos. *Ant.* 17. 271ff.). Hengel, *Die Zeloten*[2] (1976) 296-307 observes that Simon and Athronges were of exceptional stature, a Messianic trait (Ps. 89.19, where however, the sense is uncertain). It is true that a Talmudic tradition (Lam. R. ii. 2.4.) reports that R. Aqiba acknowledged Bar Kochba as Messiah because of his supernatural strength, but this is at best a tenuous argument, as is Hengel's further point that the name Athronges might be connected with Ethrog. Josephus' own description of these men as rebels who aspired to the Kingship is not only plausible in itself, but is confirmed by Tacitus' report on the same Simon, *regium nomen invaserat* (*Hist.* 5.9). The burden of proof must lie with those who wish to find 'messianic' traits in these leaders: and no evidence for their case is available.

(b) The rebel leader Menahem captured the palace in Jerusalem and behaved for a short time οἷα δὴ βασιλεύς (Jos. *B.J.*2. 434). Here again there is no hint of any religious dimension in the episode. Hengel, loc. cit., suggests that this may be the same Menahem who turns up (this time as the son of Hezekiah) in a rabbinic reminiscence as a Messianic figure who was born the day the temple was destroyed (Lam. R. 1.16 = yBer 5a 12ff.). But this again can hardly be regarded as serious evidence; cf. M. de Jonge, *Josephus - Studien* (Festschrift für O. Michel) 216-17.

(c) A leader of a Jewish revolt in Cyrenaica in the reign of Trajan called Lukuas by Eusebius, Andreas by Dio (for refs. see Schürer 1. 531). Papyrus finds illuminate this rebellion. Their editor, Tcherikover, argues that it, and therefore its leader, must have been messianic; but his argument is a *priori*, and no evidence is adduced (*CPJ* 1.86-92).

(d) Bar Kochba achieved considerable military and political successes: complete control over Jerusalem, coins and legal documents dated by 'the Year of the freedom of Israel', etc. He was acknowledged Messiah by R. Aqiba – but did he claim this for himself? bSanh. 93b states that he did, but only after 'he had reigned for two-and-a-half years'. The accuracy of the figure is immaterial. The important point is that subsequent rabbinic tradition took it for granted that no one would 'claim' to be Messiah until he had considerable achievements behind him. Something resembling a 'messianic age' would have to come into being before the question could be seriously raised. Indeed, the analogy of Sabbatai Sevi and R. Nathan suggests that it may well have been R. Aqiba who first suggested the idea (G. Scholem, *Sabbatai Sevi* (1973) 383ff.).

# Appendix III

## The Divinity of Jesus in the New Testament
### (see p.157)

The texts which may be adduced as evidence that Jesus was called 'God' or 'divine' in the New Testament are as follows:

(i) Romans 9.5: ἐξ ὧν ὁ Χριστὸς τὸ κατὰ σάρκα ὁ ὢν ἐπὶ πάντων θεὸς εὐλογητὸς εἰς τοὺς αἰῶνας, ἀμήν.

This kind of doxology inserted into a discourse is characteristic both of Paul (Romans 1.25; 11.36; 2 Cor. 11.31; Gal. 1.5; Phil. 4.20) and of rabbinic literature. The question is one of punctuation: is it grammatically connected to the preceding clause, qualifying ὁ Χριστός, or does it stand on its own? A certain answer cannot be given; but the great majority of recent commentators and translators accept the second alternative; cf., e.g., H. Lietzmann, *An die Römer* (1928) ad loc.

(ii) Titus 2.13: προσδεχόμενοι τὴν μακαρίαν ἐλπίδα καὶ ἐπιφάνειαν τῆς δόξης τοῦ μεγάλου θεοῦ καὶ σωτῆρος ἡμῶν Χριστοῦ Ἰησοῦ.

This is a similar question: does it mean 'our great God and Saviour Jesus Christ'? or 'the great God and our Saviour Jesus Christ'? The fathers unanimously (apart from the Ambrosiaster) opted for the first, and there are strong stylistic and contextual arguments on their side (cf. C. Spicq, *Les Épîtres Pastorales* (1947) 265-6). Yet an impressive array of recent commentators takes the opposite view (Dibelius–Conzelmann, 1955; Kelly, 1963; Houlden, 1976; and Wettstein, Grotius and de Wette among those of earlier centuries). The decision has usually depended on the presuppositions of the commentators. H. Meyer was one of the few Protestant scholars to take the opposite view.

(iii) 1 Tim. 3.16 ὅς (v.l. θεὸς) ἐφανερώθη ἐν σαρκί.

The v.l. is attested in the Koine, but can hardly stand as the original reading, and is easily explicable as a device to make the hymn grammatically independent (Dibelius), or as a simple error (Houlden).

(iv) Jn. 1.1: ὁ λόγος ἦν πρὸς τὸν θεόν, καὶ θεὸς ἦν ὁ λόγος.

The relevance of this is easily expressed in a syllogism:

(a) The Word was God;
(b) Jesus was the Word;     *therefore*
(c) Jesus was God.

But both premises require some qualification.

(a) At the conclusion of his discussion of the opening words of the Prologue, C. H. Dodd (*The Fourth Gospel* (1955), 280) writes that 'they are clearly intelligible only when we admit that λόγος, though it carries with it the associations of the Old Testament Word of the Lord, has also a meaning similar to that which it bears in Stoicism as modified by Philo, and parallel to the idea of Wisdom in other Jewish writers'. This analysis precludes the meaning 'The Word was (a second) God' or 'The Word was (identical with) God' (for which the Greek would be ὁ θεός: Philo is careful to maintain the distinction between θεός = divine and ὁ θεός = God Himself, Dodd loc. cit.). If, then, the Word is neither an independent god nor identical with the one God, the phrase can only mean that the word was (an expression or reflection of) God (cf. Wisdom 7.25-6), that it was (in some sense divine, i.e. of) God.

(b) The second premise is not stated explicitly in the Fourth Gospel. It is of course true that the reader is intended to understand the Logos as referring to Jesus, but this is not necessarily to say that Jesus was identical with the Word. The relationship requires a more careful articulation such as is again offered by Dodd (op. cit. 285): 'the Prologue is an account of the life of Jesus under the form of a description of the eternal Logos in its relations with the world and with man, and the rest of the gospel an account of the Logos under the form of a record of the life of Jesus'.

The premises of the syllogism now have to be rephrased in some such form as the following:

> (a) The Word was an expression of God's activity;
> (b) Jesus could for certain purposes be described as the Word.

The conclusion cannot therefore be pressed beyond a statement such as

> (c) Jesus could for certain purposes be described as an expression of God's activity.

This is certainly not what is normally meant by Divinity.

(v) John 1.18: μονογενὴς θεός (v.l. ὁ μονογενὴς υἱός), ὁ ὢν εἰς τὸν κόλπον τοῦ πατρός κτλ.

The currently accepted canons of textual criticism (*difficilior lectio* and the antiquity of the reading in $P^{66}$) would seem to impose the reading μονογενὴς θεός; but both sense and context demand υἱός (so e.g. R. V. Tasker, *The Greek New Testament* (1964) 424-5, justifying the text adopted by the *NEB*; C. K. Barrett, *The Gospel according to St. John*[2] (1977) 169). Palaeographically the change is easy to explain; if υἱός is original, we must admit that the less original reading began to be exploited for the purpose of christological debate at a very early date.

(vi) 1 John 5.20: ἐσμὲν . . . ἐν τῷ υἱῷ αὐτοῦ Ἰησοῦ Χριστῷ, οὗτός ἐστιν ὁ ἀληθινὸς θεὸς καὶ ζωὴ αἰώνιος.

Grammatically, this is again ambiguous. For a modern discussion, cf. A. Segond, *RH PhR* 45 (1965), 349-51. Most British commentators (e.g. Dodd, Houlden) follow Westcott (1902): 'The most natural reference (of οὗτος) is to the subject not locally nearest but dominant in the mind of the apostle . . . This is obviously "he that is true" further described by the addition of "His Son".'

(vii) *Unity with God* is predicated of Jesus in the fourth gospel (10.30) and forms the basis of an accusation against him of blasphemy (10.33). But the argument of the chapter is clearly intended to refute the suggestion that this unity implies *identity* with God: Jesus' answer amounts to a re-statement of the claim that he is the Son of God, and that he is a fully authorised divine agent in that the Father is in him and he in the Father (10. 37-38).

(viii) *Pre-existence* is certainly attributed to Jesus in John's gospel (1.1; 8.58; 17.24), and possibly in Paul (Col. 1.15 – though this is disputed by e.g. J. Dunn, *Christology in the Making* (1980) 38-45 – Romans 8.3 and Gal. 4.4) and Hebrews 1.2. But it is important to state clearly exactly what is implied by this. In all these cases (except John 8.58, though here, too, it may be implied) we are told that Jesus was present *at the creation of the world*. The prototype for such 'pre-existence' is undoubtedly the figure of Wisdom; and Wisdom's presence at the creation was a way of saying that no part of creation is an afterthought: it was all there at the beginning. So with Jesus. He is not an afterthought, but was part of creation. The same was believed of the Messiah, whose 'name' was there at the beginning. But no one thought of the Messiah as 'divine'. Pre-existence, in this sense, hardly implies divinity; though I would agree with, for instance, J. Dunn's recent conclusion (ib. 254-6) that it was the early application of this Wisdom-language to Jesus which was the most immediate antecedent to the development of the doctrine of the incarnation. I would not wish to deny that the seeds of a later Christology are present in the New Testament, nor that the subsequent doctrine of the divinity of Christ may have been a proper or even inevitable development. I am concerned only to show that there is no unambiguous evidence that the constraint of monotheism was effectively broken by any New Testament writer.

# Index

## PRIMARY SOURCES

1. Old Testament   2. New Testament   3. Apocrypha
4. Pseudepigrapha   5. Dead Sea Scrolls   6. Rabbinic Writings
7. Greek and Latin Authors   8. Inscriptions, Papyri etc.

### 1. OLD TESTAMENT

Genesis: *16.13*, 165, 172; *31.11*, 172; *31.11-13*, 165; *49.11*, 124

Exodus: *22.18*, 40; *23.20*, 164; *23.21*, 165

Leviticus: *11*, 39, *19.9-10*, 143; *20.10*, 55; *20.27*, 40

Numbers: *16.15*, 124

Deuteronomy: *14*, 39; *17.12*, 58f; *18.10*, 104; *18.15*, 146, 147; *18.18-20*, 59, 150, 164; *18.20*, 165; *21.18-21*, 159; *21.22-3*, 21; *21-23*, 22; *24.1*, 55

Judges: *5.10*, 125; *9.23*, 117; *10.4*, 125

1 Samuel: *16.14ff*, 117; *18.10*, 117; *25.41*, 161

2 Samuel: *10.1ff*, 162; *20.18-22*, 25

1 Kings: *11.29ff*, 130; *19.20*, 60; *22.11*, 130

2 Kings: *2.12*, 33; *4.29*, 61; *9.13*, 125; *18.37f*, 33

Nehemiah: *13.4-13*, 133

Job: *31.1*, 55; *31.9*, 55; *38ff*, 145

Psalms: *2*, 140; *2.7*, 167; *22*, 148; *22.19*, 163; *69.9*, 133; *74*, 146; *89.4*, 69; *89.19*, 175; *90*, 69; *118.25*, 126; *119.24*, 44

Proverbs: *3.11-12*, 159; *3.27*, 9; *3.27-8*, 143; *4.1*, 160; *4.4*, 159; *8.22-3*, 146; *20.22*, 56

Isaiah: *11.1*, 3; *20.1ff*, 130; *26.14*, 151; *26.19*, 151; *35.5f*, 115, 153; *40.12*, 145; *41.24*, 144; *42*, 147; *42.1*, 141; *42.1-4*, 141, 152; *42.6*, 147; *42.7*, 152; *43.15*, 144; *44.6*, 144; *50.6*, 34; *52.7*, 142, 144, 152; *52.10*, 144; *53*, 18, 23, 24, 148; *53.5*, 24; *53.6*, 23; *53.7*, 34; *53.12*, 22–4; *54.13*, 146; *56.7*, 132; *59.14-20*, 133; *61*, 143; *61.1*, 140, 141, 142, 152; *61.1-2*, 141

Jeremiah: *3.19-20*, 159; *7.11*, 132; *16.5-7*, 60; *26.7-19*, 28; *27*, 132; *31.31-4*, 146; *38.34*, 146

Ezekiel: *20.25*, 48; *24.15ff*, 60

Daniel: *2.38-44*, 144; *4.17*, 144; *4.25*, 144; *4.32*, 144; *12.2LXX*, 151

Hosea: *1.2*, 130; *6.2-3LXX*, 128; *6.5*, 134; *6.5-6*, 133; *6.6*, 134

Zechariah: *9.9*, 120, 135; *14.21*, 133, 135

Malachi: *1.6*, 159; *1.14*, 144; *2.14-16*, 56; *3.1*, 164; *3.1-3*, 133; *4.5f*, 61


### 2. NEW TESTAMENT

Matthew: *5.17-20*, 54; *5.19*, 54; *5.20*, 65; *5.48*, 65; *8.22*, 47, 59; *9.8*, 168; *9.27-31*, 115; *9.29*, 108; *9.32-4*, 115; *9.36*, 111; *10.2*, 81; *10.33*, 163; *10.40*, 162; *11.4-6*, 83, 141, 153; *11.12*, 47; *11.26-7*, 160; *11.27*, 169; *12.18-21*, 141, 152; *12.27*, 99; *12.30*, 47, 50; *12.43-5*, 109; *14.14*, 111; *14.33*, 112, 165, 172; *15.4*, 54; *15.15*, 39; *15.20*, 54; *15.24*, 162; *15.30*, 115; *15.31*, 115; *15.32*, 111, 16.6, 81; *16.16*, 165; *19.4-5*, 64; *19.9*, 54; *20.18*, 20, 22; *20.34*, 111; *21.5*, 122; *21.11*, 58, 135; *21.23*, 134; *21.46*, 58, 135; *22.35-40*, 54; *23.2*, 54; *23.3*, 65; *23.13ff*, 54; *23.23*, 64; *23.37*, 148; *24.3*, 57; *24.20*, 61; *24.36*, 169; *24.40-1*, 61; *25.13*, 87; *25.14*, 23; *26.6*, 40; *26.59-61*, 32; *26.59-66*, 20; *26.61*, 28; *26.63*, 81; *26.65*, 33; *27.3*, 20, 22; *27.16*, 18, 80; *27.40-3*, 166; *27.43*, 148, 163, 166; *28.17*, 166; *28.20*, 54

Mark: *1.22*, 168; *1.27*, 54; *1.41*, 111; *1.43*, 114; *2.1-12*, 115; *2.7*, 171; *2.8*, 106; *2.18*, 50, 62; *2,23-8*, 38, 61; *2.25f*, 51; *3.6*, 29; *3.10*, 101; *3.21*, 168; *3.22*, 168; *4.25*, 143; *5.17*, 105; *6.4*, 58, 135; *6.15*, 58, 135; *6.34*, 111; *7.2*, 50; *7.3ff*, 52; *7.10*, 54; *7.17*, 39, 114; *7.19*, 39, 40, 54; *7.32-5*, 115; *7.33*, 108; *8.2*, 111; *8.17-21*, 113; *8.22-6*, 115; *8.23*, 108; *8.28*, 58, 135; *8.29*, 82; *8.38*, 163; *9.1*, 89; *9.7*, 165; *9.10*, 151; *9.31*, 24; *9.37*, 162; *10.6-8*, 51; *10.8*, 157; *10.10*, 114; *10.17*, 45; *10.20*, 45; *10.23*, 141; *10.25*, 141; *10.26*, 141; *10.33*, 20, 22, 24, 174; *10.34*, 24; *10.45*, 24; *10.46-52*, 115; *11.2*, 122; *11.3*, 123; *11.10*, 128; *11.27*, 48; *11.28*, 131, 134, 168; *12.17*, 47; *12.29*, 157; *12.28-34*, 54; *12.33*, 36, 64; *12.34*, 47; *12.36*, 64; *13.2*, 32; *13.3*, 57; *13.10*, 87; *13.22*, 169; *13.28-9*, 87; *13.33*, 87; *13.35*, 88; *13.37*, 88; *14.3*, 40; *14.7*, 143; *14.55*, 31; *14.55-9*, 32; *14.55-64*, 20; *14.56*, 32; *14.58*, 28; *14.61*, 81, 82, 166; *14.64*, 22, 34, 174; *15.1*, 29; *15.7*, 85; *15.10*, 26

Luke: *2.14*, 127; *2.26*, 80; *2.47*, 163; *2.49*, 163; *4.16-30*, 140; *4.18*, 141; *4.18-19*, 141; *4.32*, 168; *4.43*, 162; *6.11*, 22; *6.15*, 46; *6.18-19*, 108; *6.20*, 141; *7.13*, 111; *7.22*, 83, 141, 153; *9.20*, 80; *9.26*, 163; *9.27*, 89; *9.48*, 162; *9.60*, 59; *10.4*, 61; *10.22*, 160; *11.24-6*, 109; *11.47*, 148; *12.9*, 163; *12.13-14*, 52; *12.37*, 88; *12.40*, 87; *12.46*, 87; *12.51-3*, 61; *12.55-6*, 87; *13.15*, 51; *18.32*, 174; *19.30*, 122; *19.37*, 122, 125; *19.38*, 145; *19.39*, 125; *20.1-2*, 134; *20.16*, 163; *21.5*, 57; *21.33-4*, 169; *22.25*, 46; *22.69*, 138; *22.71*, 21, 174; *23.2*, 33, 80; *23.19*, 85; *23.35*, 80, 81; *23.41*, 175; *23.51*, 31; *24.19*, 58, 135

John: *1.1*, 176, 177; *1.18*, 177; *1.48*, 106; *2.18*, 134; *2.19*, 28; *2.22*, 122; *2.25*, 106; *3.2-3*, 83; *4.18*, 106; *4.25*, 147; *5.1-9*, 38, 115; *5.16*, 38; *5.17*, 62; *5.18*, 19, 171; *6.6*, 122; *6.15*, 105, 144; *7.30*, 19; *7.48-9*, 78; *8.58*, 177; *8.59*, 19; *9.1-7*, 38; *9.1-7*, 115; *9.2-3*, 117; *9.6*, 108; *9.16*, 38; *9.32*, 115; *10.11*, 24; *10.20f*, 78; *10.30*, 177; *10.31*, 19; *10.33*, 157, 177; *10.37-8*, 177; *10.38*, 113; *11*, 27; *11.4*, 122; *11.53*, 34; *12.13*, 145; *12.14*, 122; *12.15*, 122; *12.16*, 122; *12.49*, 162; *13.20*, 162; *13.28-9*, 122; *16.12*, 122; *17.24*, 177; *18.30*, 26; *18,31*, 19; *18.36ff*, 128; *18.37*, 20; *19.7*, 171; *20.24*, 81; *20.28*, 166; *20.30*, 100; *21.2*, 81

Acts: *1.6*, 145; *1.7*, 169; *2.36*, 137, 151; *3.14*, 138; *3.17*, 22; *3.18*, 80; *3.22*, 164; *4.25*, 127; *4.27*, 139, 140, 152; *5.30*, 21; *5.38-9*, 59; *5.39*, 174; *6.11*, 53; *6.14*, 28; *7.52*, 138; *7.56*, 138; *10.14*, 36; *10.37f*, 9; *10.38*, 139, 140; *10.39*, 21; *13.27*, 22, 174, 175; *13.27f*, 174; *13.29*, 21, 174; *13.33*, 167; *14.11*, 156; *14.14*, 33; *19.14ff*, 109; *21.21*, 53; *21.31*, 130; *22.14*, 138; *23.7*, 28; *25.25*, 174

Romans: *1.3f*, 166; *1.4*, 138, 167; *1.25*, 176; *4.25*, 24; *8.3*, 177; *8.19*, 74; *8.32*, 23; *8.38*, 117; *9.5*, 176; *10.4*, 53; *11.36*, 176; *13.8*, 65; *14.14*, 39; *15.18f*, 98

1 Corinthians: *3.11*, 139; *6.1ff*, 25; *8.5*, 155; *10.25*, 39; *12.9-10*, 98; *13.12*, 146; *15.25*, 117

2 Corinthians: *4.4*, 117; *11.31*, 176; *12.12*, 98

Galatians: *1.5*, 176; *2.20*, 24; *3.13*, 21; *4.4*, 177; *4.10*, 41
Ephesians: *1.21*, 114; *5.2*, 24
Philippians: *2.5-11*, 99, 167; *2.8-9*, 148; *3.5-6*, 45; *4.20*, 176
Colossians: *1.15*, 177; *2.15*, 114; *4.11*, 81
1 Thess.: *4.15*, 88
1 Timothy: *3.16*, 176; *6.13*, 14
Titus: *2.13*, 176
Hebrews: *1.2*, 177; *2.4*, 98; *4.14*, 34; *5.8f*, 159; *7.26*, 34; *12.2*, 14; *13.16*, 9
1 Peter: *2.18-25*, 22; *2.23*, 24; *2.24*, 21; *4.12*, 88
2 Peter: *3.7*, 68
1 John: *5.20*, 177
Revelation: *20.4*, 69

### 3. APOCRYPHA

2 Esdras: *7.28*, 69, 79; *9.3*, 69; *12.32*, 79; *14.48(syr)*, 69
Tobit: *4.3-4; 60; 4.7*, 143; *5.2*, 161; *6.14*, 60; *14.9ff*, 60
Wisdom of Solomon: *2*, 166; *2.12-20*, 148, 163; *2.13*, 163; *2.16*, 163; *2-5*, 148; *3.7*, 151; *5.1-7*, 148; *5.5*, 138; *5.15*, 138; *7.25-6*, 177
Sirach: *4.3*, 143; *9.5*, 55; *23.9ff*, 56; *24.23*, 146; *28.1-5*, 56; *30.1*, 159; *48.8*, 152; *48.10*, 61
1 Maccabees: *2.28-9*, 61; *4.46*, 134; *13.51*, 125; *14.41-2*, 134
2 Maccabees: *2.22*, 56; *7*, 151; *7.9*, 151; *9.12*, 148, 171; *9.28*, 171; *10.6*, 125; *10.7*, 125

### 4. PSEUDEPIGRAPHA

Jubilees: *4.30*, 69; *20.4*, 55; *23.13ff*, 69; *50.17*, 37
Psalms of Solomon: *3.13*, 151; *17.3f*, 144; *17.23*, 144; *17.36*, 79, 144; *18 tit.*, 79; *18*, 136; *18.6-8*, 79, 144; *18.10*, 127
4 Maccabees: *5.33*, 56
Sibylline Oracles: *3.47*, 144; *3.176*, 144; *3.49-51*, 124; *3.63ff*, 69
1 Enoch: *42*, 146; *48.10*, 79; *51.3*, 147; *52*, 69; *52.4*, 79
2 Enoch: *33*, 69
3 Enoch: *48C 7*, 45, 160
Assumption of Moses: *10.1*, 144
2 Baruch: *29.3*, 79; *39.7*, 79; *70*, 69; *70.9*, 79; *72.2*, 79
Testaments: Test. Iss. *6.1*, 69; Test.Lev. *2.10*, 146

### 5. DEAD SEA SCROLLS

Community Rule: *1QS 5-8*, 46; *1QS 9.11*, 144, 147
Messianic Rule: *1QSa 2.12*, 79
Psalms: *1QH*, 148; *1QH 18.14*, 152
Damascus Document: *CD 4.19ff*, 56; *CD 6.1*, 152; *CD 6.3ff*, 147; *CD 9.1*, 26; *CD 10-11*, 37
War Scroll: *1QM 6.6*, 144; *1QM 11.7*, 152
Nahum Commentary: *4QpNah 1.6-7*, 12
Blessings of Jacob: *4QPatr.Bless.*, 124
Melchizedek Document: *11QMelch*, 152
Temple Scroll: *11QTemple 64*, 21, 26

### 6. RABBINIC WRITINGS
Mishnah
Berakoth: *1.5*, 79; *5.1*, 104; *5.5*, 161; *9.5*, 121, 129
Terumoth: *8.12*, 26
Shabbath: *7.2*, 38; *10.1-5*, 38; *22.6*, 38
Shekalim: *1.3*, 129
Yoma: *8.6-7*, 38
Sukkah: *4.5*, 126
Taanith: *3.8*, 169
Megillah: *3.3*, 129
Hagigah: *1.1*, 121
Ketuboth: *10.5*, 53
Sotah: *9.15*, 70, 79, 86
Baba Metzia: *2.11*, 160

Sanhedrin: *6.4*, 21; *6.5*, 174; *7.2*, 28; *7.4*, 159; *7.5*, 33; *7.11*, 40, 104; *8.1-4*, 159; *11.2*, 40
Makkoth: *3*, 28
Shebuoth: *3ff*, 55
Abodah Zarah: *2.3*, 39
Aboth: *1.1*, 41, 51; *1.13*, 31; *2.11*, 56; *3*, 44; *5.11*, 56
Tamid: *5.1*, 154
Zabahim: *4.7*, 125
Tosefta
Sanhedrin: *14.12*, 40; *14.13*, 59
Babylonian Talmud
Berakoth: *33a*, 104; *34b*, 100, 104
Shabbath: *12a-b*, 38
Yoma: *86b*, 86
Sukkah: *37b*, 126
Hagigah: *3a*, 100; *6a*, 121
Baba Metzia: *59b*, 112
Baba Bathra: *14b-15a*, 146
Sanhedrin: *41a*, 20; *43a*, 31, 40, 59; *93b*, 175; *97a-98a*, 69f; *98a*, 122; *99a*, 69; *99b*, 160
Aboda Zarah: *8b*, 20
Jerusalem Talmud
Berakoth: *1.3*, 154
Sanhedrin: *1.1*, 20
Midrashim
Leviticus Rabba: *37.2*, 126
Lamentations Rabba: *1.16*, 175; *2.24*, 175
Sifre Deuteronomy: *6.7*, 160; *21.22*, 155
Maimonides: *1.3.6.14(9)*, 25

### 7. GREEK AND LATIN AUTHORS
*Acta Pilati*: 40
Aelian: *Var. Hist. 21.19*, 156; *12.59*, 9
Aristobulus: (Eus. *Praep. Ev. 8.10*), 102
Aristophanes: *Pluto 683ff*, 115
Aristotle: *Eth. Nic. 1160b*, 159; *Pol. 1259a*, 159; (*Wiener Gnomologikon*), 10
Arnobius: *2.11*, 113
Arrian: *4.12*, 155
Bardesanes: *Patr.Syr. 2.612*, 69
Barnabas: *15.4*, 69
Cicero: *Pro Ligario: 9.33*, 50
Clement of Alexandria: *Exc. e Theodoto 4.24*, 88; *Stromateis 3.6.28ff*, 103
Clement of Rome: *1 Clem 42.1*, 139
Ps. Clement: *Recog. 1.161*, 48
Dio Cassius: *54.3.7*, 13; *78.18.4*, 105
Dio Chrysostom: *36.42ff*, 68
Diogenes Laertius: *7.142*, 68; *7.156f*, 68; *8.5*, 150; *8.58f*, 103
Diognetus: Ep. of: *10.6*, 10
Dionysius Hal.: *Ant. Rom, 2.56.2f*, 102
Empedocles: *fr. 115-19*, 156
Epictetus: *Diss. 3.13.4*, 68
Eusebius: *Contra Hier. 6*, 102; *Praep. Ev. 8.7.13*, 53; *8.10*, 102; *9.27.6*, 157
Firmicius Maturinus: *3.1.10f*, 69
Galen: *Nat. Fac. 3.7*, 107
Hermas: *Vis. 5.2*, 172
Hermetica: *CH 13.1.3*, 160
Herodotus: *2.55-7*, 102; *2.73*, 102; *2.142*, 68; *2.156*, 102; *4.95f*, 102; *4.105*, 102
Hyperides: *6.21*, 156
Iamblichus: *Vita Pyth. 8*, 106; *17.73*, 60; *28*, 106, 156
Ignatius: *Eph. 18.2*, 139
Irenaeus: *Contra Haer. 5.28.3*, 69
John Chrysostom: *Hom. in Rom. 14.5*, 75

Josephus: *Vita 10*, 41; *Contra Apionem 1.1*, 69; *1.41*, 146; *2.178*, 41; *2.198*, 43; *2.218*, 150; *Bellum Jud. 1.91*, 12; *2.75*, 13; *2.119*, 49; *2.135*, 56; *2.163*, 150; *2.241*, 13; *2.253*, 13; *2.259-61*, 112; *2.261-5*, 69; *2.316*, 33; *2.397*, 27; *2.400*, 27; *2.421*, 27; *2.434*, 175; *2.444*, 13; *3.351ff*, 93; *3.374*, 150; *5.194*, 132; *5.402*, 132; *5.545*, 60; *6.288-309*, 110; *6.300-5*, 27; *6.312*, 124; *Antiquitates 1.13*, 69; *1.104-8*, 102; *1.106*, 68; *1.158*, 102; *3.180*, 157; *4.202*, 21; *4.238*, 28; *8.34*, 157; *8.187*, 157; *8.354*, 60; *9.111*, 125; *10.35*, 93, 157; *13.288*, 47; *13.297f*, 52; *13.370*, 80; *16.43*, 53; *17.14*, 53, 93; *17.271ff*, 175; *17.285*, 13, 85; *17.354*, 102; *18.9*, 85; *18.18f*, 43; *18.23*, 46, 50, 85; *18.23-5*, 85; *18.116*, 14; *19.297*, 80; *20.97-9*, 69; *20.102*, 85; *20.167-70*, 69, 102, 112; *20.196*, 80

Justin Martyr: *1 Apol. 13*, 157; *Dial. 48*, 158; *48f*, 172; *55*, 157

Justinian: *Digest 48.19.28.15*, 12

Lucian: *Alexander* 103; *4*, 105; *24*, 100; *Philops: 26*, 100; *31*, 109

Manilius: *1.73ff*, 68; *4.832ff*, 68

Origen: *Contra Celsum 1.19*, 68; *1.28*, 108; *De Principiis 1.2.6*, 159

Panaetius: *fr. 64-9*, 70

Philo: *De op. mundi. 170*, 157; *De Migr. Abr. 89f*, 37; *Quis rer.div.haer. 261*, 93; *De Vita Mosis 1.155f*, 102; *1.158*, 157; *2.22*, 39; *De Decalogo 18f*, 48; *107*, 171; *111*, 171; *119*, 162; *119f*, 171; *De Spec. Leg. 1.68-70*,

129; *2.224ff*, 159; *2.227*, 159; *2.232*, 48; *2.234*, 159; *3.151f*, 21; *3.182*, 56; *4.73*, 9f; *De Praemiis 165*, 70; *De aet. mundi 8*, 68; *Leg. ad Gaium 298-305*, 85; *302*, 16; *Hypothetica*, 53

Philostratus: *Vita Ap. Tyan. 1.2*, 102, 106, 156; *1.13*, 60; *1.19*, 106; *4.45*, 100, 102; *5.13ff*, 102

Ps. Phokylides: *22f*, 143

Plato: *Timaeus 22d*, 68; *37d*, 68; *Phaedo 71e*, 151

Pliny; *Ep. 10.97.1*, 16; *Nat. Hist. 31.18.24*, 102

Plutarch: *Camill. 6*, 102; *Cato Minor 12*, 125; *Coriol. 37*, 102; *Marius 36*, 102; *Q. Conv. 4.1.3 (663A)*, 108; *Moralia 219E*, 156

Polybius: *2.17*, 102; *2.56*, 102; *3.47f*, 102; *16.12*, 102

Satyrus: ap. D.L. *8.58f*, 103

Seneca: *De Benef. 6.16.2*, 107

Solon: *fr. 13.61f*, 107

Suetonius: *Aug. 52*, 155; *Cal. 32.2*, 13; *Vesp. 4*, 69; *7*, 108; *Dom. 10.1*, 13

Tacitus: *4.81*, 108; *5.9*, 175; *5.13*, 69, 124

Thucydides: *1.126*, 102; *5.26*, 102

## 8. INSCRIPTIONS, PAPYRI ETC

*Cat. Codd. Astrol. 4.114-18*, 69
*Edict of Germanicus*, 9
*Inscr. Graecae 4.951f*, 100
*Corp. Inscr. Jud. 2.1404*, 53
*Pap. Mag. Graec. 7.768*, 114
*Corp. Pap. Jud. 86-92*, 175

# MODERN AUTHORS

Aulen, G., 46

Baeck, L., 78
Bammel, E., 20, 27
Banks, R., 39, 56, 61, 94
Barbel, J., 172
Barbour, R., 8
Barnett, P., 85
Barrett, C. K., 82, 177
Benoit, P., 34
Berger, K., 48, 59, 78, 147, 149, 151, 163
Bergmann, J., 143
Bertram, G., 127
Beyer, H., 170
Blenkinsopp, J., 124
Blinzler, J. 18, 31, 174
Bloch, E., 76, 97, 116
Bolkestein, H., 10, 143
Boll, F., 160
Borg, M., 46
Bornkamm, G., 155
Bovon, F., 18
Bowersock, G., 102, 155
Bowker, J., 6, 40, 58
Brandon, S. G. F., 14, 15, 130
Braun, H., 42
Brown, R., 167
Bühner, J. A., 161f
Bultmann, R., 13, 50f, 56, 66, 88, 99f, 120, 123, 136
Burkitt, F. C., 126
Burney, C., 72
Burridge, K., 67

Cadbury, H. J., 126, 137, 139
Caird, G. B., 71
Carcopino, J., 159
Carmignac, J., 150
Carroll, J., 73
Casey, M., 83, 170
Catchpole, D., 30, 174
Cavallin, H., 150
Charlesworth, M., 155
Cohn, H., 15, 31, 38
Cornelius à Lapide, 159
Conzelmann, H., 24, 32, 39, 89, 138
Cullmann, O., 88, 91
Cumont, F., 68

Dahl, N., 5, 139
Dalman, G., 170
Danby, H., 51, 79
Daniélou, J., 172
Daube, D., 25, 38, 48, 55
Davey, N., 109
Davies, W. D., 49, 51, 77f
Deissmann, A., 3, 80
Delling, G., 98, 103
Derrett, J. D. M., 26, 40, 53, 123, 125, 129, 131, 133f, 146, 155, 159, 161, 170
Desroche, H., 77
Dibelius, M., 120, 176
Dietzfelbinger, C., 56
Dodd, C. H., 58, 61, 64, 88, 126, 133, 145f, 156, 160, 176f
Dodds, E. R., 103
Donahue, J., 33

Dunn, J., 91, 160, 168, 177f
Dupont, J., 53
Duprez, A., 115

Eichrodt, W., 48, 89, 143f, 154, 165, 172
Eliade, M., 68
Eppstein, V., 134

Falk, Z. W., 26, 28, 39, 161, 171
Festinger, Riecken and Schachter, 90
Festugière, A. J., 100, 160
Fiebig, P., 100
Finkelstein, L., 42
Fischel, H., 148
Flusser, D., 38, 174
Focillon, H., 72
Franklin, E., 89
Friedrich, G., 152

Gächter, P., 160
Gager, J., 67
Gardavsky, V., 97, 119
Genest, O., 34
George, A., 167
Georgi, D., 102
Gerhardsson, B., 113, 164
Giblet, J., 46, 85
Grant, M., 99
Grant, R., 102
Gray, J., 60
Grundmann, W., 136, 139
Gundry, R., 164

Hacker, K., 55
Haenchen, E., 13, 34, 120, 130, 133
Hahn, F., 79, 128, 136, 165
Hanson, P., 75
Harnack, A., 66
Harvey, A. E., 19, 22, 31, 38, 113, 146, 158, 161ff, 170
Hengel, M., 4, 12, 13, 46, 60, 67, 132, 146, 156, 158, 163, 175
Held, H., 165
Hennecke, E., 110
Hiers, R., 89
Holladay, C., 157
Horsley, R., 85
Horst, P. van den, 10
Hoskyns, E., 109
Houlden, J. L., 176f
Hull, J., 104, 107-9, 114

Jackson, B., 56
Jacobs, L., 49, 78, 154
Jeremias, J., 24, 50, 61, 110, 114, 121, 129, 135, 137, 141, 144, 149, 159f, 164, 168
Jonge, M. de, 79, 175

Kee, H. M., 46
Kegel, G., 151
Kelly, J., 12, 176
Kermode, F., 72
Klappert, B., 24
Klausner, J., 77, 79, 124
Klostermann, K., 169
Knox, W. L., 68, 124, 126
Koch, D., 113
Koch, K., 91
Kopp, C., 3
Kramer, W., 139
Kümmel, W. 66, 83, 88, 91, 135, 169
Kuhn, H.-W., 3, 13, 124f

Lampe, G., 113
Lang, M., 115
Latourelle, R., 101
Lauterbach, J., 44, 93
Légasse, S., 102
Leivestad, R., 58
Lietzmann, H., 176
Lifshitz, B., 53
Lightfoot, R., 132
Lindars, B., 24, 83, 138
Lindblom, J., 73
Lochman, F., 97
Lohmeyer, E., 127, 132
Lohse, E., 126, 128, 160
Long, A., 68
Lowy, S., 53

Machoveč, M., 76, 97
McCasland, S., 99, 110
McKane, W., 92
MacRae, G., 98
Marshall, I. H., 78, 121, 163
Mayer, G., 49, 150
Meyer, B., 117
Meyer, H., 176
Meyer, R., 43, 134
Milik, J., 152
Mitchell, B., 71
Montefiore, C., 64
Moore, G. F., 42, 51, 70, 127, 145f, 150, 154f
Moule, C. F. D., 56, 137, 163
Mowinkel, S., 92

Neusner, J., 44, 49, 93, 150
Nickelsburg, G., 151
Nicklin, T., 123
Nineham, D., 6
Nock, A. D., 9, 108, 156
North, C., 146
Noth, M., 164

Pancaro, S., 37
Perrin, N., 79
Petuchowski, J., 78
Petzke, G., 102
Popkes, W., 21, 23, 25

Rabinowitz, L., 26
Rad, G. von, 143f
Reicke, B., 57
Rengstorf, K., 162
Ridderboos, J., 117
Robertson, A., 3
Robinson, J. A. T., 88
Roloff, J., 49
Ruppert, L., 148
Russell, D. S., 70, 75, 77

Safrai, S., 48, 104, 169
Schillebeeckx, E., 2, 57, 137, 167
Schoeps, H., 149
Scholem, G., 77, 146, 175
Schürer, E., 20, 37, 41, 43, 98, 150
Schweitzer, A., 63, 83
Schweizer, E., 165
Segal, A., 155
Segond, A., 177
Senior, D., 163
Sherwin-White, A., 16, 30

Silver, A., 69
Smalley, S., 139
Smith, Morton, 100
Spicq, C., 176
Stauffer, E., 66, 123
Sticker, B., 68
Stommel, E., 60
Stone, L., 158
Stuhlmacher, P., 140, 152
Suggs, M., 54

Tasker, R., 80, 177
Taylor, L. R., 155
Taylor, V., 20, 121, 123, 127
Tcherikover, V., 175
Telford, W., 157
Thackeray, H. St. J., 29, 150
Theissen, G., 63, 105
Tiede, D., 108

Vaux, R. de, 28
Vermes, G., 21, 26, 38, 43, 46, 48, 83, 93, 104, 127, 141, 152, 154, 163, 166, 169
Vester, B., 121
Viviano, B., 31

Weber, H.-R., 12
Weinreich, O., 100, 103, 108
Westcott, B. F., 177
Westerholm, C., 44, 49, 55
Wettstein, J., 33, 176
Whitley, C., 73, 92
Wieder, N., 147
Wilckens, U., 146, 174
Wiles, M., 2
Wilson, B., 67, 90, 101
Winter, P., 18, 41, 98, 174
Wolfson, H., 167

# SUBJECTS

*abba*, 168f
agent, agency, 161ff
agents, in the O.T., 162
Alexander the Great, 156
Allenby, General, 121
angel, 165
anointed, *see Christ, christos*
anointing, 141
Antiochus IV Epiphanes, 156n
antitheses, 52ff
apocalyptist, 57
Apollonius of Tyana, 100, 103, 156
Aristarchus, 68n
astrology, 102f, 106
authority, of Jesus, 134, 148, 150f, 167f, 170, 172f

Barabbas, 80
Bar Kochba, 70
Bethphage, 124
Bible, inerrancy of, 5
blasphemy, 22, 29, 40, 155, 170ff
borrowing, law of, 123f
burial duties, 59ff

capital charges, 19, 40, 170ff
charitable giving, 143
Christ, *christos*, 33, 79ff, 135ff
Cicero, 17
cleansing of the Temple, 129ff
concession, 48
constraints, notion of, 6
'Court of the Gentiles', 132
courts: competence of, 25ff; procedure of, 17, 30f
credulity, 101ff
'crisis', 73f, 90
cross, superscription on, 13
crucifixion, 4, 11ff

Decalogue, 154
Dedication, festival of, 125f
deification, 155f
demon-possession, 99

'disconfirmation', 90
dissimilarity, criterion of, 8, 59n
'dissonance', 73n
divinity: of emperor, 155f; of Jesus, 157f, 168, 173, 176ff; of philosophers, 156
divorce, 53

education, Jewish, 41ff
Eighteen Benedictions, 127
Elijah, 60f
Empedocles, 103, 156
end of the word, 68ff
ending: in experience, 72f; of stories, 71ff
entry into Jerusalem, 120ff, 145
Essenes, 42f
*euangelion*, 142
*euergetēs*, 9, 46n
exorcism, 108f, 114f, 117f

fasting, 50, 62
father, as teacher, 160
father-son relationship, 158ff
fatherhood of God, 168ff
'fence around the law', 56n
form-criticism, 2, 4f, 49n
fulfilment, 56

Great Year, 68

*haber, haberim*, 44f
*haereseis*, 41
'handing over', 23ff
Hanina ben Dosa, 104, 107
healing, gift of, 107f
healing miracles: of Jesus, 108ff; Jewish, 104; pagan, 103f
herald, in Isaiah, 141
Honi, 104, 107, 169
*hosanna*, 126
Hume, David, 102n

inerrancy, of Bible, 5

innocent suffering, 148
'interim ethic', 63

Jannaeus, Alexander, 12
Jesus: and the law, 36ff; and Pharisees, 47ff; and the sabbath, 37ff, 61f; and sects, 46; and time, 66f; as Messianic pretender, 79; as a prophet, 57ff, 131f, 134f; as a rebel, Zealot etc., 14f, 46f, 84ff; as Son of God, 158ff; as a sorcerer, 40, 59, 98; as a teacher, 41ff, 93f; certainly known facts about, 6; his authority, 134, 148, 150f, 167f, 170, 172f; his birth, 167; his compassion, 111; his miracles, 98ff, 110ff, 118; his supernatural foresight, 122; his transfiguration, 165
Jesus son of Ananias, 27f
Josephus, 41f
Judas of Galilee, 46, 65

Kaiser Wilhelm, 121
Kingdom, the, 76, 83, 86ff, 91, 128, 143ff

Law: Jesus' attitude to, 36ff; Jewish, 36f; Roman, 159n; as revelation, 145f
laws: of borrowing, 123f; of food, 39f; of sabbath, 37ff; of sons' obedience, 159

Maccabees, 56, 61, 86, 125, 151
Magic, 105
*mal 'ak yhwh*, 165
Mark, the gospel of, 113
Marxism, 75f, 96f, 118f
*matsar*, 23
Matthew, gospel of, 53f, 113
*mebasser*, 152
'men of deed', 104, 107, 169
Messiah, 79, 101, 111, 121 127f, 135ff; suffering, 137
messianic age, 69
messianic pretenders, 85, 175
messianism, 67, 77ff, 85
miracles: of Jesus, 98ff, 110ff, 118; Jewish, 104, 111f; pagan, 103, 115
monotheism, 154ff
Mount of Olives, 124, 134
mystery, of God, 145

Nakdimon, 100n, 107
Nazareth, 3
new age, 115ff, 143ff

obedience, of son, 159
omen, 110n
oracle, 124
oral tradition, 51f, 55
ossuary, 3

Panaetius, 70n
*paradidonai*, 23ff
paradise, 116f, 143
paradox, of Jewish religion, 146
'paradoxical works', 98
Passover, 40n, 126
Paul, 45n, 53, 139
'People of the Land', 42, 45
persecution, 88
Pharisees, 42, 44; 'houses' of, 49, 51; 'philosophy' of, 49
Philo, 16

Philostratus, 100, 102f, 106
pilgrimage, 121
polygamy, 53
Pontius Pilate, 12, 16f
poverty, 143
'power', of healing, 108
prayer, men of, 104, 107
prophet, 57ff, 94f, 131, 134f, 148, 152
prophets, Old Testament, 73, 89, 92, 130f
psychic knowledge, 106
Pythagoras, 103, 150n, 156

rainmaking, 100, 104, 107
raising the dead, 100
*raz*, 146n
rebellious elder, 19n, 40
Reign of God, *see* Kingdom
requisition, right to, 123
resurrection, 138, 150f, 166f
revelation of God, 145ff

sabbath, laws of, 37ff, 61f
Sadducees, 43, 45f, 52
Scripture, authority of, 5
sectarianism, 42f, 45f
Sermon on the Mount, 52ff, 63
Servant, in Isaiah, 23ff, 141, 149
*shema*, 154
Simon Maccabaeus, 125, 129
social anthropology, 67, 77, 101
son: as agent, 161ff; as learner, 160; obedience of, 159
Son of God, 158ff
Son of Man, 33, 83
son–father relationship, 158ff
sorcery, 104f
*stibades*, 125
Stoics, 68
story, in the Bible, 71ff
suffering servant, 23ff
synagogue, 53

Tabernacles, festival of, 125f
*Tefillah*, 127
Temple, 129ff; administration of, 134; pilgrimage to, 48
Testimonium Flavianum, 41n, 98n
*theios anēr*, 157n
*titulus*, 13
Tolstoy, 72
Torah, *see* Law, Jewish
transfiguration, 165
transmigration, 150
trial: before Pilate, 17ff; before Sanhedrin, 21, 30f

utopia, 116

Verres, 17
Vespasian, 104
vindication, 138, 151
virgin birth, 167n

Wisdom, 92f, 146f

zeal, 45
Zealots, 46f, 85